The Emergence and Evolution of Markets

The Emergence and Evolution of Markets

Edited by

Horst Brezinski

and

Michael Fritsch

Technical University
Bergakademie Freiberg, Germany

European Association for Comparative Economic Studies

Edward Elgar
Cheltenham, UK • Lyme, US

Published by
Edward Elgar Publishing Limited
8 Lansdown Place
Cheltenham
Glos GL50 2HU
UK

Edward Elgar Publishing, Inc.
1 Pinnacle Hill Road
Lyme
NH 03768
US

A catalogue record for this book
is available from the British Library

Library of Congress Cataloguing in Publication Data
The emergence and evolution of markets / edited by Horst Brezinski and
    Michael Fritsch.
        European Association for Comparative Economic Studies.
        Includes index
        1. Capitalism—History. 2. Markets—History. 3. Post-communism
    —Economic aspects.   I. Brezinski, Horst Dieter, 1947–   .
    II. Fritsch, Michael.   III. European Association for Comparative
    Economic Studies.
    HB501.E557 1997
    330.12'2—dc21   97–25024
                                                                        CIP

ISBN 1 85898 659 1

Printed and bound in Great Britain by Hartnolls Limited, Bodmin, Cornwall

Contents

List of tables

List of figures

Contributors

Wladimir Andreff, *University of Paris, France.*

Jozef M. van Brabant, *Department of Economic and Social Information and Policy Analysis of the United Nations, New York, USA.*

Horst Brezinski, *Technical University Bergakademie Freiberg, Germany.*

Junior R. Davis, *Heriot-Watt University, Edinburgh, UK.*

Michael Fritsch, *Technical University Bergakademie Freiberg, Germany.*

John Garland, *University of Kansas, Lawrence, Kansas, USA.*

Silvio Goglio, *University of Trento, Italy.*

Michael Keren, *Hebrew University, Jerusalem, Israel.*

Ellen C. Krupa, *Wissenschaftszentrum Berlin, Germany.*

Karl Lohmann, *Technical University Bergakademie Freiberg, Germany.*

Larry Neal, *University of Illinois, Urbana-Champaign, Illinois, USA.*

Lucjan T. Orlowski, *Sacred Heart University, Fairfield, Connecticut, USA.*

Karl-Ernst Schenk, *University of Hamburg, Germany.*

Harm G. Schröter, *Free University of Berlin, Germany.*

Mechthild Schrooten, *German Institute of Economic Research, Berlin, Germany.*

Wim Swaan, *Hungarian Academy of Sciences, Budapest, Hungary.*

Foreword

This book contains a collection of contributions to the 'Third Freiberg Symposium on Economics', which took place at the Technical University Bergakademie Freiberg, Germany, from September 1-3, 1994. In addition, contributions presented during research seminars at the Freiberg faculty of Economics and Business Administration in 1994 and 1995 were chosen for publication in this volume.

The topic for our third conference manifested itself while we were discussing the findings of our second Freiberg Workshop which was concerned with the creation of new and small firms especially in economies in transition. One of our findings was that bottom-up privatization as well as top-down privatization are important prerequisites for the coming-up of markets. Yet, the process of transformation aims at the establishment and continuous development of markets. Therefore, the articles presented in the foregoing volume will focus on the question of the emergence and evolution of markets.

First concepts of the market in theory and reality are discussed and contrasted with other forms of coordination such as hierarchies and networks. In addition, we considered it promising to concentrate on a historical assessment of the development of markets in general, and the stock market in particular. In doing so we wanted to find out about the factors determining the emergence and evolution of markets which, initially, were not designed at the desks of economists. Moreover, we expected to gain insight into the problems connected with the creation of markets in transforming countries.

One of the conclusions drawn in this book which is based on theoretical as well as empirical analysis of the transformation process is that formal institutions, such as the implementation of the liberalization of prices, of privatization, and a new legal structure do not per se generate efficiently performing markets. Corresponding changes in the value systems of individuals have to take place in order to arrive at the economic behavior needed for markets to yield the expected results.

We also discovered that the necessary knowledge about the functioning of markets depends on the existence of informal rules, hidden information and interdependencies between economy and society which are difficult to identify by means of the traditional economic theory. In identifying and acknowledging these deficits, the book may close an important gap in the research on economies and societies in transition, provide direction for future research and caution us to give definitive answers in regard to the transition of post-socialist countries once and for all.

The editors gratefully acknowledge the invaluable help provided by Hermann Fink and Danielle Schons in checking language and style of the articles, many of them written by non-native speakers. Special thanks go to Jana El Hassan and Kerstin Ulbricht for providing the photo-technical version of this book.

Freiberg

Horst Brezinski
Michael Fritsch

1 Markets in economic theory and reality: introduction and overview

Horst Brezinski and Michael Fritsch

Markets are of central importance to the coordination of individual activities in the real world; they also play a major role as an explanatory concept in economic theory. Economists possess a variety of well-elaborated analytic tools to deal with markets from a static or in a comparatively static perspective. However, our knowledge concerning market dynamics is still rather deficient. We still do not know very much about questions of how markets emerge, how they mature and in what way their evolution depends on specific conditions. This deficit becomes particularly obvious with regard to the post-socialist countries of Eastern Europe where a change from the old regime, dominated by central-bureaucratic planning, to a more decentralized coordination based on market relationships is taking place. The experience in these countries clearly shows that this transition is not easy at all. Abolishing the central planning system and allowing for a free exchange of goods and services is only a starting point for the establishment of a market economy. Obviously, much more is needed to implement a well-functioning market system.

The contributions to this book all deal with the development of markets. They focus on general aspects in the explanation of market evolution as well as on empirical examples from capitalist countries and from the post-socialist economies of Eastern Europe. Part 1 contains three contributions that treat general aspects. First, Horst Brezinski and Michael Fritsch, in their contribution, give an introduction to the 'state of the art' of economic theory with regard to market evolution and name a number of open questions. They stress the 'embeddedness' of markets into a certain transaction 'culture' and provide an introduction to a number of issues related to the implementation of a market system in the former socialist countries. Silvio Goglio then describes the development of markets as a coordination device from the Middle Ages until today. He gives a number of historical examples that demonstrate how the organization of exchange depends on cultural as well as economic factors. Goglio shows that in Europe modern 'markets' in the very sense the term is used nowadays are quite a recent phenomenon and emerged no earlier than during the industrialization process of the 19th and the late 18th centuries. Trying to explain this development, he crystallizes out a number of factors that stimulated the evolution of a market system. In the third contribution of Part 1, Michael Keren analyzes the transition from hierarchy to markets by means of a model based on network relationships that focusses on the retail sector. He stresses the importance of this sector in the transformation process, and shows that this sector tends to remain underdeveloped and an obstacle to a rapid transition.

1

The contributions in Part 2 deal with experiences with some specific markets trying to draw general conclusions concerning market evolution. Larry Neal analyzes the emergence and the historical development of the stock market. He concentrates on the Amsterdam stock exchange and the London banking sector of the 17th and 18th centuries. Stock markets are of a central importance for a well-functioning market system and, therefore, represent a salient feature of the economies in transition. Based on his analysis, Neal draws a number of conclusions for the emerging stock markets in the post-socialist countries. Karl-Ernst Schenk examines patterns of evolution and institutional change in the newly emerging markets of telecommunications services. He shows that, initiated by technological change that led to the obsolescence of government-protected 'natural monopolies' in some parts of the telecommunications sector, the implementation of competitive elements has spread from market segment to market segment as well as from country to country. In Schenk's analysis, technological innovation in radio transmission has provided only the necessary conditions for such developments. He concludes that the building up of expectations about advantages for some major players in the market as well as the formation of interest coalitions played an important role in the shake-up of the incumbent institutional setting in the telecommunications sector in order to create more competition. Ellen C. Krupa studies factors that impede the market success of a new, superior product generation based on a new technological paradigm using the example of chlorofluorocarbons (CFCs) in household refrigerators. Very early international agreements made clear to the CFC producing and consuming industries that this market would be phased out in the near future. However, instead of exiting these markets and developing CFC-free products, for a long time many firms showed themselves reluctant to act. According to Krupa's analysis, the oligopolistic structure of the respective markets has been a major reason for the slow reaction by the incumbent firms. In Germany, basic change has been initiated rather quickly when an outsider introduced the new product generation A small East German company was faced with the threat of being closed down.

Part 3 focusses on the emerging market systems in post-socialist countries. Wim Swaan, in his contribution, analyzes the role of knowledge and transaction costs in the creation of markets in post-socialist economies. He argues that in the transition process economic actors face considerable transformation costs that work as a barrier to behavioral change. These transformation costs may be broadly divided into the costs of reorganizing existing firms and the costs of establishing transactions. Swaan shows how, possibly, deficient transaction skills as well as the lack of appropriate institutions supporting transactions determined the reaction of firms to the disintegration of the party-state hierarchy. Obviously, these factors work as severe impediments to the increase of the inter-firm division of labor and the emergence of a well-functioning market system. Junior R. Davis examines the evolution of food markets in Bulgaria. These markets came into existence with the liberalization of prices and the abolition of subsidies for the production of most kinds of food. In this early stage, food markets in Bulgaria were rather 'informal', i.e. they were characterized by high barriers to entry and a severe lack of transparency. Despite this general liberalization, the prices for some basic products were monitored and maintained under some degree of control by the government, mainly to prevent unjustified price increases and, thereby, to assure a certain level of food consumption. However, this projected price system does not seem to have worked well because the prices for monitored goods increased more than those for the non-monitored produce. Davis discusses a number of possible causes for this phenomenon and concludes that there is no alternative to stimulating competition and to complete liberalization by abolishing remaining price controls.

The subsequent contribution by Jozef M. van Brabant deals with the transformation of the banking system in the post-socialist countries of Eastern Europe. The development of a well-working banking sector is a core issue in the implementation of a market economy, particularly since bank intermediation of intertemporal resource allocation is critical in greasing the wheels of market-based operations. Van Brabant analyzes various approaches in coming to grips with the 'old debts' of state-owned production units, the problem of recapitalizing banks. He also discusses the difficulties of instilling commercial rationality into the behavior of existing banks. He shows that the conversion of the banking sector in these countries requires not only the establishment of new rules and institutions but also, at least equally important, the accumulation of 'tacit' knowledge that can only be generated by learning from doing. Van Brabant points out that this will be an arduous and very time-consuming task. John Garland studies the emergence of markets in the transforming economy of Kyrgyzstan, one of the Central Asian republics of the former Soviet Union that gained independence in late 1991. In terms of population, Kyrgyzstan is a rather small country and it is economically lagging far behind most of the other former Soviet republics. In the beginning of the transformation process Kyrgyzstan experienced a collapse of economic relations with its main trading partners that resulted in a considerable decline of its GDP. Garland analyzes the problems Kyrgyzstan has in establishing a market economy and in finding its place in the international division of labor. He concludes that a market economy will emerge much more slowly in Kyrgyzstan than in most other post-socialist countries, mainly because there are no significant entrepreneurial pre-war capitalist and technological traditions to build on. Finally, Lucjan T. Orlowski deals with recent developments in international currency derivatives, i.e. financial instruments that enable firms engaged in international trade relations to hedge the risk of unfavorable appreciation or depreciation of a single currency. On the basis of an overview of the evolution of markets for such derivatives and with reference to the Polish example, he asks under which conditions the currencies of the countries in transition of Eastern and Central Europe might be involved in these markets. Orlowski argues that, currently, the very limited volume of respective contracts will not guarantee a proper pricing mechanism. Moreover, a high degree of price instability invites speculative transactions and destabilizing attacks on exchange rates. Therefore, building derivative security markets in transition economies will have to be preceded by a strengthening of underlying security markets, whose success strongly depends on the ability of the economic authorities to reduce inflation.

The papers collected in this volume very clearly show that liberalization, privatization and corresponding changes of the formal institutions alone by far do not suffice to implement a 'market economy' which leads to satisfactory results. Even if the system of legal rules and government institutions is changed very quickly, as, for example, in the case of East Germany, the economic agents need time to learn the new 'rules of the game', to experience the application and operation of these rules in order to be able to predict the outcome of their actions and to adjust to the changed structure of incentives (cf. Brezinski and Fritsch, 1995). Moreover, a well-operating market economy is characterized by private-sector institutions and hybrid forms of relationships that correspond to the prevailing rules and lead, in many different ways, to a reduction of transaction costs. In addition, the evolution of the corresponding institutions and arrangements is a time-consuming process. We know that these issues are of importance for a smoothly functioning market economy but, unfortunately, our knowledge concerning factors involved still is very incomplete. It is quite far from enabling us to give advice on how to accelerate the evolution of markets and the corresponding transformation processes. The social sciences, particularly economics, are just beginning to recognize these issues and to direct attention to them. The analyses compiled here are only a first step in this direction. There is, however, still a long way to go.

References

Brezinski, Horst and Michael Fritsch (1995); Transformation: The Shocking German Way; *Moct-Most*, 5:4, 1-25.

PART 1

GENERAL ASPECTS

2 Spot-markets, hierarchies, networks, and the problem of economic transition

Horst Brezinski and Michael Fritsch

1. The problem

Transition in post-socialist countries after the fall of the Iron Curtain is commonly described as a process leading from a command economy to a market economy as quickly as possible (Lavigne, 1995). From the perspective of a very popular economic model (Coase, 1937; Williamson, 1985, 1989) this is the step from the hierarchy form of organization to a market. One problem in this description is that it might appear to be too simple because all real economic systems are based on a mix of different coordination mechanisms (Kornai, 1992). On the one hand, the socio-economic systems in the former socialist countries did not rely on pure hierarchical coordination while, on the other hand, there have never been societies in the West in which everything was decided by the market mechanism. But, even if we accept this simplistic description and agree on the perception that transition leads to the market economy and, thus, to the emergence of markets as the dominating coordination mechanism, the theoretical support for the transformation of non-market economies into capitalist ones is less solid than is often assumed (Gros and Steinherr, 1995). Fundamental questions have to be solved: What is a market and how does it work? Our knowledge of this issue is rather unsatisfactory, a deficiency strongly reflected in the problems we face when trying to give advice to the post-socialist countries on how to manage the transition from a centrally planned economy to a Western type of market economy. We are particularly lacking a dynamic theory of the market and of market evolution.

Much has been said about legal preconditions for the evolution of markets (e.g. clearly defined property rights that are enforceable at reasonable cost) and about the macroeconomic conditions that seem to be helpful in the formation of a market economy. This article simply assumes that these problems have been solved to a satisfactory degree. Our aim is to provide an outline of the questions associated with the transition to a market economy which go beyond these issues. What other difficulties do we have to expect, how can they be solved, and what advice can we give? These are questions which are not only relevant for the process of transformation in the post-socialist countries. The answers to these questions may also be expected to have some bearing for Western-type market economies, developing countries, as well as for the further progress of the economic theory of the market. The foregoing contribution concentrates on some important issues that are of specific interest to the questions raised above. We will start with the 'life-cycle' model of a market and draw a number of conclusions for the emerging markets in Eastern Europe (Section 2). In Section 3 we will then deal with the standard economic theory of a market which we call a 'neoclassical market' or a 'spot-market' (Section 3). The shortcomings of this model of a market lead to the so-called 'network approach' that has become rather popular in the social sciences only recently. Building on a critical discussion of the network approach and its implications (Section 4) we will attempt to present an overview on markets and hierarchies in socialism (Section 5). Section 6 formulates some conclusions and hypotheses on the emergence of markets in post-socialist countries. Finally, the outlook provides a brief agenda for further research.

2. Ecology of firms during a market-life cycle

The market is an institution which is essentially dynamic: it changes over time as well as with its environment. The standard approach to describe and analyze the emergence and evolution of markets is the well-known 'life-cycle' model: markets for certain goods come into existence, grow, shrink, and die after the product has been completely substituted by its successor (cf. Jovanovic and MacDonald, 1994; Klepper and Simons, 1993).[1] This life-cycle model has implications for the development of the population of firms in a market (firm-ecology) as well as for the intensity and the characteristics of competition during the process of market evolution. It is part of our theoretical knowledge about markets that may be directly applied to the transformation process in the post-socialist economies.

Figure 2.1 Paths in the number of entries, exits, and firms during the market-life cycle

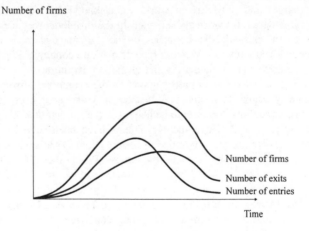

---

1 It should be noted that this life-cycle model does not apply to certain goods such as many kinds of services which are provided in interactive process according to the specification of the customer. The money market, too, is an exception where the life-cycle model does not apply. See Tichy (1991) for details.

Figure 2.1 shows the number of firms operating in a market as well as the number of entries and exits during the market-life cycle. The first firm in the market has a monopolistic position which - in most cases - will soon be contested by competitors entering this market. In the early phases of the market life-cycle there is a considerable degree of concentration on the supply side which will probably allow for some extra profit. The lower the barriers to entry the faster the population of firms in the market will grow and induce an increase in supply and a decrease in prices and profits. Having reached the maximum number of suppliers, markets enter the so-called shakeout phase during which a large number of suppliers will be eliminated (see Klepper and Graddy, 1990; Klepper and Simons, 1993); only a relatively small number will survive for a longer period. Empirical analyses of such market-life cycles indicate that there might be entries into the market even after the shakeout has already begun. However, during that phase entry declines to a negligible level. By contrast, there is a considerable share of exits from the market over the entire life-cycle.[2] The fact that in the later stages of the life-cycle there is a relatively small number of suppliers in the market does not necessarily imply that output will be correspondingly low. Typically, at that stage of the market life-cycle the product is highly standardized and is produced in large numbers while the minimum optimal size of a firm is relatively big; accordingly, barriers to entry are also relatively high.

This life-cycle model has some important implications for the developing market economies in Eastern Europe.[3] The first implication is that in setting up a market economy some monopolistic or oligopolistic tendencies which may lead to exploitation of the demand side are inevitable in the early stages of a life-cycle. One cannot simply jump into the more developed stages of the market life-cycle and leave the early phases out. In many cases it may take a considerable period of time for a sufficient number of suppliers to be established on the market and a 'workable' form of competition to emerge.

From this might be concluded that some kind of price control will be necessary in the young markets of Eastern Europe to prevent exploitation and extra profit. But this would only be an attempt to cure symptoms caused by the small number of suppliers in the market and to return to the discrepancies of the former socialist system. Experience in Western market economies with such controls shows that they are not suited at all to

---

2 However, this life-cycle model which is quite well-suited to describe the evolution of industries may not directly be transferred to national or regional economies, because, in contrast to most markets, regions have no such life-cycle. In the development of regions cyclical fluctuations caused by dominating industries might occur in the region experiencing such a life-cycle, but, at least in the real world of developed countries, regional economies do not emerge and die in the way markets do. See Fritsch (1996) for details.

3 Of course, there is a considerable discrepancy between the assumptions of the life-cycle model and many markets in post-socialist countries. Many of the newly emerging markets are for standard goods that have been produced there for some time. But this is not a really severe objection to the above conclusions. If a market for a standard good emerges that may be produced by many suppliers then we could expect a faster growth in the number of competitors than in a market for a 'real' innovation where the pioneering firm often has some know-how advantages that makes it hard to compete against. It should also be noted, that in many cases it is a problem to judge in what respect a given product is really 'new'.

produce satisfactory results. Considerable regulation may be necessary in so-called 'natural monopoly' cases. But a natural monopoly is a rare exception and not the rule. Moreover, one should be very cautious in applying such measures because, as experience shows, once they are implemented such regulative measures are very hard to abolish. Consequently, one should wait and see whether the problems of market power and exploitation will not eventually vanish soon. The main response to the phenomenon of market power in the early stages of market development should be to lower entry barriers (for domestic as well as for foreign firms) in order to induce a fast rise in the number of competitors. This increased competition will solve the problems of market power and exploitation (cf. Hansen, 1994). All measures that enhance entrepreneurship and competition are suited to cope with the problems of market power during the early phases of market development.[4]

While high numbers of entries into markets are a relatively new phenomenon in post-socialist economies, this holds true, to a much larger degree, for market exits. It has to be recognized that entries and exits are main characteristics of a functioning market and that it would be rather alarming if there were no entries and exits at all, or only entries and no exits. Experience in Western market economies shows that a relatively high number of entries is not viable and that many of the new firms have to exit rather early (Freeman, Carroll and Hannan, 1983; Brüderl and Schüssler, 1990; Brüderl, Preisendörfer and Ziegler, 1992). Therefore, it might be argued that we are building our economic well-being on the bleeding bodies of entrepreneurs that have failed. Yet, this is simply the normal price to be paid to get the system working. Economic policy should, therefore, resist the temptation of trying to prevent exits. On the contrary, it should assist necessary exits so that the resources used by these firms are made available to the market again. Otherwise, the efficiency gains to be expected from markets will be limited (Montias, Ben-Ner and Neuberger 1994).

3. The economic standard model of markets and hierarchies

The life-cycle model which may be applied to the development of many markets ignores a central question: What is a market and how does it work? A market is commonly defined as a set of social institutions that brings together buyers and sellers by announcing time, location, price as well as type and quality of a product to be voluntarily exchanged between different actors (Goglio, 1997; Hodgson, 1988, 174; Stiglitz, 1993, 13). In general, there are several actors on both sides of a market competing with each other and, furthermore, a large number of exchange transactions of a specific type that regularly take place. Because market contracts involve the exchange of property rights, these rights can be seen as a prerequisite to the proper functioning of a market, i.e. some property rights are generally accepted or enforceable at a reasonable cost. The market is an institution which helps to organize these exchanges by providing relevant information.

---

4 For issues of entrepreneurship in Eastern Europe see the contributions in Brezinski and Fritsch (1996).

The standard model of economics which describes and analyzes markets is that of perfect competition. Major shortcomings of this model are that it deals only with a very special type of market, the so-called 'spot-market', and that costs of transacting are completely neglected (North, 1990). In such spot-markets both parts of the exchange process take place simultaneously at a specific point in time, actors do not have any future obligations, and there is no uncertainty concerning the quality of the goods that are exchanged. Therefore, trust or reputation of actors are not required in such markets. Interaction needs no history and no future; it is impersonal.[5] However, only very few markets in the real world come close to this spot-market model. Spot-markets are rare exceptions. Most economists are aware of these weaknesses of their standard model. However, despite its unrealistic assumptions the spot-market model has been quite fruitfully applied to many 'real world' problems and in the absence of a more realistic alternative model which might lead to better results, it is still common practice in economics to build on this spot-market model.

The opposite of the spot-market is commonly called 'hierarchy'. Hierarchy is a system in which everything happens according to the order of a central agency that has the power to dictate: Thus, relationships are characterized by a certain asymmetry. In mainstream economics, firms serve as a standard example of hierarchies and, of course, so do the socialist 'command economies'. Yet, there is a problem in the hierarchy approach, a difficulty that is similar to the model of the spot-market: in the real world, we rarely find such hierarchies. In firms, for example, there is often competition between people and/or between departments, and the behavior of firms in many real-world cases has to be seen as the result of a number of decentralized decisions that may be influenced by top management only to a limited degree.

In standard economic theory the so-called 'transaction-cost approach' has become famous for dealing with the question of whether a certain good or service should be bought in a market or whether it should be provided internally, i.e. through the hierarchical form of organization. The initial version of this approach, as proposed by R. Coase (1937, 1989) and O.E. Williamson (1985, 1989) spot-market and hierarchy were the only alternatives. In recent years, however, the transaction-cost approach has been successfully applied to a number of interfirm relations which are located somewhere between the extremes of pure spot market and pure hierarchy.[6] Thus, the analytical tools of mainstream economics lead us to conclude that the spot-market is only one of several forms of the allocation mechanism that characterize a market economy.

---

5 For a detailed analysis of these implications of the 'spot-market' model see Macneil (1974 and 1978).

6 On the basis of this approach we may explain and analyze many real-world phenomena such as long-term R&D cooperation among firms, strategic alliances, cooperation and competition in industrial districts or in rather complex forms of supplier relations like those in the automobile industry (Saxenian, 1994; Fritsch, 1992, and the contributions in Grabher, 1993).

4.   The 'network' approach: 'embedded' markets

For several years the so-called 'network' approach to socio-economic behavior has gained increasing attention in the social sciences (Albach, 1994; Grabher, 1993; Hakansson and Johanson, 1993). The term 'network' approach characterizes several schools of research which aim at analyzing the 'social' dimension in the relationship between actors. The network approach evolved mainly in non-economic disciplines of the social sciences, e.g. sociology, political science, and social geography. Possibly, this variety of scientific cultures is one reason for the heterogeneity of concepts and definitions that characterize the discussion. The term 'network' itself is a good example of this diversity. In the relevant literature, one may find a large number of varying definitions of what the respective author understand to be a network and, frequently, these definitions also prove to be vague.[7]

One issue in the debate on the network approach is how far this approach is compatible with economic theory and the transaction-cost approach (cf. Johanson and Mattson, 1987). It is neither possible nor useful or enlightening to describe this discussion here in detail. However, it can be concluded that at least a considerable part of the phenomena that are dealt with in the network literature may be successfully analyzed on the basis of the economic approach to social behavior. This may be done particularly by combining the standard economic model with the transaction-cost approach. From this perspective, the non-spot markets of the real world appear to be 'embedded' not only in a legal framework which secures basic property rights, but also in specific types of social relations or a 'culture' of exchange (see Granovetter, 1985). Such an exchange culture encompasses, above all, often unwritten rules of behavior, which are commonly respected in a market. It also contains sanctions for actors who defect from these rules and behave opportunistically. In many cases such cultures need considerable time to develop. They normally emerge in markets where there is only a limited number of actors that know each other well and where defection from rules can easily be detected and sanctioned. Frequently, there are major socio-economic barriers to entry into such embedded markets. This may be either due to the fact that the main actors in the market belong to a specific ethnic group or that it is simply difficult to be accepted as trustworthy by the market participants, or that one needs specific tacit knowledge which is not easily accessible (cf. for example Carr and Landa, 1983). Clearly, trust and reputation are of central importance in such so-called 'relational' contracts. The past and the future matter, and a main reason for rational egoists not to behave in an opportunistic way is simply that they want to secure the once-established exchange relationship in order to make similar contracts in the future. Obviously, irreversible investment and the danger of sunk costs play a significant role here.

The main advantage of embedded markets is that they allow the economic units the sourcing out of activities to subcontractors that would have to be kept inside if there were only spot-markets. Embedded markets provide for an increased range of goods

---

7 See for example Aldrich, 1979; Antonelli, 1992; Hakansson and Johanson, 1993; Knoke and Kuklinski, 1982; Powell, 1990; Tichy, 1981, and Grabher, 1993.

allocated by the market mechanism. This, in turn, will induce a decrease in vertical integration, an intensified division of labor, and a higher degree of specialization which will probably result in welfare gains. Unfortunately, we still do not know much about the evolution of embedded markets and of exchange cultures in such markets. We also lack knowledge on the public and private institutions that are appropriate to stimulate the evolution of such markets.

There is, however, an important shortcoming which the model of perfect competition *and* the network approach have in common: they are both static approaches and, thus, not particularly suited to deal with such dynamic phenomena as innovation, growth, and market development. Nevertheless, the network approach may be a helpful tool to explain how and why markets develop into new organizational forms.

5. Markets and hierarchies in socialism

The socialist economies were not pure hierarchical systems. The classical socialist system was predominantly based on a bureaucratic (hierarchical) coordination and - to a lesser degree - on market coordination. This is illustrated by Table 2.1 which shows the input-output flows between the units of the various social sectors and makes clear that there was some kind of market coordination (Kornai, 1992 and 1995). There existed formal and informal markets. These markets differed from Western markets according to the culture, history and embeddedness. They emerged due to the specific characteristics of the socialist system.

Table 2.1 The role of bureaucratic and market coordination in socialism

Supply of specific social sector	Demand of specific social sector				
	1 State-owned firm	2 Cooperatives	3 Formal private sector	4 Informal private sector	5 Households as buyers of consumer goods and services
1. State-owned firms	B+IM	B+IM	B+IM	IM	B+FM+IM
2. Cooperation	B+IM	B+IM	B+IM	IM	B+FM+IM
3. Formal private sector	IM	IM	FM	IM	FM
4. Informal private sector	IM	IM	IM	IM	IM
5. Households as sellers of labor	B+FM	B+FM	FM	IM	IM

Note: The meanings of the symbols are as follows: B = bureaucratic coordination, FM = formal market coordination, IM = informal market coordination

The organizational form of the central hierarchy led to an imperfect coordination (Montias and Rose-Ackerman, 1981). Vertical channels of information dominated. Since it was costly and time-consuming to transmit all available information to the higher levels, much of the information was lost or distorted on its way up in the hierarchy. On the other hand, the lower levels, e.g. the enterprises, were flooded with information from above. Consequently, plans became inconsistent and forced managers to benign plan violation and, thus, to engage in hidden market activities (Brezinski 1985, 365). Besides plan inconsistencies there were blank spaces in the plan leaving some decisions to the managers of the enterprises and/or to the population (Haffner, 1978, 100). These blank spots in the plan concerned consumer goods for which the individuals had a choice among various kinds. To some extent it applied also to the labor market and to the kolkhoz markets. In addition, central planning was not as total as the leadership would have liked it to be. Consequently, there was room for market-type relations, especially in the consumer goods sector and the labor market. These relations were far from market relations in capitalist systems. The state controlled or limited such activities by imposing severe restrictions on the property rights in the enterprise sector. In general, private persons were neither allowed to control the assets of enterprises nor to appropriate the usufruct, nor sell or otherwise dispose of the enterprise. Even the small private enterprises faced an excavation of the private property rights. Socialist policy aimed at the creation of an egalitarian income distribution. Those who still were rich had to face heavy sanctions if their behavior deviated from the socialist norms. Because of these restrictions, the weak market relations had no major influence upon the allocation of resources.

The various reforms which began in 1956 continued particularly in the late sixties and focused on a market socialism which - varying from country to country - gave rise to official consumer goods markets and to parallel markets in the underground economy (Dallago, 1990; Andreff, 1993; Brezinski 1995). The parallel markets were seen as a relief from obvious shortcomings of the hierarchical coordination by central planning. These market forms, however, were not identical with spot-markets and also lacked the specific features of the real markets in Western economies. The Eastern markets were characterized by shortages, inputs except for labor were hardly available; demand for output exceeded supply. Only a minimum of capital was invested. Entrepreneurship was more or less non-productive (cf. Baumol, 1990; Arzeni, 1996) and consisted of entrepreneurs that were mainly aiming at arbitrage profits. The system of fixed prices of the socialist economies constituted the minimum price and, thus, reduced the entrepreneurial risk to zero. Barriers to entry to the market were high. Consequently, entrepreneurs benefitted from a monopoly situation and had only weak incentives to be innovative. Summing up, market activities deviated very much from markets in capitalist economies. They could hardly be regarded as a nucleus of a market economy (Brezinski, 1992; Brezinski and Fritsch, 1996; Arzeni, 1996).

6.   The process of transition

The question of how to manage the transition of the socio-economic system in the post-socialist countries to a Western type of market economy involves numerous problems that belong to the core of economic theory. Consequently, it is of central importance to analyze these processes not only in order to be able to assist and to ease the transformation process but also to gain valuable insight into the dynamic properties of specific markets and of entire socio-economic systems.

It has been argued that some important aspects of the transition to a market economy may be dealt with on the basis of the life-cycle model. This approach allows the conclusion that problems of market power and exploitation likely to appear in the early stages of a market can be overcome by lowering in some way the barriers to entry into the market or by encouraging entrepreneurship. It is also of importance to recognize that exits from the market are a quite normal phenomenon in a well-operating market mechanism and that economic policy should not try to prevent such exits. In some cases, there will probably be a need for competition-policy measures. But, in the early stages of this process, one should be rather cautious in applying such measures. The quality of a market mechanism should not be judged before a market has fully emerged. Clearly, there will be numerous 'imperfections' in the early phases of a market and markets may need considerable time until they produce satisfactory results. However, there is the danger that regulations may cure only temporary symptoms and that, as is known from experience, such measures, once implemented, are very difficult to abolish.

A second important issue that has been largely neglected by mainstream economics is the embeddedness of markets and the role of a market culture. In most real-world markets, unwritten rules, reputation and trust are highly important. The emergence of embedded markets which offer an opportunity for relational contracting takes time. Yet, even the establishment of new relations, i.e. the finding of suitable partners for transactions, may involve considerable transaction costs.[8] Most Western enterprises which look for investment opportunities in Eastern Europe have now realized that they can only successfully set up promising projects if their plants can be embedded into a framework of supplier relations in the respective country. Therefore, a certain degree of market coordination may be seen as a prerequisite for foreign direct investment that might be conducive to the desired transformation of the previous socialist economies (cf. Swaan, 1997). This may help to explain why in the recent past the process of foreign direct investment has developed so slowly in countries such as Poland.

The evolution of a market economy might be described as a process in which in the early stages market transactions are mainly of a spot-market type. With the emergence of a true market culture embedded exchange relations will begin to play an increasing role. This description, however, implies a start from scratch. By contrast, the

---

8 Swaan (1997) illustrates this problem of establishing transactions after the disintegration of the old system by "a hypothetical situation in which all consumers from Paris would be replaced by Londoners, while all producers, wholesale and retail companies from Paris would be replaced by companies from the Milano area. For quite some time Paris would be dominated by chaotic conditions and a serious fall in output as actors would lack any frame of reference to base their decisions upon."

emergence and evolution of markets in the post-socialist countries starts out from a specific level of economic activities. The old system had been based on long-established social and economic relations between actors that might well be described as 'networks'. This fact raises the question whether and to what extent this old 'social capital' can still be used and to how a brutal start from scratch, i.e. the total depreciation of this social capital, can be avoided. It also appears to be legitimate to ask whether certain networks, e.g. nomenclatura or mafia-type organizations, may be an obstacle to the process of erecting real markets.

Of central importance, finally, is, what means may stimulate the emergence of efficient markets. Experiences gained these days in the post-socialist countries will also prove to be relevant for economic policy in developed Western market economies which aim at increasing the efficiency of this system.

7. Outlook for future research

From our analysis we may derive the following agenda for future research which obviously will not have to concentrate on the prerequisites for the establishment of a market in post-socialist countries. On the contrary, the emergence and the dynamic evolution of markets will have to be analyzed in different contexts (e.g. regional, socio-economic, technological, political or historical). Current economic theory appears well-suited as a point of departure, and may well provide a number of hypotheses to be tested.

Some of the issues that seem of crucial importance for such research could be:

* the evolution of markets, market relations, competition, and allocative efficiency during the life-cycle;
* the evolution of rules, norms, and market culture in terms of efficiency and competitiveness;
* the role of economic policy in these processes aiming at minimising unavoidable market imperfections;
* possible market and policy failures;
* the evolution of institutions conducive to efficient markets.

Economics as a science is based on the conviction that the decentralized exchange of actors in general will lead to more welfare than central planning and bureaucracy. This agenda of research which definitively has to concentrate on the microeconomic sphere (Lavigne, 1995) could probably lead to a better understanding of markets as a mechanism of allocation and may help to improve our theory.

References

Albach, Horst (1994) *The Transformation of Firms and Markets - A Network Approach to Economic Transformation Processes in East Germany*, Stockholm: Alquis & Wiksell.

Aldrich, Howard (1979) *Organizations and Environments*, Englewood Cliffs: Prentice Hall.

Andreff, Wladimir (1993) *La crise des économies socialistes: la rupture d'un système*, Grenoble: Presses Universitaires de Grenoble.

Antonelli, Cristiano (1992) The Economic Analysis of Information Networks, in Antonelli, Cristiano (ed.) *The Economics of Information Networks*, Amsterdam: North Holland, 5-28.

Arzeni, Sergio (1996) Entrepreneurship in Eastern Europe: a critical view, in Brezinski, Horst and Michael Fritsch (eds) *The Economic Impact of New Firms in Post-Socialist Countries: Bottom Up Transformation in Eastern Europe*, Aldershot: Edward Elgar Publishers, 53-59.

Baumol, William J. (1990); Entrepreneurship: Productive, Unproductive, and Destructive; *Journal of Political Economy*, 98, 893-921.

Brezinski, Horst (1985) The Second Economy in the Soviet Union and its Implications for Economic Policy, in Gaertner, Wulf and Alois Wenig (eds) *The Economics of the Shadow Economy*, Berlin, New York: Springer, 363-376.

Brezinski, Horst (1992); Privatization in East Germany; *Moct - Most*, 2, 3-21.

Brezinski, Horst (1995) "Schattenwirtschaft, Osteuropa", in Nohlen, Dieter (ed.) *Handwörterbuch: Politik und Wirtschaft*, München: Hanser, 665-670.

Brezinski, Horst and Michael Fritsch (1996) The bottom-up strategy to transformation: summary and policy conclusions, in Brezinski, Horst and Michael Fritsch (eds) *The Economic Impact of New Firms in Post-Socialist Countries: Bottom Up Transformation in Eastern Europe*, Aldershot: Edward Elgar Publishers, 253-262.

Brüderl, Josef and Rudolf Schüssler (1990); Organizational Mortality: The Liability of Newness and Adolescence; *Administrative Science Quarterly*, 35, 530-547.

Brüderl, Josef, Peter Preisendörfer and Rolf Ziegler (1992); Survival Chances of Newly Founded Business Organizations; *American Sociological Review*, 57, 227-242.

Carr, Jack L. and Janet T. Landa (1983); The Economics of Symbols, Clan Names, and Religion; *Journal of Legal Studies*, 12, 135-156.

Coase, Ronald H. (1937); The Nature of the Firm; *Economica*, 4, 386-405.

Coase, Ronald H. (1989) *The Firm, the Market, and the Law*, Chicago: University of Chicago Press.

Dallago, Bruno (1990) *The Irregular Economy and the Black Labor Market*, Aldershot: Dartmouth.

Freeman, John, Glenn R. Carroll and Michael T. Hannan (1983); The Liability of Newness: Age Dependence in Organizational Death Rates; *American Sociological Review*, 48, 692-710.

Fritsch, Michael (1992) Unternehmens-"Netzwerke" im Lichte der Institutionenökonomik, in Boettcher, Erik, Philipp Herder-Dorneich, Karl-Ernst Schenk and

Dieter Schmidtchen (eds) *Jahrbuch für Neue Politische Ökonomie*, 11, Tübingen: Mohr/Siebeck, 89-102.

Fritsch, Michael (1996); Turbulence and Growth in West-Germany: A Comparison of Evidence by Regions and Industries; *Review of Industrial Organization*, 11, 231-251.

Goglio, Silvio (1997) The concept of market from a historical point of view, in this volume.

Grabher, Gernot (1993) Rediscovering the social in the economics of interfirm relations, in Grabher, Gernot (ed.) *The Embedded Firm - On the socioeconomics of industrial networks*, London, New York: Routledge, 1-31.

Granovetter, Mark (1985); Economic Action and Social Structure: The Problem of Social Embeddedness; *American Journal of Sociology*, 6, 481-510.

Gros, Daniel and Alfred Steinherr (1995) *Winds of Change - Economic Transition in Central and Eastern Europe*, London, New York: Longman.

Haffner, Friedrich (1978) *Systemkonträre Beziehungen in der sowjetischen Planwirtschaft*, Berlin: Duncker und Humblot.

Hakansson, Hakan and Jan Johanson (1993) The network as a governance structure: interfirm cooperation beyond markets and hierarchies, in Grabher, Gernot (ed.) *The Embedded Firm - On the socioeconomics of industrial networks*, London, New York: Routledge, 35-51.

Hansen, Knut (1994); Wettbewerbsschutz in Mittel-/Osteuropa - Zum Beitrag des Kartellrechts für den Übergang zur Marktwirtschaft; *Wirtschaft und Wettbewerb*, 44, 1002-1012.

Hodgson, Geoffrey M. (1988) *Economics and Institutions*, Cambridge: Polity Press.

Johanson, Jan and Lars G. Mattson (1987); Interorganizational Relations in Industrial Systems: A Network Approach Compared with the Transaction-Cost Approach; *International Studies of Management and Organization*, 17, 34-48.

Jovanovic, Boyan and Glenn M. MacDonald (1994); The Life-cycle of a Competitive Industry; *Journal of Political Economy*, 102, 322-347.

Klepper, Steven and Elizabeth Graddy (1990); The Evolution of New Industries and the Determinants of Market Structure; *Rand Journal of Economics*, 21, 27-44.

Klepper, Steven and Ken L. Simons (1993) *Technological Change and Industry Shakeouts*, Pittsburgh: Carnegie Mellon University.

Knoke, David and James Kuklinski (1982) *Network Analysis*, Beverly Hills, London, New Delhi: Sage.

Kornai, Janos (1992) *The Socialist System*, Princeton: Princeton University Press.

Kornai, Janos (1995) *Highway and Byways - Studies on Reform and Postcommunist Transition*, Cambridge, Mass. and London: The MIT Press.

Lavigne, Marie (1995) *The Economics of Transition*, London: Macmillan.

Macneil, Ian R. (1974); The many futures of contracts; *Southern California Law Review*, 47, 691-816.

Macneil, Ian R. (1978); Contracts: Adjustment of Long-term Economic Relations under Classical, Neoclassical and Relational Contract Law; *Northwestern University Law Review*, 72, 854-905.

Montias, John M., Avner Ben-Ner and Egon Neuberger (1994) *Comparative Economics*, Chur: Harwood Academic Publishers.

Montias, John M. and Susann Rose-Ackerman (1981) Corruption in a Soviet-type Economy: Theoretical Considerations, in Rosefielde, Steven (ed.) *Economic Welfare and the Economics of Soviet Socialism*, Cambridge: Cambridge University Press, 53-83.

North, Douglass C. (1990) *Institutions, institutional change and economic performance*, Cambridge, Mass., Cambridge University Press.

Powell, Walter (1990); Neither market nor hierarchy: Network forms of organization; *Research in Organizational Behavior*, 12, 295-336.

Saxenian, Annalee (1994) *Regional Advantage*, Cambridge, Mass.: Harvard University Press.

Stiglitz, Joseph E. (1993) *Principles of Micro-Economics*, New York: W.W. Norton.

Swaan, Wim (1997) Knowledge, transaction costs and the creation of markets in post-socialist economies: preliminary remarks, in this volume.

Tichy, Gunther (1991); The product-cycle revisited: some extensions and clarifications; *Zeitschrift für Wirtschafts- und Sozialwissenschaften*, 111, 27-54.

Tichy, Noel (1981) Networks in organizations, in Nystrom, Paul C. and William H. Starbuck (eds) *Handbook of Organizational Designs*, I, New York and Oxford: Oxford University Press, 225-249.

Williamson, Oliver E. (1985) *The Economic Institutions of Capitalism: Firms, Markets, Relational Contracting*, New York: The Free Press.

Williamson, Oliver E. (1989) Transaction Cost Economics, in Schmalensee, Richard and Robert Willig (eds) *Handbook of Industrial Organization*, I, Amsterdam: North-Holland, 135-182.

3 The concept of market from a historical point of view[*]

Silvio Goglio

1. The notion of market

'Market' is today one of the terms most frequently used in the economic and political lexicon, both in descriptions of modern Western economies and in proposals for the institutional and organizational restructuring of the countries of the Third World and the ex-Soviet bloc. It is a usage which undoubtedly comprises a good deal of validity, but it also contains a number of analytical inaccuracies, a certain historical confusion, and a latent - but nevertheless powerful - cultural ethnocentrism.

Analytically, the concept of *market* may refer to several, only apparently associated, phenomena:

- a specific *organization*[1] which governs transactions: primitive and peasant markets, the wholesale markets for certain goods, stock markets, specialized auctions, etc.;
- a complex *institution*[2] which has evolved over time into a dense network of rights, incentives and behavioral norms; it may more properly be called a *market system* or *economy;*
- a culture which extols the advantages deriving from the coordination of economic transactions according to the principles of free exchange;
- a *stylization* of free exchange relations, i.e. an ideal mechanism which generates Pareto-optimal solutions.

A *market-as-organization* coordinates a number of agents who cooperate within an already-given structure of the division of labor. It may assume patterns which vary according to the institutional system, to the rights and incentives that derive from it, to the goals that individuals set for themselves, and to the characteristics of the goods and services exchanged. Participation is less binding than in other organizational forms,

---

[*] This article summarizes a number of hypotheses and conclusions set out in Goglio (1994), to which the reader is referred for more detailed arguments and bibliographical references.

1 By 'organizations' I mean networks of social relations, contracts in particular, explicitly created by people to achieve their goals, while their resources, information and expertise are pooled and risk is shared.

2 'Institutions' are sets of interrelated rules governing given aspects of social life which are acknowledged (sanctioned) by all or some members of society. Institutions are founded on norms. By defining rules of behavior, institutions regulate the relationships among individuals, i.e. their rights and duties, and hence the costs and benefits of social action. They thus provide a detailed map of the advantages deriving from known types of exchange, i.e. of their incentives and deterrents.

because contracts tend to comprise a restricted number of transactions and because the market's inner dialectic favors *exit*.[3] Its efficiency stems from the provision of high-powered incentives - that is, property rights on profits and losses - whereas other organizations offer only low-powered ones (cf. Williamson, 1986).

Since the market relies mainly on prices to convey information, it limits the information required to make a choice, and restricts the complexity of the context of exchange. This operation, however, may be imperfect, as demonstrated by the systematic occurrence of market 'failures'.[4] The inability of prices to control the peculiar nature of the cognitive processes and the inter-individual communication necessary to activate economic exchange may mean that the contract fails to give sufficiently clear specification to the terms of every transaction: namely nature, subject, time and conditions.

As an organization, the market involves operational and transaction costs which accrue unequally to the participants in the exchange. If, in order to reduce the risks of opportunistic behavior consequent on uncertainty, these costs prove greater than those deriving from other organizations, the latter will be preferred.[5] In general, the market becomes less viable - i.e., transaction costs will be higher - the more knowledge and rationality are scarce, the more the resources involved are specific and therefore limited, and the more private interests prevail over observance of the law in contractual relations (cf. Williamson, 1986).

Market contracts may in fact leave broad margins of uncertainty, thereby creating disincentives for exchange. They thus require the backing of an ideology and an ethic which create a motivating and reassuring environment, as well as measures of contract enforcement. For the market to function, therefore, non-market organizational apparatuses are necessary.

A market system comes about when the coordination of essential economic elements (final and intermediate goods and services, capital goods, financial capital, labor, land and information) relies largely on interconnected markets. This is a pragmatic mechanism which arose concurrently with the nation-states and which is now expanding - albeit with some difficulty - into an ever broader international market. However, it is not exhaustive. On the one hand, primitive and/or less developed economies make scant use of it, while, on the other hand, a large proportion of exchanges in market economies themselves are carried out within other organizational forms. These organizational forms, moreover, do not always regulate transactions among themselves via the market. Nevertheless, the market system is the device most commonly employed by the modern

---

3 As the term is used by Hirschman (1970).

4 A 'market failure' is a situation in which the transaction costs arising from use of the market are greater than those deriving from alternative organizational forms.

5 These preferences are never definitive, however, because "the costs of carrying out exchange transactions through the price mechanism will vary considerably, as will the costs of organizing these transactions within the firm": for instance, "most inventions will change both the costs of organizing and the costs of using the price mechanism." Coase (1937, 45f., note 31).

industrial world, given its ability to reduce and to localize information and calculation (cf. Simon, 1981).

Obviously, there are no perfect market systems. Firstly, because individual markets cannot be perfectly competitive and transmit information perfectly. Secondly, historically, the reality of market systems is that prices and the allocation of land, labor, and capital have been influenced by factors extraneous to the economic system. For instance, even in conditions of great geographical mobility and high labor turnover, emotional, relational, cultural, political and technical factors are still decisive in the labor market. These are factors which endow the parties involved (often, but not always, employers) with informal and formal power that hinders every attempt to bargain on an equal footing, thereby attenuating the effects of mobility on supply and demand.

Certain institutional and structural conditions must be fulfilled for a market system to develop. A first condition is the transferability and alienability of private property. This gives rise to the greater specialization of such property and to the narrower concentration of its consequent benefits and costs.[6] A second condition is that individuals must feel that they are, to some extent, protected against behavior which seeks private gain at collective expense. Such reassurance requires institutional and cultural guarantees that asymmetries in knowledge, information and power will not render excessively unequal situations permanent. Institutional guarantees, in particular, should ensure that deviant behavior will be punished and that opportunism will be deterred, if possible, or that it will at least be curbed. Cultural guarantees, which rest on assumptions that are not necessarily scientifically proven, should induce individuals to regard market relations as by and large advantageous and trustworthy. These two sets of guarantees obviously operate jointly, and they reciprocally influence each other.

A culture may be viewed as a set of categories, interpretative schemata, and values. It constitutes, that is, a reference framework within which phenomena can be located and interpreted, and courses of action plotted. The term *market culture* refers to that body of scientific analyses, ideologies and beliefs which interpret economic and social reality and base such interpretation on the concept - more or less ambiguously defined - of 'market', thereby justifying certain types of behavior and organization. By postulating the market as the central form of economic organization, it tends to generalize its characteristics to the entire economic system; that is, it envisages a clear division of economic roles among players and views market exchange as tying specialized players together, with competition as the only incentive to productivity, and an external law (of the state) as the only efficient guarantee that the system will work properly.

This alleged *conceptual centrality* of the market generates the notion that this form of organization is 'natural'; and equally natural, in the sense of innate and spontaneous, is the behavior on which it rests. Research on the motivations for such behavior therefore loses significance, to the advantage of scientific demonstration of its advantages. It is the existence of exceptions that instead requires explanation. The justification for

---

6 "Under public ownership the costs of any decision or choice are less fully thrust upon the selector than under private property." Alchian (1977, 146).

alternative organizational forms, however, is based on market features and on the 'external' constraints that prevent it from working efficiently. One may also infer, as most of liberal historiography has done, the *historical centrality* of the market, as a substantially teleological process whereby every given historical pattern is interpreted as one further shift closer to a natural center of gravity, rather than as the outcome of randomness and incremental evolution.

Although this approach has the undoubted advantage of breaking economic behavior down into its constituent elements, it fails to account for the actual behavior of complex organizations and for the most important economic structural changes that occurred, for example, in the last century. This is because it tends to reduce the household to a mere unit of consumption and the supplier of productive factor services. Moreover, this approach reduces the firm merely to its productive function, ignoring a complex organizational structure that is analogous to a community with internal institutions, agreements, norms, customs and composite goals. Finally, this approach reduces the state (or, more generally, public organizations) to a mere guarantor of compliance with market agreements and fails to account for the state's expression of an alternative economic vision.

In economic theory, by *perfectly competitive market* is meant an idealized set of relations which governs exchange. The distinctive feature of this mechanism is that it provides Pareto-optimal solutions for allocative, productive and distributive problems. This theoretical representation, as furnished by general equilibrium theory, is the only rigorous solution to the problem of the optimal organization of an economy. The argument that the chasm between the actual solution and possible historical realizations of the market is unbridgeable constitutes the most persuasive evidence against the contention that free market exchange is generally superior to other institutional and organizational forms. And, it must be remembered, that it only requires imperfect knowledge and/or information and/or computation, i.e. transaction costs, for this unbridgeable gap to spread (cf. Coase, 1937). The conditions that ensure the optimal (only in the Paretian sense) economic regulation based on free exchange, therefore, can never be entirely fulfilled. Any historical configuration assumed by the market must inevitably be 'imperfect' with respect to these idealized optimal conditions. These imperfect solutions (and which are not perfectible beyond a certain limit) are, therefore, in competition against other, equally imperfect, organizational and institutional solutions.

Theoretical analysis of the market and the market culture have common origins in laissez-faire utilitarian theory and in the writings of the classical economists. The link, however, is only partial: on the one side stands the solution to an abstract problem while, on the other, an ideology. Their common origins do not mean that the solution to the problem is part of the ideology itself. Indeed, what is ideological, and as such is part of the market culture, is the use to which the results of the theory can be put. Using the solution demonstrated to be optimal in a particular abstract context as a benchmark for assessment of real alternative solutions to the market is based in ideology alone.

2. The conditions that generated the modern market

Throughout most of human history, economic behavior has been confined to a non-economic context, and coordinated by institutions and organizations which have been mainly communitarian, cultural and political in nature, such as kin, the religious apparatus, the fief, the state, and so on. Economic destiny was a collective fact. Solidarity, which came about through symmetrical and redistributive behavior, was an essential component of society and economic behavior was tied more to status than to individual interest.

The predominant economic cultural environment was encapsulated by the term *moral economy*,[7] that is, the conception of economic survival as a collective problem. It originated from the fear that, in a context in which output was just enough to ensure survival, opportunism, uncertainty and asymmetries in knowledge and power would threaten the survival of the community itself. Individual affirmation through economic competition was viewed as a zero sum game which might endanger the group.[8] At the institutional and organizational level, the social system was culturally conceived (which is not to imply that it was always such in reality!) as a defense against both an external predator, a not easily identifiable alien, and an internal one. This gave rise to the rigid regulation of economic exchanges designed to prevent individual gain at the expense of the community.

Since profiting at the expense of the opposite party by exploiting his/her need was expressly forbidden, an increase in demand was not allowed to induce an increase in price. Equivalences were therefore essentially a question of custom and tradition, in that the transactions in which they were used were motivated by a form of solidarity, that is, by the necessity that the economic units should compensate for active and passive surpluses to guarantee their survival.[9]

A typical expression of a cultural context of this kind was the concept of 'just price', an equivalence fixed by the authorities "according to determinants relevant to the concrete social situation" (Polanyi, 1977, 72). This was the price deemed to be just relative to the equilibrium of a given society, so that equivalences reflected advantages tied to status and, consequently, those incomes "required to maintain existing social relations and values" (Polanyi, 1977, 71). The just price made it possible to lift "the

---

7 The term "moral economy" was first used by the historian E. P. Thompson, as a merging of certain concepts from cultural anthropology with political economy, Marxist in particular. In Thompson's definition - which was probably more narrow than that used here - an economic system is 'moral' when the interests of the family and of the community prevail over the acquisitive instincts of individuals. Cf. Thompson (1971).

8 Great fortunes were amassed by individuals outside their own group by means of warfare, pillage or trade. This is a context in which labor productivity is not regarded as important, and the productivity of the land is regarded as practically constant. A typical case of a society rigidly organized on these principles was, until a few years ago, the Bedouin tribes of the Arabian and North African desert.

9 This exchange, which restores self-sufficiency to economic units, is explicitly mentioned both in the Jewish Old Testament and in Aristotle's Politics, where it is called 'natural commerce'. Cf. Polanyi (1977, 68-69).

tribal ban on transactions by criminating the stigma of gain, with its disruptive implications",[10] and allowing the advantages of exchanges to be reaped without subverting the social order.

If more thorough analysis of the process of market formation[11] is to be conducted, however, it is not enough to show that, in the past as well, physical sites called markets existed, that they used money, and that they talked about prices, to demonstrate the existence of organized institutional structures conceptually similar to those of today, or even to those hypothesized in economic theory. Market, price and money often assumed meanings other than those conventionally attributed to them, and they belonged to social and economic mechanisms different from modern ones. Forgetting this may provoke misunderstanding of these economies, as well as the social foundations on which they rested.[12]

Given that communications systems and forms of payment were limited, the market of antiquity was primarily the physical site of exchange and consequently also the activity that went on there[13] in compliance with the rules deemed appropriate by the authorities. Prices were rarely left free to fluctuate. These relationships were part of an exchange administered with fixed equivalences established by agreements and/or tradition. There is an evident difference here from the modern concept of market, which not only requires that demand and supply should lead to price formation, and that buyers and sellers should be interchangeable and independent of other institutions and status situations, but also, and especially, that the social system should be coherent with these presuppositions.

Marketplaces were born with very restricted dimensions and purposes, with often precarious physical structures, in order to facilitate the exchange of consumption goods -

---

10 Polanyi (1977, 74): "From the early Assyrian trade colonies, the laws of Eshnunna and the Code of Hammurabi, down to the Mishna and the Babylonian Talmud of some 2 500 years later; indeed, up to the time of Thomas Aquinas, if not considerably longer, the just price remained the only rate at which transactions were deemed legitimate." The last and most sophisticated justification for the just price was formulated by the Scholastics.

11 The two most familiar explanations of market formation are those proposed by Adam Smith and Karl Polanyi. According to Smith, "the division of labor at a local and regional level generates the need for markets"; therefore "market trade is universal insofar as scarce goods are always allocated by some system in which supply and demand are brought into equilibrium by the relative values attached to goods of different scarcity". According to Polanyi, "markets are initiated by long-distance trade contacts" and market trade is "a rather 'unnatural' human activity that requires certain specific conditions to develop forces exogenous to the domestic economy: trade is compartmentalized to begin with at places where economic maximization will not threaten the social order." Hodges (1988, 77).

12 For instance, "In primitive trade, the path to economic equilibrium lay not across the play of autonomous individuals and firms fixing a price through the parallel contentions of buyers and sellers. It began rather from the interdiction of competition within the community of either, traversed a structure of institutional arrangements that with varying facility brought together partners mutually obliged to be generous, upon separating those not so inclined, to negotiate in the end an analogous 'price'. The similarity to market trade appears when abstraction is made of all this." Sahlins, quoted in Hodges (1988, 13).

13 In Latin, the word *mercatus* referred both to the activity and the place of commerce. City squares of medieval origin bear the names of markets still today: "Haymarket", "Fishmarket", etc.

food especially - within less affluent social groups. They therefore performed a function greater than self-consumption or centralized distribution. Very often these marketplaces were created and protected by the authorities, which regarded them as instruments of alimentary and economic policy, ensuring that they conducted exchange properly while rigidly controlling conditions of entry to them and their operation.[14]

An example is provided by central and northern Italy in the Middle Ages. In the pre-communal age, the prices of many goods were fixed within the feudal organization by the landed seigneury, which controlled production and distribution. These prices, "often traditional and fixed once and for all, belonged to a system of social relations founded on the exercise of power" (Tucci, 1983, 335). When the commune achieved political and economic dominance, "integration with the productive activities of the countryside assumed different forms, but relationships did not substantially change". It was now the city that "monopolized distribution and used the prices of food and labor to control the production factors, adjusting the system's mechanisms by means of mercantilist policies. The rates of exchange between agricultural products and artisan and industrial products were influenced by powerful corporatist organizations, and the labor supply was disciplined accordingly" (Tucci, 1983, 335). Consequently, the oscillations in supply due to the weakness of the agricultural system were subjected to the rigidity of demand, which required prices to be kept as constant as possible. The outcome was that "the expenditure of a considerable part of the population was more decisively determined by political prices than by market ones".[15]

What we have here, therefore, are mixed economies controlled by aristocracies which wielded twofold power: over the urban population by regulating the labor market and nonagricultural wages, mostly in exporting sectors and over the countryside by regulating the prices of the foodstuffs upon which the urban labor force depended. In a social organization of this kind prices were the expression of a system of control. Together with the parallel practices of tax exemption, of import subsidies, and of public purchasing, they constituted an instrument of central planning which pervaded numerous sectors of political and social life.

The expansion of behaviors and forms of economic integration based on free market exchange has been a slow and difficult process, one that has been anything but "natural". It has required not only the overthrowing of previous institutions and organizations, but a recasting of cultural context as well.

It has been a process entailing, first, the freeing of humankind from the fear that its collective survival is at risk. This liberation was a product of major structural changes, notably the agricultural revolution, the industrial revolution and the transport revolution, which greatly reduced threats to the community. Second, a massive operation of social engineering has been necessary. The laissez-faire doctrine hostile to intervention by the state resulted, as Polanyi observed, in neglect of the fact that "the emergence of national

---

14 According to Polanyi (1977), this was also the case for the marketplaces of Ancient Greece.

15 Tucci (1983, 330). In the mid-14th century, the city of Florence monopolized the food supply, "granting a certain amount of freedom to commerce only in periods of surplus"; that is, when this was to the advantage of the system.

markets was in no way the result of the gradual and spontaneous emancipation of the economic sphere from the governmental control. On the contrary, the market has been the outcome of a conscious and often violent intervention on the part of government which imposed the market organization on society for noneconomic ends".[16] Finally, institutional change has created a specific culture base grounded on individual values and rights, however much these may be constrained by correctives which take account of common rights.

Although the self-regulating market undoubtedly made it possible to eliminate a series of cumbersome rigidities, inertias and restraints in pre-industrial society which were at odds with and constrained the new productive system, it led to the triumph of individualism and to the crisis of social solidarity.[17] This explains why, geographical differences notwithstanding, the development of market systems has been neither a linear nor a progressive process; it has been hampered by rethinking and fierce opposition. And needless to say, nothing even approaching a pure market society has ever been accomplished.[18]

Acceptance of this manner of coordinating economic exchange and its underlying culture has never been total. Indeed, approval of it varies widely even within market societies themselves. Not for all goods and factors is the market system deemed conducive to collective well-being. Anti-individualistic community relations have frequently been encouraged in order to moderate it. After a period of comparative neglect, at least since the beginning of the last century until the First World War, the social question - which is ultimately about the distribution of wealth and property - has once again become an issue of major importance.[19] The moral obligation thus arises that all citizens (belonging to the community, to the region, to the state, and even beyond) must be provided with a socially guaranteed 'minimum' that prevents some of them from being caught up in a spiral of poverty and forming a caste of pariahs on the margins of the "affluent" society. This necessarily entails altering one of the fundamental features of the current form of the market by intervening in the social conditions of risk (Meade,

---

16 Polanyi (1968, 250). Whereas in situations of reciprocity, of autarky and of redistribution, economic relationships are regulated by the status of the parties concerned, i.e. by manifold and stable functions, in the market, relationships are regulated by contracts worked out for specific transactions. For this to be possible, the economy must be detached from the institutions and organizations of which it was previously a part.

17 Typical of a society in which it is evident that wealth results from labor and its specialization, and that productivity can be increased by competition and technical and organizational innovations, this rests on the assumption that "every human activity and almost every feature of the natural world can be readily categorized according to its potential place in a market system". Almost inevitably, the demands of the market disrupt the harmony of the ends of all human activity, "subordinating all other ends of an activity to the terms of a real or hypothetical exchange". Hence derives the difficulty of analyzing many aspects of economic organization (e.g. the economic role of the household) because production, exchange and consumption must be kept sharply distinct. Cf. Reddy (1984, 12-13).

18 Contrary to what Polanyi (1968) believes.

19 "The triumph of free exchange in Europe was as spectacular as it was short-lived, and it was speedily replaced not only by a revived protectionist policy against foreign competition, but also by efforts to reduce competition on internal markets", (North, 1984, 120).

1989, xii) and reviving certain essential values of the moral economy in order to search for new solutions.

3. Why did deregulation start in the eighteenth century?

Until 1300, in Europe, less than half of output was exchanged in specialized sites, such as markets held in village squares (usually once a week), markets in city squares (more frequently), and occasional large-scale trade fairs as international market squares. Although it was possible to discern the first signs of the labor and land markets, these were not comparable in size to those for manufactured goods, agricultural produce and raw materials, all of which were controlled by the political, municipal or corporative authorities (Dalton, 1974, 242).

Lacking in most of society was the stimulus and sanction of competition. In particular, quality/price ratios were different from those that would arise with the market. Distribution may have been much less unequal than might be deduced from the distribution of monetary incomes and more egalitarian than in a market system with a corresponding level of income. Social aspects predominated in transactions. For instance, mechanisms of reciprocity were deliberately imprecise, and systematic transfers, disguised as variable cost transactions, were made to weaker members of the community. This greater distributive equity could have had deleterious effects on development, giving rise to a rate of growth of output and productivity below that potentially achievable by the system, because it dispersed resources and created disincentives to attempts to increase productivity and production under the stimulus of profit.

The rise of nation-states partly altered this situation by fostering the numerical growth of local markets.[20] However, as Polanyi observed, this did not bring any radical change: "the towns raised every possible obstacle to the formation of that national or internal market for which the capitalist wholesaler was pressing" (Polanyi, 1968, 65); moreover, as Polanyi concluded, "the 'freeing' of trade performed by mercantilism merely liberated trade from particularism, but at the same time extended the scope of regulation" (Polanyi, 1968, 67). But to prevent misunderstanding of this picture of Europe between the fifteenth and nineteenth centuries, it is important to stress "the distinction between a Self-Regulating Market System and a number of markets more or less free to regulate themselves, but in sum not constituting a Self-Regulating System".[21]

---

20 "In no case did long-distance trade give way to regional marketing. Instead, peasant markets appear to have been formulated as a calculated political strategy, as part and parcel of the dynastic aspirations embodied in the new nation states" (Hodges, 1988, 95).

21 Neale (1957, 370). "Taking this period ... we find that typically product markets tended insofar as they could to approximate the Self-Regulating Market, but were subject to controls of varying efficiency and importance, while Factor Markets in the economist's sense had not come into existence, except for the Capital Market. The situation was logically (and in this case historically) a stage between non-supply-demand-price Market Places and a supply-demand-price Self-Regulating Market."

Throughout the period leading up to the Industrial Revolution, demand, given the importance of self-consumption, was restricted and difficult to specify. The greatest spender and generator of demand was still the state. "Since the real income of wage-earners declined in the early modern period, it is not possible to state without qualification that they created a growing market, given the fall in the purchasing power; on the other hand, the increase in numbers in urban centers certainly boosted consumer demand. Since the bulks of goods entering international trade, particularly in textiles, were luxury items catering to the needs of the elite, the expansion of trade was itself a guide to demand; few traded where consumers could not buy." (Kamen, 1984, 91)

This situation was reflected in the scant importance of money in everyday life.[22] The monetary economy was still in the process of formation, and in rural areas it was still rudimentary: "credit may well have played a larger part than cash transactions in the ordinary activities of agricultural producers" (Kamen, 1984, 67) and "the peasantry paid their dues in the shape of labor services, and received their wages in kind rather than cash".[23] Nor did the upper rural classes, who were principally concerned about increasing their landed property or about accumulating credit, have many relations with money, whose distribution remained "confined largely to the urban and the upper trading classes, and was excluded in general from the lives of the common people and the countryside" (Kamen, 1984, 68).

One of the major obstacles against the growth of a market system in the modern sense was raised by the guilds and the food institutions. After emerging in the twelfth century with the rise of new social classes, the guilds introduced new and diverse forms of labor exploitation based on a combination of class solidarity with the control and mediation of social conflicts within the world of artisan production.[24] Subsequently described as bulwarks against market forces, to contemporaries guilds were a defense of moral correctness. "No one thought of guilds as aimed at preventing the differentiation of a distinct social function (entrepreneurship); instead they saw any deviation from guild production standards as morally suspect, as fraudulent behavior aimed at fooling the customer." (Reddy, 1984, 35f).

One of the chief reasons for the stubborn defense of the guilds, even when they were economically outmoded, was that membership in them conferred a status independent of

---

22 The tendency to economize on money increased its purchasing power and favored those who supplied goods and services under market conditions or who at any rate had a monetary income (cf. Grossi, 1990, 14).

23 Kamen (1984, 68). "Barter and exchange still had inordinate importance in some regions, and in entire areas (such as in Sweden) metallic money was not used as a medium of exchange." (Ibid., 67).

24 "From the point of view of productive development, it is evident that the internal protection provided by the crafts guilds, various forms of solidarity and welfare, the restrictions imposed by the standardization of products and control over supplies, prices and wages, were all elements essential for the expansion of the artisan economy in conditions of an underdeveloped labor force and social inferiority to aristocrats and merchants" (Cammarosano, 1978, 499). Consequently, "in no case can one accept, as an interpretative criterion, the back-dating performed in the eighteenth and nineteenth centuries", when this organization was described as feudal and inefficient. There is a danger that feudalism may be considered "as a distinct method of production which characterized eleven (or more) centuries of European economic history" (ibid., 508).

occupation: destroying the guild created isolated and defenseless individuals.[25] Until 1600, "it was in the local communities that the social life and solidarities of a European were concentrated" (Kamen, 1984, 16). As observed by Kamen, "whatever the nature of the bond, the sense of 'belonging', the feeling of 'solidarity', was always intense and profound. Community feeling, of a sort seldom experienced today in our more individualistic world, was indeed perhaps the most powerful social force in early modern Europe. All human activity was judged by norms created by the community." (Kamen, 1984, 17). In short, according to Kamen, "the community and the village assembly played a crucial role in all aspects of economic and social life."[26]

Food policy, too, was a complex and heterogeneous institutional structure set up to distribute foodstuffs.[27] Like the cities of antiquity, those of the Middle Ages and the Renaissance city were particularly sensitive to the problem of food supply, since it was a danger to their autonomy. To avert this threat, the cities of northern Europe developed systems to regulate local markets. Although the Italian cities also used these means, their greater political and economic power enabled them to exert direct control over the countryside and its agricultural production.[28]

Intervention by the authorities in the food trade, especially commerce in corn, was "designed to restrict initiatives by private individuals, producers and merchants" (Zanetti, 1964, 42) by forbidding exports, attracting outside production, eliminating intermediaries, imposing transparency (all bargaining was to be conducted in the market square), stabilizing prices in the city market (towards a 'just' price rather than a political one, i.e., by fixing a ceiling price which to a certain extent reflected the real situation), and releasing public reserve stocks[29] in order to cushion against fluctuations in the external market. However, although the various Italian and European food supply systems may have resembled each other, the forms taken by the bodies administering the market in various localities displayed "specific features according to political and social equilibria and to productive capacities" (Malanima, quoted in Guenzi, 1978, 358, note 57).

"The right to be fed had solid political origins. The burghers of medieval Europe had fashioned a clanking, cumbersome but operative system of inspection and control." (Tilly, 1975, 428). The inspiration behind legislation intended to prevent the rise of intermediaries and the activities of speculators by bringing peasant and city-dweller into direct contact, was wholly the urban consumer's need to obtain supplies at low prices:

---

25 "A life of work is a complex, multidimensional experience" which falls outside market categories: hence the attachment to the corporation which comprised such experience (Reddy, 1984, 330).

26 Kamen, 1984, 18.

27 Provisioning policy comprised all agricultural products as well as cattle (cf. Pult Quaglia, 1982, 192).

28 Cf. Miskimin (1975, 77-81). "From the earliest years of their formation, the communes included in their statutes norms intended to improve the exploitation of landed property" by imposing specific crops and soil-management methods (cf. Zanetti, 1964, 40). "In no case was [the price] determined by the simple interplay of demand and supply, on either the market of origin or of arrival." (Fazio, 1990, 664).

29 Stocks were accumulated by taxation, the confiscation of private hoards, external purchases using public money or subscriptions.

"It could work quite effectively so long as cities were small enough to supply themselves from their own immediate hinterlands, and so long as they retained political and economic control of the hinterland" (Tilly, 1975, 429).

Also the nation states, caught up as they were by the expansion of the great cities, of the urban proletariat and of the government apparatus, soon found themselves forced to intervene in the production and, especially, distribution of food until nearly the nineteenth century.[30] Although this was initially an extension of the procedures adopted by the cities, methods and motivations later diversified. The growth of an urban, mercantile and manufacturing population required the creation of an agricultural surplus and its diversion to the cities. The creation of a state apparatus (army, bureaucracy) required in turn that the state should assume greater responsibility for food supplies. Control over the production, consumption and distribution of foodstuffs was made necessary by the fact that the bulk of a country's resources were of agricultural origin.

By the eighteenth century, the market economy was still not firmly established in Europe. Although in decline, the guilds continued to operate on the continent. In food supply, "state regulation predominated, substantially uniform in all countries, under every type of political regime, from the early beginnings of the commune to the eighteenth century almost in its entirety" (Zanetti, 1964, 40). The most significant exchanges were therefore very far from responding to the ineluctable laws of the market. The crisis of this organizational system was provoked, not by the laissez-faire thinkers, but by profound structural changes. Factors contributing to this new order included increases in population, prices and international trade, as well as the end to absolute shortage brought about by the agricultural, industrial and transport revolutions.[31]

Change in the organization of the food economy required at least three centuries, from 1500 to 1800, to be accomplished. Demand addressed to the city markets increased owing to the growth of the urban population[32], of its proletarian component, and of state-employed workers. Increasing proletarianization in the countryside, villages and towns was a consequence of the shrinking of agricultural land. Although this was often relative proletarianization (families with little land, rather than none), a greater proportion of the population came to depend on the city market for sustenance. This phenomenon shifted the distribution of income in favor of the wealthy classes, given that they consumed a smaller proportion of the food supply.[33] Satisfaction of demand "occurred mainly through changes in the social organization of production" (Tilly, 1975, 417), especially by bringing further land under cultivation, introducing new crops, using

---

30 Tilly (1975, 443f). "State-making, the maintenance of public order and the control of the food supply ... depended on each other intimately" (ibid., 396).

31 When conditions changed, "in one way or another, all the European statemakers allied themselves with the promoters of commercialized, productive, capitalist economy" (Tilly, 1975, 414).

32 This was a phenomenon that principally affected the small cities and towns; the large cities started to expand after 1800.

33 The growth of rural industry was obviously encouraged both by the greater availability of labor consequent on proletarianization, and by the redistribution of income in favor of the wealthy classes, although the latter were unable to generate an economic system based on mass consumption. Cf. Miskimin (1977, 85).

more intensive farming methods, increasing the division of labor among exporting sectors, and diverting foodstuffs from local consumption to other markets. Already in the sixteenth century corn was widely sold on international markets, although the prices were then filtered through the food provisioning systems of individual countries. "The predominance of changes in organization, property, and control [was] crucial", for in the long run it led to the destruction of the rural world and to the subordination of agriculture to the international market.[34] In general, the greater or lesser resistance raised by rural society against its incorporation into the national market depended on the profitability of alternative uses of the land, on their possibilities of application within existing community organizations, and on the capacity to react to change permitted by existing institutions (Tilly, 1975, 404).

That this was not a straightforward and natural process is illustrated by the fact that "the food riots prevailed in most European countries until well into the nineteenth century" (Tilly, 1975, 385). These riots exploded "as the effective demand for grain to feed cities and armies extended into agricultural regions previously little involved in production for the market." In their various forms, therefore, they were a clear manifestation of "the struggle for control over the existing supply of food" (Tilly, 1975, 387). These often violent protests were provoked by the perception that consolidated rights were being violated, and they were an appeal to tradition against the new economic agents and against the speculators. The most severe conflicts "occurred not so much where men were hungry as where they believed others were unjustly depriving them of food to which they had a moral and political right. The dissolution of the peasant community removed the chief defenders of those rights. The food riot vanished as the peasants lost their struggle against the penetration of capitalism into the countryside", that is, with the dissolution of the rural communities. (Tilly, 1975, 389f). However much the development of private trade may have made distribution more rapid, cheaper and more extensive (Tilly, 1975, 430) - by concentrating control over trade into the hands of a relatively small number of professionals and making it more difficult for consumers to purchase food directly from the producer - it was long perceived as a violation of "moral sensibilities as well as local interests" (Tilly, 1975, 432).

This reversal of situation accelerated even more rapidly when the advance of the industrial revolution required complex and specific plants: "the factory system, which at first seemed to involve little more than some additional overseas trading stations of the usual kind, soon induced a process of institutional change of a very different magnitude." (Polanyi, 1977, 1; see also Polanyi, 1968, 75). Given the increasingly massive investment in the new industrial system, an institutional system was required which would alter society in a multitude of ways. It would create a labor market in order to ensure the unrestricted use of manpower, its concentration into the new factory system, and control over production by the entrepreneur; it would expand demand in order to absorb increased output; it would lead to the formation of a land market in order to

---

34 Tilly (1975, 418). "Through a number of different paths, the agrarian transformations of early modern Europe led to a greatly increased demand for marketed food on the part of agricultural workers" (ibid., 407).

adjust agriculture to new alimentary and industrial needs, and the land to new infrastructural exigencies; and it would expand the financial market in order to yield the resources necessary for increased scale, first commercial and then productive.

The separation of the entrepreneur's function entails specific property and resource-utilization rights that give him broad, although not total, control over production and the use of labor, so that the productive process can be altered and costs minimized. Radical transformation, therefore, was required of the decision-making process in the use of resources, and the exclusion from it of artisans and their guilds.[35] This transformation combined with the simultaneous formation of the labor market resulting from elimination of the previous communitarian and agricultural society to uproot workers and herd them into the cities, transforming them into units of commodity-labor and revolutionizing the social organization of production.

The expansion of final demand and of exchange among sectors entailed the disappearance or curtailment of selfconsumption and of exchanges in kind, in the form of both barter and payment of the return on factors.[36] It was thus necessary to increase the productivity of land and labor, so that the conditions could be created for the positive elasticity of supply to the prices of agricultural products and for the transfer of labor from the agricultural sector (Federico, 1984, 252, note 29).

These processes could not have come about without redefinition of the economic role of the state, reducing its redistributive functions and increasing those that ensured compliance with contractual rules. The suppression or marked attenuation of the sense of community implicit in these functions could not have occurred without redefinition, however unsatisfactory, of the social pact.[37]

4.   What can be learned from history?

History teaches that what appears to be economically rational depends on the conditions and therefore on the goals of society. The paradigm proposed by the market culture, at least in its most inflexible forms, clashes with more than a century of historical and

---

35 Even during the period of the putting-out system, the producer merchant never exerted any significant influence over production, which was controlled by the guilds and agricultural laborers. As long as development was confined within the limits of the organization then current, there arose no clear entrepreneurial vision of a productive process geared to the predominant purpose of realizing monetary profit. Cf. Reddy (1984, 46-48).

36 "It is generally probable that the process of 'mercantilization' reduced or eliminated an '*a priori* preference for own-consumption' present in its initial stages." This was because outlets increased and the functioning of the market improved, thereby enhancing its advantages and reducing its risks, with a wider range of purchasable goods available and increased demand for money." Frequently (although not in the majority of cases) these processes were, partly or entirely, the outcome of activity by individuals external to peasant farms in the strict sense." An important role was played by intermediaries (merchants, hoarders) and lenders in stimulating the supply of products for sale (Federico, 1985, 209).

37 "The appearance of rules governing market exchange ... was ... the result of the drastic simplification and standardization of social relationships, of the proliferation of a doctrine of indifference and independence which was grafted onto an already existing doctrine of equality." Grossi (1990, 6).

anthropological research, which has scaled down the importance of organizations taking the form of the competitive market and radically reinterpreted their genesis. The rise of market economies in Europe was contemporaneous with the bourgeois revolution, the agricultural and industrial revolution, the spread of machines, the development of transport, the end of the threat of famine, and the consolidation of the nation states.

On the other hand, contemporary market societies - some more, some less - show signs of the constant evolution of the institutional and organizational structure of their economies. This can be discerned, for instance, in the redefinition of the role played by households, firms, associations, central state organization, and peripheral state organization. The cultural and institutional trends that one observes today in Western countries are contradictory and not easily generalized: increasingly pluralist control of the state with more complex equilibria; a redefinition of rights to use resources, in particular property rights, a symptom of pressures for the redistribution of income and wealth and their alternative use; the demise of a dominant ideology which resolves tensions in the economic sphere.

If the foregoing analysis is valid, one may deduce that a haphazard "transplant" of organizational institutions, without taking account of the cultural substratum to which they are to be applied, may be dangerous as well as irresponsible. On the one hand, if the traditional cultural system and its values proves unable to accommodate new solutions, or unable to adapt for this purpose, and if new cultural values fail to emerge and/or find acceptance, a social malaise definable as a state of anomie will arise. The context will become more unstable and less controllable, and lead, if the causes are not dealt with, to stagnation, social apathy and/or pathological behavior. This latter will take the form of unregulated clashes between ideological opposites and social groupings, violent flashpoints, authoritarian political backsliding, forms of power and social control parallel or antithetical to official ones.

However, even if there is no basic incompatibility, the risks are considerable. The process of cultural and institutional evolution which generated the market systems of antiquity lasted for more than a century, with frequent crises of values, agitations and political and social breakdown. The briefer and more concentrated the period becomes, the greater the risks, because a society which grows and changes at a speed greater than a physiological maximum looses its cohesive force and therefore its capacity for goal-fulfillment, and perhaps even for survival.

Finally, despite its essential unity, the system of the market countries contains marked *differentiations* stemming from the diversity of their histories and of their endowments of physical, human and cultural resources. If we accept that diversity is a decisive factor in the form and pace of development, granting the importance of common elements, it follows that not all countries are confronting development with equal economic and social mechanisms. Which model should be proposed?

References

Alchian, Armen A. (1977) Some Economics of Property Rights, in Alchian, Amen A. (ed.) *Economic Forces at Work*, Indianapolis: Liberty Press.

Cammarosano, Paolo (1978); L'economia italiana nel'età dei Comuni e il 'modo feudale di produzione': una discussione; *Società e storia*, 2.

Coase, Ronald H. (1937); The Nature of the Firm; *Economica,* November.

Dalton, G. (1974); Peasant Markets; *The Journal of Peasant Studies*, 1.

Fazio, I. (1990); I mercati regolati e la crisi settecentesca dei sistemi annonari italiani; *Studi storici,* 31.

Federico, G. (1984); Azienda contadina e autoconsumo fra antropologia ed econometria: considerazioni metodologiche; *Rivista di storia economica*, 2.

Federico, G. (1985); Autoconsumo e mercantilizzazione: spunti per una discussione; *Società e storia*, 8.

Goglio, Silvio (1994) *Dall'organizzazione allo sviluppo*, Quaderni del Dipartimento di Scienze Giuridiche, University of Trento

Grossi, F. (1990) *Espansione del mercato nelle economie nazionali*, Third International Karl Polanyi Conference, novembre, Milano.

Guenzi, A. (1978); Un mercato regolato. pane e fomai a Bologna nell'età moderna; *Quaderni storici,* 37.

Hirschman, Albert O. (1970) *Exit, Voice and Loyaltv*, Cambridge, Mass.: Harvard University Press.

Hodges, Richard (1988) *Primitive and Peasant Markets*, Oxford: Basil Blackwell.

Kamen, Henry (1984) *European Society, 1500-1700*, London: Hutchinson.

Meade, James E. (1989) *Agathotopia*, Milano: Feltrinelli.

Miskimin, Harry A. (1975) *The Economy of Early Renaissance Europe, 1300-1460*, Cambridge: Cambridge University Press.

Miskimin, Harry. A. (1977) *The Economy of Later Renaissance Europe, 1460-1600*, Cambridge: Cambridge University Press.

Neale, W.C. (1957) The Market in Theory and History, in Polanyi, Karl (ed.) *Trade and Market in the Early Empires. Economies in History and Theory*, New York: The Free Press.

North, D.C. (1984) La seconda rivoluzione economica negli Stati Uniti, in Segreto, L. (ed.) *La rivoluzione industriale tra il Settecento e l'Ottocento*, Milano: A. Mondadori.

Polanyi, Karl (1968) *The Great Transformation*, Boston: Beacon Press.

Polanyi, Karl (1977) *The Livelihood of Man*, New York: Academic Press.

Pult Quaglia, Anna M. (1982); Sistema annonario e commercio dei prodotti agricoli: riflessioni su alcuni temi di ricerca, *Società e storia*, 15.

Reddy, William M. (1984) *The Rise of the Market Culture. The Textile Trade and French Society, 1750-1900*, Cambridge: Cambridge University Press.

Simon, Herbert A. (1981) Economic Rationality: Adaptive Artifice, in *The Science of Artificial*, cpt. II, Cambridge, Mass.: MIT Press.

Thompson, E.P. (1971); The Moral Economy of the English Crowd in the XVIIIth Century; *Past and Present*, 50.

Tilly, C. (1975) Food Supply and Public Order in Modern Europe, in Tilly, C. (ed.) *The Formation of National States in Western Europe*, Princeton: Princeton University Press.

Tucci, U. (1983) Prezzi ed autoconsumo nel Medioevo italiano, in Romano, R. and U. Tucci (eds) *Storia d'Italia. Annali 6. Economia naturale, economia monetaria*, Torino: Einaudi.

Williamson, Oliver E. (1986) *The Economic Institutions of Capitalism. Firms, Markets, Relational Contracting*, New York: The Free Press.

Zanetti, D. (1964) *Proklemi alimentari di un econonzia preindustriale*, Torino: Boringhieri.

Comment on Silvio Goglio

Harm G. Schröter

Silvio Goglio's most important point is only to be underlined: the concept of the modern market is a human creation, or better, still is in the process of its creation. It is based on a set of human values and rules, worked out by the author. Wherever such rules and values did not emerge as in Europe, no dynamic development of the economy took place. Know-how and means in terms of technology, capital, organizational capabilities etc., concentrated to a much larger extent, were in China or India. It was Europe however, which created the institutions for a dynamic economy. This is still valid today: where these preconditions of behavior will not emerge, a modern market will not develop. During a whole generation, foreign economic aid to the Third World paid no attention to such preconditions for markets and, therefore, was doomed. What is to be learned from European history in this sense?

According to Goglio the change from the old static medieval economy to the new dynamic market system came about because of profound structural changes, while laissez-faire thinkers where less important. The principle key to markets still developing today lies in the emergence of modern market relations during industrialization. Below, we will explore the roots of this change.

The feudal system was not a market system, although the latter developed within the former. In order to get an idea as to what extent the market emerged, we will need indicators, the best one of which is the use of money. Indeed, the first in need of money were the state and the gentry for luxury goods and efforts of warfare. However, the mercenary and the smith, who received the money, spent it and again brought it into circulation.

Recent research shows that the use of money was much more widespread in late medieval and early modern times than thought before (North, 1994). The bulk of this trade was carried out locally, i.e., with little state intervention (Mathis, 1992, 42). Local trade represents the use of money by ordinary people. The discussion of 'industrialization before [the] industrialization' has brought forward an abundance of evidence on the long but steady evolution of market relations from the 16th century onwards (Kriedke, Medick and Schlumboom, 1992, 70-255). Old and established institutions tried to control these new forces and succeeded to a certain extent. But neither administrative rules nor stocks of goods piled up for market intervention could prevent the trebling and quadrupling of prices for grain in the whole of Europe e.g. between 1760-1774. Such movements of prices had little in common with the feudal concept of a 'just price'. They represented the breakdown of the old order, still restricted to a certain sector and period; on the other hand this marked the limits of the power of established institutions.

Regional development was very different in Europe. There was little change in the eastern and south-eastern parts, while certain regions, such as England, Northern Italy, the Netherlands etc. showed considerable progress at times. Furthermore, regions in which the state was able to exert a thorough control of all the commercial activities of its subjects, such as Spain and Portugal or Russia, showed little sustained progress.

Variation was not restricted to regions. At the same time as branches of industry stagnated, others deviated from this blockage. New established crafts, such as the printers', never submitted to any guild. True, the guilds had largely succeeded in controlling the development of their specific branch in towns, but externally they lost their grip. In central Europe market development took place by non-guilded outdoor-workers in villages. Such homeworkers received the yarn they needed for weaving from a trader who took the cloth. The outdoor-weavers never owned their product; they received wages in cash in contrast to the craftsmen. The market emerged through by passing old institutions. Another example is the enclosure movement in Britain which had already started in the 13th century. The first information on it is from legal proceedings. Through various judgements the courts tried to prevent steps that acted against the old feudal order. With the enclosures, landowners hedged in their property to let the sheep graze on it. Wool was more profitable than other agricultural activities. Of course, the precondition of such a profitability was an established market for cloth, cloth not only for the gentry but for the common man. To sum up, market development took centuries. It was hampered by established institutions; in various parts of Europe, though, it could not be blocked as (for instance) in China. In market development, state demand represented an important factor, but not the dominant and not the decisive one.

It has been suggested by Goglio that the emergence of modern markets and that of the nation-state occurred instantly. In some cases, such as Italy, this was clearly the case. However, the majority was different. The English, the French, the Spanish, the Polish or Russian nation-state was formed long before modern market forces became strong within their specific territory. Other nations, e.g. Czechoslovakia, industrialized before they became independent as a nation-state. Chronological parallels in the development of nation-states and market economies occurred rather by chance. This is important information for today's development of markets. If no such link in history has been made, we can expect territories, which today are inhabited by people of mixed nationalities, to have the same hope for development as those with one homogenous people. Economic history provides no argument to advocate ethnically coherent entities. Mixed ones have at least equal, if, because of variety, not better, chances for the development of markets.

Market dynamics came about with industrialization. And here there are still unsolved historical problems: What was the precondition for which development? Technical innovation, growth of population, a new quality of investment, different economic rules etc., many different issues are intertwined. However, some points have been settled. Abundance of labor promoted the process of industrialization, but was not a precondition. The structural shortage of labor in the United States did not prevent industrial growth, the US were the second industrial nation after Great Britain. Education on the other hand was decisive. Where general education, e.g. literacy, was low, market development was small, too. Finland, Japan or Korea, all countries where education was not only highly valued, but received considerable investment, provide us with examples of a late but successful industrialization.

Furthermore, social and economic modernization in the agrarian sector represented a precondition for the emergence of markets. Serfdom and all other forms of personal dependency had to be abolished, and freedom of movement had to be granted. Land had to become private property. Consequently, land could be sold and bought freely, and crops were no longer decided upon communally. The same legislation hit everybody. Legal differences had to be levelled, property-rights had to be considered regardless of status. According to Senghaas, where these conditions were given, like in west, central and northern Europe, markets emerged, while those regions with no agricultural modernization, like Eastern Europe or Latin America, stagnated (Senghaas, 1985). In various cases modernization of social institutions and rules as well as legislation clearly represented a precondition for the emergence of markets.

Finally we face examples in which the emergence of markets was a reaction arising from institutional change, while in other cases market relations forced their way through the opposition of established institutions. In this process the role of laissez-faire thinkers was important. They were sensitive of the blockades by which old institutions prevented the emergence of markets. They had a vision of how to overcome such constraints. But the laissez-faire thinkers only represented a certain aspect of all the varieties of ways of new thinking. The precondition for their laissez-faire ideas was the development of a new perception of the world and a trust in mankind.

Scientists such as Copernicus or Newton, who shook established thinking, philosophers such as Descartes, who justified the new approach, geographers such as Mercator, who showed the usefulness of science for shipping, as well as many others provided the necessary basis for a profound change of thinking. Furthermore, in those cases where the old order was shaken not by certain authors but by "profound structural change", this change had mental preconditions as well. Any deviation from the old order needed justification, in those days even more than today. There, too, the precondition for the emergence of markets was a change in social values, not only by a small minority - who would have ended in prison - but by at least a considerable part of the population envolved. The precondition for the emergence of markets is, as Goglio has shown, a set of mental and social human values, which is perceived as just by the majority of people.

References

Kriedke, P., H. Medick and J. Schlumboom (1992); Sozialgeschichte in der Erweiterung - Proto-Industrialisierung in der Verengung? Demographie, Sozialstruktur, moderne Hausindustrie: eine Zwischen-Bilanz der Proto-Industrialisierungs-Forschung; *Geschichte und Gesellschaft*, 18, 70-255.

Mathis, Franz (1992) *Die deutsche Wirtschaft im 16. Jahrhundert*, München: Oldenbourg.

North, Michael (1994) *Das Geld und seine Geschichte vom Mittelalter bis zur Gegenwart*, München: Beck.

Senghaas, Dieter (1985) *Von Europa lernen*, Frankfurt/M.: Suhrkamp.

4 From hierarchy to markets: an evolutionary perspective of the transformation process[*]

Michael Keren

1. Introduction

When bureaucratic allocation ceases, the role of the distribution sector, particularly of retail, undergoes radical change. It is this change which this paper examines through an evolutionary perspective. To the evolutionary approach a network aspect is added in this paper, thereby gaining a better understanding of the role of the organizational structure.

The economy is a network of agents, tied together by hierarchies and markets. These ties may be stronger when the agents belong to the same organization, but in all cases the agents are bound to one another through links of routines, of internalized rules of response to incoming impulses. The impulses which the agents receive depend on the environment in which they function. And the environment is largely system-dependent, and the planned-centralized economy of socialist days in Eastern Europe is quite different from that of a Western market economy. The transition economy is neither, but it is moving in the direction of the Western market. Its speed of convergence may depend on the efficiency of trade and the distribution sector, and the aim of this paper is to contribute to our understanding of this sector's role in this process. This sector is referred to as retail below, but the reader should note that wholesale and other parts of distribution - e.g., those parts of distribution which are concerned with foreign trade - are omitted only to simplify the argument.

The retail sector links producers to consumers. It does so in the obvious manner when it distributes output among consumers. But this is not the aspect with which this paper is concerned. Here the focus is on the informational dimensions of retailing. The retailer learns in an immediate manner the needs and preferences of consumers, as revealed in the market place, while the producer has only indirect ways of assessing them. It is in the retailer's interest to convey the knowledge he gains to the producer, who can then adjust his production profile to the benefit of both (and of the consumers). This natural link is severed in centralized planning: vertical communications gain priority, and horizontal messages are relegated and used mainly to avert calamities: this is further discussed below.

Following this brief introduction, Section 2 presents the model of the economy, while Section 3 analyzes the working of the planned economy. Section 4 looks at the production activity of the firm and at its internal information flows. Transition is analyzed in Section 5, and the longer term evolutionary trend is developed in Section 6.

* I am grateful to Wladimir Andreff and to Hans-Jürgen Wagener for detailed comments on a previous version of this paper.

Section 7 concludes with a few lessons that this network-evolutionary perspective supplies.

2. The model

We focus on just two groups of agents in this paper: on the producing firm and its internal structure and on the retailing organization. Other actors, the planning organization, input-supplying enterprises and the consumers themselves, remain in the background. The system that binds them together starts off by being a centralized, planner-coordinated network. With transition the planner is removed, and coordination becomes horizontal and decentralized. The different games played by the actors under these two environments are the subject of the paper.

Consumer tastes. The consumers are distributed in several taste clusters. At each point of time, tastes are given, but in between they are changing randomly. The clusters are characterized by size, x, and by the exact specification of their preferences, ρ. Preferences, ρ, measured in radian, should be considered a state variable, tracked in its movements over time by the retailers. The movement of ρ can be seen as Brownian motion, so that knowledge of its position at any point of time is relevant for the future, but this relevance decays over time. The size parameter x_i may signify the measure of consumers who purchase, say, a sports car, while ρ_{it} denotes the passing fashion which may favor certain classes of colors, given gadgets, and other qualities that are in constant flux. Consumers will also buy models that do not embody all the desired qualities, but they will be ready to pay less for them:

$$(1) \qquad p_{it}(\rho_i) = 1 - d(\rho_i), \qquad d(\rho_i) = \frac{1}{\pi} |\rho_i - \rho_{it}|,$$

where p is the price the consumers are willing to pay for quality ρ, and $d(\rho)$ is the radial distance of the supplied quality from the one preferred at t. Observe that when the supplied good is at ρ_{it} its price $p(\rho_{it}) = 1$, and when it is at the greatest possible distance from ρ_{it}, i.e., $\rho_i = \rho_{it} \pm \pi$, $p(\rho_i) = 0$. There may be some overlap in tastes between different clusters, so that a product of quality ρ may fetch a positive price in several taste clusters.

The producer is a monopolist, both before and after transition. His production costs, it is here assumed, are unaffected by his choice of ρ: thus ρ may signify here a quality such as color, rather than speed or reliability. The number of different qualities, different ρ's, produced by an enterprise may naturally affect costs. Evolutionary forces enforce different objectives on the firm under the two regimes, and these affect both its working structure (though not its formal structure) and its ties to the outside world. Under the centralized system resource allocation is determined by the *planner*: he decides the output that is to be directed to each of the I clusters of consumers, as well as the flow of inputs from the firm's suppliers. See Figure 4.1, where the number of taste-clusters, I, equals 3. The planner's role, though kept in the background, is highly important for the molding of the environment. He fulfills the role of the market in a capitalist economy, and has to balance supply and demand in all markets of the economy. Because of the enormity of his task, his time is highly valuable, and, to prop up the authority of his plan, he has to be the final arbiter of the careers of the cadres engaged in the productive sphere. In other words, he is the principal in the agency game that he play with his subordinates: see below. Being responsible for balance in the economy, he is highly sensitive to any glaring imbalances that might develop.[1]

Incentives: The planner, in his capacity as the principal, can tie incentives only to those aspects of the agent's activities that are visible to him. The problem is that much of the agent's activities is not transparent, and not all dimensions of his action are equally measurable. Some, like the quantity produced, are usually statistically verifiable, while the qualitative aspects are hard to evaluate. They can be assessed indirectly by the customers who are affected by them. But their feedback is suspect, because they have their interests may be to pin their own failures on their suppliers. However, the cause of a serious breakdown can usually be traced, and the party considered responsible can be punished and made an example of. The basis of the bureaucratic incentive system is, therefore, judgment in accordance with two dimensions of performance. The first is quantitative: did the enterprise fulfill its production target? The second dimension is used only when there is a major breakdown, when the guilt can be pinned on somebody. Thus the qualitative dimension may come into play when shoddiness becomes a cause of such a calamity. As far as the enterprise is concerned, punishment for poor quality is stochastic. When it comes to retailing, here the added value of the trading sector is all a matter of the quality of service: the quantities which the sector supplies are, usually, those that have been purchased (disregarding the routine depreciation and losses in transport and trade). Hence in this sector it is only the qualitative dimension of performance which may come into light: thus trade, as distinct from production, will usually not attract high powered incentives. Some of the effects of this difference will be touched upon in the closing sections of this paper.

The retailer links the producing enterprise to the market. In this highly simplified model, he represents the distribution sector at large, including, in particular, wholesale trade. For simplicity it is assumed that in a market economy each cluster of consumers is supplied by a different retailer, and in a planned economy - by a single retailing organization. The retailer, who is 'nearer' the consumer than the producer, is capable of seeing today's choice of ρ by his cluster; retailers differ in their ability to estimate the expected change in consumers' tastes tomorrow. These variations in the ability to understand the market is the main basis of evolutionary selection among the retailers in this paper. Another element in the goodness of tracking of consumers' tastes is the effort the retailer exerts: since ρ follows Brownian motion, the more frequently one samples changes in ρ, the closer one follows it. Assume that ρ^{rt} is an unbiased estimate

---

1 This does not stand in conflict with the extensive literature that ascribes to leading members of the nomenklatura an interest in excess demand for given commodities, from which they can profit personally. Glaring shortages become political issues which focus attention on the 'guilty' party, and are therefore to be avoided.

of retailer r of ρ_{it}, the market's future taste, and that $d(\rho^{rt})$ is the expected distance of ρ^{rt} from ρ_{it}, as defined in (1). Then

(2) $$d(p_{rt}) = \phi(e_{r,t-1}|\alpha_r) \qquad \phi_e, \phi_{e\alpha} < 0$$

where $e_{r,t-1}$ is the retailer's input of effort in the previous period, and α is a measure of r's inborn mercantile efficiency. The role of the selection process should be to weed out low-α retailers.[2] The single period utility function of all retailers is standard,

(3) $$u^r = y^{r,t+1} - e^{rt} \geq \underline{u}^r$$

where y is r's income in the coming period and $\underline{u}^r$ is r's reservation utility. Observe that linearity of u in y assumes risk-neutrality on the part of the agent.

The structural characteristics of the actors do not depend on the economic environment. What does depend on the environment is their play: it is a function of the game being played, and the rules of the game are set by the environment that is, by the economic organization. These need not be formally set rules; quite often they are the rules enforced informally by environmental conditions, and this may be the case even when formal rules may exist.

Figure 4.1 The centralized economy

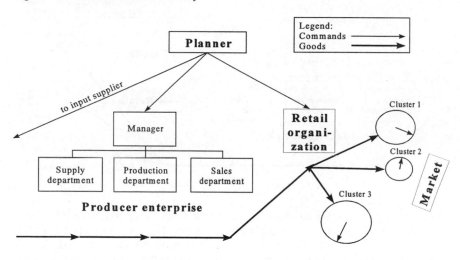

---

2 The inborn efficiency parameter, α, should be thought of, in a wider model, as a multidimensional vector. Individuals of different α-vectors could have comparative advantages in different lines of activity. High-α individuals should therefore be thought of in the present context as agents with a high comparative advantage in retailing.

Figure 4.1 shows the basic structure of the planning organization, and the flows of commands and goods in it. The framed rectangles represent organizational units: the arrows of commands originate with the planner and are directed to the three organizations that participate in the game, the (hidden) supplier, the producing enterprise (whose departments are specified in the Figure), and the distributing retail organization. The heavier arrow at the bottom shows the flow of the goods, from the input supplier, to the supply department in the enterprise, to the production department which transforms inputs into outputs, to sales, and then to the retail organization which distributes the output to the three clusters of consumers. The latter are represented by circles, with arrows that show, clock-like, the current values of ρ_1, ρ_2, and ρ_3.

The new regime removes the planner from the scene: it is assumed that imports as alternatives to the locally produced input flow gradually become available, and the availability of inputs becomes less of a concern to the producing enterprise.[3] The retail organization is also dissolved and replaced by private retailers, each of whom specializes in supplying a cluster of consumers. He need not be alone in supplying his cluster: competition among retailers is possible. Figure 4.2 illustrates the transformed regime.

Figure 4.2 The market economy

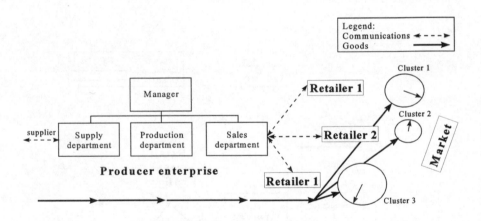

In Figure 4.2 the planner has disappeared and the single retail organization has been replaced by three retailers. The vertical command arrows have been replaced by double-sided horizontal communication arrows. The change in the flow of goods is less discernible: the flow now runs from the sales department to the three retailers; the intra-

---

3 The foreign commercial institutions are initially no better organized than those of the internal market, and the emergence of imports as a regular alternative to local supplies is a matter of time. Nevertheless, the hurdle imports have to pass can be expected to start to decline with the beginning of transition.

enterprise arrows have been omitted. But the quality of that flow may be affected - and this is the topic of the following sections.

3. Planned retail and the death of demography

The choice of a single retailing organization under the planning system is not accidental: the planner's time is precious, and it is highly desirable to reduce the number of units that communicate with him on a regular basis. The costs of this are several: the obvious one is the monopoly position enjoyed by the single retailer. Of no lesser importance is the fact that, in the absence of competition, the single retailer becomes indispensable. These two costs are discussed below in reverse order.

Indispensability means that the organization is secured against death. Being the only one in the field it cannot be simply abolished. It can be reorganized and in the history of the socialist economies reorganizations in areas which are considered ancillary to production may possibly have been more common than even reorganizations in the productive sphere. But these reorganization can never do away with one basic fact: the single retailer cannot simply be abolished. It is also administratively extremely difficult to replace him by an entirely new organization, because the required specific human capital can be found only in the single organization. To all intents and purposes the irreplaceable organization is assured of indefinite existence. And irreplaceability entails the soft budget constraint.

Monopoly position raises the specter of monopoly prices. But this need not be the principal effect. Indeed, prices are administered by the planner who may keep them low. But the value of the service granted by the monopolist, the retailer in this case, may be minimal. Furthermore, the stake-holders in the organization will tend to divide its surplus among themselves: costs will tend to equal revenues. To mention just once possible illegal activities, the latter may also try to avail themselves of some of the difference between the official price of the good and its black market value, by selling it under the table or exchanging it for other scarce goods.

How can the planner fight against these phenomena? What is the reward structure he can offer this organization to improve its performance? In many ways he is has very few instruments at his command, mainly because his information about the retailer's activities is quite skimpy. As was mentioned in Section 2, his habitual tests of performance break down here: the quantity reported sold will usually equal that produced. If unsold inventories accumulate, the blame can be put on the producer who does not supply what the market demands. Queues can be blamed on the insufficiency of supplies. Only unequal availability, queues in one market and surpluses in another, can be pinned on the distributor. But this will become a factor only if the cries of protest from the public become intense enough, more intense than those of other sufferers.

Does the retailer have any incentive to learn about the markets' developing tastes, and to transmit this information to the producer? This depends on two factors: on the communication links between producer and retailer, and on the interests of the producer in the use of this information. The former, as Figure 4.1 shows, are very long and often clogged. There are also direct lines from retailer to the sales department of the enterprise, omitted from the Figure, but, as is argued below, the information which arrives through them at the producing enterprise is not likely to affect production decisions.

The producing enterprise is plagued by supply problems. The reason why this is an integral part of the centralized economy lies outside the domain of this paper, and is here accepted as fact. These supply problems as well as production breakdowns in the enterprise are the main factors that may hinder plan fulfillment, i.e., satisfactory economic performance, and information that flows in from the supply and production departments obtains priority in the manager's office. Little attention is paid to messages from the retailing side, because adjustment of the goods to market conditions is very low on the agenda. This can be examined by following Domar (1974) and looking at alternative incentive structures. Let y^R be the income of the head of the retailing organization. Then suppose

$$(4) \qquad\qquad y^R = \begin{cases} y(p_{it} \cdot x_{it}), & x_{it} \geq \underline{x}, \\ 0 & \text{otherwise,} \end{cases}$$

where $y' > 0$, i.e., the bonus increases as the value of sales rises. This bonus equation seems to offer the retailer incentives to do his best to raise the revenue for each unit sold in his market cluster, by increasing p (since, by assumption, the quantity sold is not in his hands). But his efforts to obtain a good reading of the market are of use to him only if the producer reacts to them, i.e., if he adjusts the quality of his goods to market tastes in order to increase profits.[4] Even if the retailer were to come up with very accurate estimates of consumers' tastes, only if the firm were to follow his retailer's advice and adjusts its product range as suggested by him, only then would the retailer be able to raise his income (and his good name in the bureaucracy, an aim masked by the simple bonus-incentive equation (4)). Hence we have to examine the interplay between the retailing organization and the producing enterprise, or better, the game played inside the enterprise: would the sales department give an ear to the retailer, and would it influence production decisions?

4.   The firm as a network

To gain a better understanding of the reactions of the firm to outside impulses we have to look at the interplay between the various departments during the production process.

---

4 In the case also in the seller's market ruling in the planned economy this might not seem to be relevant. But this is not so: the seller's market has been taken into account here by the assumption that the quantity sold was given. The assumption that quality is costless, i.e., that the choice of qualities that are nearer the consumers' tastes do not require any more resources, means that there is no gain from producing low quality. It may be claimed that with the fix-price regimes of Eastern Europe higher quality does not pay, but the assumption here is that the characteristics of quality-adjusted goods change sufficiently to justify a new price.

To do this the production process has to be specified and, if possible, a production function derived. To be meaningful, the assumed process and function have to allow for uncertainty and take account of the involvement of superior bodies in the solution of production problems.

The basic production process assumed here is very simple: the output of Q requires the input of X and labor, L. In general one unit of X is needed per unit of output, but there is a range where some labor can be substituted for X (e.g., by reducing wastage and using scrap). The problems that arise in production have their roots in the uncertain arrival rate of the inputs, and in the possibility of machinery breakdowns. Both are stochastic processes, independent of one another. An example of a possible specification of production under such conditions is given below.

Suppose the flow of intermediate inputs allotted to the firm is planned at the rate of x per week, but that it is in fact a random process ξ which follows, say, a Poisson distribution, whose mean is x. Let $f(\xi,x)$ denote the density of ξ and $F(\xi,x)$ its cumulative distribution. Production capacity, given ξ, is given by the following function:

$$(5) \qquad \bar{q} = \begin{cases} \min\,[q_M, L_0], & \xi \geq q_M, \\ \max\,[\sqrt{\xi L}, q_M], & q_m \leq \xi \leq q_M, \\ \xi, & \xi \leq q_m, \end{cases}$$

where $L_0 = q_m$ and, most important, the manager's attention is required whenever ξ falls below some critical value, say q_M. Capacity, $\bar{q}$, defines the maximum output available out of given inputs. Panel a of Figure 4.3 illustrates the capacity function of (5). Two isoquants, for $\bar{q} = q_M$ and $\bar{q} = q_M/2$, are illustrated in the Figure: both start with a horizontal line from the right, where $L = \bar{q}$, but when $\xi = \bar{q}$ we have a curved segment (where labor can be substituted for the missing intermediate); lastly, at $\xi = q_m$ or $q_m/2$ the isoquant becomes vertical (and no substitution is possible). The first two segments are solid lines; the third is dashed. The heavy line $L_1 A$, where $L_1 = q_M 2/q_m$, illustrates the change of capacity and the increasing requirements of the L-input as ξ declines from above q_M to q_M, then to q_m - when labor has to be substituted to maintain the level of $\bar{q}$. Up to this level, when capacity is maintained at q_M, the line is solid. When ξ falls below q_m, the line becomes dashed, as the capacity $\bar{q}$ declines in proportion to ξ, even though L is maintained at the higher level of L_1.

Actual output depends on the proper operation of the firm's equipment, i.e., on the level of capacity utilization, γ, $\gamma \in [0,1]$:

$$q = \gamma \bar{q}$$

where γ is stochastic. A possible density of γ, $g(\gamma)$, given here as an example:

$$g(y) = (e-1)e^{y-2}, \qquad 0 \leq \gamma \leq 1.$$

Let the distribution of γ, be $G(\gamma)$. Again, unless managerial attention is provided, wherever γ declines below some critical value, say γ_m, output declines to zero. The two factors may be interrelated: with a more secure flow of inputs, more robust equipment can be installed, which may reduce the loss of capacity.[5] But this, of course, is a matter of time, not something to change with the initiation of transition.

Figure 4.3 The firm's production function

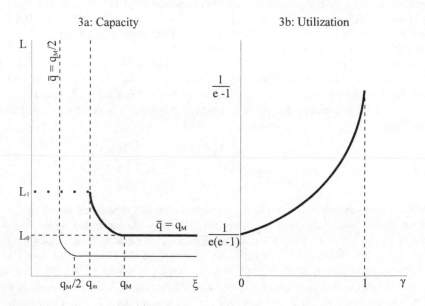

There are two points where decisions have to be taken under this technology: first, it has to be decided whether managerial attention should be directed toward inputs and production whenever ξ and γ assume low values. The second is how much labor should be employed in the firm: L_1, which would supply sufficient reserves when ξ declines to produce the maximum amount of output, or L_0, just enough to produce q_M when supplies of inputs are sufficient? Much depends, of course, on the choice between profits and production target fulfillment, on the firm's payoff function. And payoff depends on the planner's reaction to the firm's choice: since he does not want any breakdown in the chain of supply, output is of greater importance, and output will have precedence in the firm's decisions. If this is the conclusion, then $L=L_1$ and we have overmanning, a partial and typical component of excessive costs in Eastern Europe. It also tells us that managerial attention will be deflected away from product improvement and development, away from market satisfaction, toward input and production problems. In fact, only during $[1-F(q_M)][1-G(\gamma_m)]$ of all weeks will the manager's attention be free to

---

5 Compare this to 'putting out fires', in Radner and Rothschild, (1975).

listen to what his sales department has to tell him about changes in market tastes. But the development of new market-satisfying models takes time, and requires the attention of the manager (and possibly the production manager) for a fairly extended period of time; being elsewhere occupied most of the time, product development will be very lengthy and the models will be based on old and relatively irrelevant information, on tastes of some period past.

This affects the incentives of the retail organization in the collection of information on market tastes: any input to the sales department of the producing enterprise has a low probability of being made use of in the design of new products. Consequently effort expended in gathering this information is probably lost. This explains why there is little reward for this activity in the centralized economy.

A final question that arises with respect to the producer is the scope of production, i.e., the number of different clusters that the firm chooses to supply with specific models. This too is environment dependent. If we assume that an increasing number of models produced increases the firm's production costs, but at the same time allows it to supply more clusters with goods which fit best their demands, then we can obtain a simple condition for the optimal scope of the competitive profit maximizing firm. In the case of the planned economy, where there is no external competition and profits do not count for much - the incentive is to run as few distinct models as possible and offer the same model to as many taste clusters as possible.

5. Transition

The end of the planner's existence does not yet guarantee the beginning of transition to a functioning market regime. A hardened budget constraint that makes profits the determinants of continued existence and growth is also necessary. But suppose that the budget has hardened - what type of relations should develop between the producer and the retailer?

It should be borne in mind that transition is a dynamic process, and all that can be done here is to present a few snapshots of the situation at selected points of time during that process.

Let us examine first the interests of the producer. Over time imports become more easily available, and the concern about inputs recedes (see footnote 3). As this happens, and as a response to the developing competition, input quality too may improve, and production problems become less pressing. Profits gain importance and markets become the main constraint.[6] The producer, who had previously spurned the links with the market, is now dependent on the retailer, who is the only one who feels the taste of the market and can transmit it to the enterprise. The latter will use this information, which is now a primary tool to raise profits (or, in a wider model, to increase his market

---

6 Observe that the supplier of the inputs, who stands along the sidelines of the analysis, is plagued by similar problems. He too begins to be assured of inputs of more reliable quality, and he too becomes pressed to pay more attention to the quality of his output.

share). What the retailer has in it for himself is his commission, which may be affected by the price he manages to get thanks to his success in sizing up the market. The situation in which the two parties find themselves is a typical agency condition, in which the firm, as the principal, has to supply incentives to the retailer, an agent, to gather the needed information.[7] The assumptions based on the consumer's demand will be maintained: the quantity demanded in cluster i is fixed at the given level of xi, and the only variable the actor can influence is the price p_i. Using (1) and assuming that the retailer receives a commission of s_{rt} per unit sold, and an income of $y = sx$, and denoting by π the producer's profits, the firm's maximand in this last link in its operation, becomes

$$(6) \qquad \max \pi_{it} = p_{it} x_i - y_{rt} = (p_{it} - s_{rt}) x_i = [1 - d_r(\rho_{it}) - s_{rt}] x_i$$

To simplify we assume that the commission is linear in the value of sales, i.e., in the price p,

$$s_{rt} = c_r + b_r p_{it},$$

where b and c are non-negative constants. The retailer has been assumed to be risk neutral in (3), and it is a well-known result that, for risk-neutral agents, $b_r = 1$ and, obviously, $c_r < 0$. We can therefore view the agent as lessor of the market, who buys all the firm's output of model i produced for market i at $-c_r > 0$ per-unit and resells it for p_i.

Examining the retailer's response, his objective function is (3), i.e., his maximand is

$$(7) \qquad u^{rt} = y^{r,t+1} - e^{rt} = (1 - d + c) x^i - e^{rt} = [1 - \phi(e^{rt} | \alpha) + c] x^i - e^{rt}.$$

The retailer's optimizing effort level solves

$$(8) \qquad -\phi_e(e | \alpha) x^i = 1,$$

where, by (3), $\varphi_e < 0$ and $\varphi_{ea} < 0$. It is easy to see that

$$\frac{de}{d\alpha} = -\frac{\phi_{ea} x^i}{\phi_{ee} x^i} > 0, \qquad \frac{de}{dx} = -\frac{\phi_e}{\phi_{ee} x^i} > 0.$$

As an example take

$$\phi(e | \alpha) = A - \alpha \sqrt{e},$$

---

7 An alternative formulation has been suggested by Hans-Jürgen Wagener: the retailer could be viewed as the principal with the producer the agent who has to be supplied with incentives to supply goods of the desired quality. This rendering, which would provide an answer which differs mainly in the distribution of the surplus between the parties, would be preferable for the case of the single retailer - who is likely to pocket most of the surplus. It would be unwieldy in the case of many retailers.

where A is a constant, and

$$\phi_e = -\frac{\alpha}{2\sqrt{e}} = 1.$$

This, by (7), leads to

$$e = \frac{(\alpha x^i)^2}{4}, \qquad \text{and} \qquad d = \phi(e|\alpha) = A - \frac{\alpha^2 x^i}{2}.$$

Thus effort increases with α, the innate ability level of the agent, and with the size of the market. The larger the market and the more able the agent, the closer he is likely to guess consumers' true tastes. And the expected error of measurement declines with both α and x. All that remains is to divide the total cake between the producer and the retailer, and this cannot be done at this stage of bilateral monopoly, where the retailer may have the stronger hand. This is why we find at the early stages of transition cases of profiteering by those who find those markets where scarcities are the sharpest. This is true for the early stages of transition, where the market is still highly splintered, and opportunities for huge arbitrage profits abound. Enterprising salesmen who interject themselves between producers and markets are still rare. Although even this benefits consumers, the visible signs may be the great profits that flow into the pockets of the middleman, and in a society where the term speculator has been the sharpest expression of abuse, this phase does not earn heaps of praise.

Suppose, however, that another competing retailer joins the market, and that the producer now sells through both outlets. The first question that arises is what specification the producer will select for his goods, now that he is getting different advise, say ρ_{1t} and ρ_{2t} from his outlets. At the start he does not know whose is better, and uses the mean of the two estimates. However, to split sales between the retailers he may use their harmonic mean, promising retailer r a share z_t of sales,

$$(9) \qquad z_{rt} = \frac{\dfrac{1}{d_{rt}}}{\dfrac{1}{d_{1t}} + \dfrac{1}{d_{2t}}} \ x_i = \left[1 - \frac{d_{r,t}}{d_{1t} + d_{2t}} \right] x_i, \qquad r = 1, 2.$$

(where $-r$ refers to 2 when $r=1$ and to 1 when $r=2$). Checking again the two risk-neutral agents' reactions to the fixed price of c per unit sold, it easy to use (7), suitably modified, to find the condition

$$(10) \qquad -\phi_e (e^r | \alpha^r) z^i = 1, \qquad r = 1, 2.$$

Thus the smaller extent of the market reduces effort, but a better ability may raise it. It is impossible to tell whether effort levels would be raised or lowered, though the latter may be more likely. However, we have here a better sample: the expected value of the mean of both estimates lies closer to the true mean. Furthermore, the inconclusive outcome of the two-sided monopoly disappears, and it should be easier here to estimate $p+c$, the commission paid to the retailers, or $-c>0$, the price pocketed by the producing enterprise. To keep both retailers in the market, the producer has to pay them so that the utility of both will not fall below $\underline{u}$. Using (3), this amounts to

$$p^i + c^i = \min_r [\underline{u}^r + e^r] / z^r , \qquad\qquad r = 1, 2.$$

Thus the higher the reservation wage and the effort level of the least efficient agent, the greater the commission that has to be paid the retailers. Here, with greater competition in the market, the retailer reduces his share of the surplus and assumes the more modest role of that has been assumed above.

Over time $z_{it}(\alpha)$ will tend to grow with α, as can be clearly established from the market sharing equation (9). As a result, after a while z_{it}, in any given market, will be ranked by α, and become fairly stable as long as circumstances do not change. As the number of retailers in any market grows, the producer will be able to ask himself whether it might not pay him to exclude the least efficient ones from the market. The benefit the producer gets from any additional agent declines, and the benefit of those with a very low α may become negative. At that point it will pay producers to reduce the commission to a level that may reduce the low-α agents' utility below their reservation level.

Proposition 1:   In the steady state, in any market i, the market share of retailer r, $z_r(\alpha)$, and his utility level, u^r, will be an increasing function of α_r.

Proof: Let us rank the agents in any market i by their α, such that $r>s$ only if $\alpha_r \geq \alpha_s$. It is simple to show that if $r>t$, then $z_r>z_t$:

$$z_{rt} = \frac{\dfrac{1}{d(\alpha_r)}}{\displaystyle\sum_{s=1}^{n} \dfrac{1}{d(\alpha_s)}} x_t = \frac{\displaystyle\prod_{s\neq r} d(\alpha_s)}{\displaystyle\sum_{s=1}^{n} d(\alpha_s)} x_t$$

When $d_r<d_t$, the numerator of z_r is greater than the numerator of z_t. Furthermore, differentiation of z_r with respect to α_r and α_t provides

$$\frac{dz_r}{d\alpha_r} = -\frac{\phi\alpha_r}{d_r} z_r > 0 , \qquad \frac{dz_r}{d\alpha_r} = \left[\frac{1}{d_r} - \frac{1}{\displaystyle\sum_s d_s} \right] \phi_t z_r < 0$$

It is easy to show that the utility level of agents is positively related to their ability level α. In other words, a scale of $(e,y\,|\,\alpha)$ and $u(\alpha)$ is established for each market. Suppose now that different ladders of $u(\alpha)$ are established in different markets. It is easy to show that there will be a tendency of agents to move between markets, so as to equalize $u(\alpha)$

throughout the economy. This is a tendency, no more, because changes take place all the time which draw different markets apart.

6. Evolution: survival of the high-α agents

Suppose now a new agent enters, whose ability level is higher than that of all previous agents: he can enter in any market, but unless he has an affinity to any specific trade (which we have assumed away in the utility function (3)), he will choose to enter where he perceives that his ability can earn him the highest rewards. This will usually be in large markets, where the large market share which his ability can earn him is worth more in terms of income. This indicates that low ability agents will find that smaller clusters can serve as protected niches, where stronger predators will not find it worth their while to enter.

The model is not yet complete: very-low α agents will tend to have very low incomes in this model. If we divide all tasks in the economy to those that require initiative and decision-making, and those that require other skills, then for each agent there will be a threshold that will make him leave the entrepreneurial field and undertake his alternative skill as his means of earning a living. Thus high-α agents will tend to congregate in tasks which require entrepreneurial skills, while low-α agents will be squeezed out.

Observe that the centralized economy lacks any means of selection of characteristics suitable for efficient retailing. This has two consequences. Using our notation, it has no way of weeding out low-α agents in retailing. It also has no way of rewarding successful retailers. Hence those with higher α's will tend to look for avenues of advancement where their contribution will be recognized, e.g., in industry and the party. As a result there is a tendency for adverse selection of low-α managers in the retailing field in particular and the whole distribution sector in general.

7. Conclusions

The centralized economy has no place for high ability in marketing. This is not just for reasons of ideology: there are strong reasons why this should be so:

- The planner has no way of rewarding good performance in the field, because it is opaque to him: he cannot distinguish between good and bad marketing.
- Even if the retailer would fulfill his task of conveying to the producers his best estimates of the development of market tastes, the probability that the latter would make any use of this information is very low. This is partly because of the third reason.
- The market is a sellers' market, and consumers have few sanctions they can apply against poor supplies.

This is why any evolutionary forces are completely emasculated in this field. Furthermore, since the scope for able management in retailing is so limited, able and ambitious recruits to the labor force tried to build their careers in more exciting sectors, e.g., heavy industry or even politics. The effects of the neglect of marketing on the whole civilian sector were ruinous: the technological backwardness of the European socialist countries has its roots in the severance of the communication link between the producing sector and the market, i.e., the total neglect of the retail sector.[8] It is therefore of paramount importance that this sector be rebuilt as fast as possible.

There are political obstacles to the growth of trade in general and retail in particular. The contribution of this sector to the national economy is not properly understood. The view that there are 'productive' and 'unproductive' sectors is deeply ingrained into the economic thought of Eastern Europe. In fact this may have a much wider currency: it can be found in many 19th century writings, and has been transmitted to us by Marx, not developed by him. Therefore commerce is often called, pejoratively, speculation. And speculation is obviously 'unproductive', or even theft: since the contribution to the economy which originates in the unification and widening of markets is not recognized, all the speculator does is to appropriate to himself 'surplus value' which should accrue to society in general. There is indeed an element of speculation in entrepreneurial trade in the early stages of transition: because the markets under state planning are so fragmented, the transfer of resources from one to the other can be highly profitable. But the unification of the markets is highly useful to society, and these high 'speculative' profits disappear once the markets have been unified, and all that remains as a source of profits is the task of distribution and of gauging the markets.[9]

References

Domar, Evsey (1974); On the Optimal Compensation of a Socialist Manager; *Quarterly Journal of Economics,* 88, 1-18.

Radner, Roy and Michael L. Rothschild (1975); On the Allocation of Effort; *Journal of Economic Theory,* 10, 358-376.

---

8 A similar tale can be told with regard to the export sector, but this does not belong to this paper.

9 As Wladimir Andreff has rightly suggested, in amassing riches speculators also perform the role of 'primitive accumulation'.

Comment on Michael Keren

Wladimir Andreff

Michael Keren's contribution points at the role of retail trade in the evolutionary process of transformation from central planning to market economy. Indeed the author focuses on what seems to us a crucial - though rather neglected in the literature - issue concerning transitional economies today. The conclusion sounds very accurate when it is stressed that the retail trade sector must be re-built as fast as possible during the transformation process towards a fully-fledged market economy. The discussant being in tune with the general train of thought conveyed by the paper, the comments are consequently brief and marginal, and do not dissect in minute detail each equation of the stimulating two agent model. Three comments refer to the underlying assumptions of the model and two remarks attempt at following up the suggested analysis on specific points.

1. Concerning the hypotheses lying behind Michael Keren's model, it is a little bit surprising that no kind of wholesale transaction has been taken into account in modelling either a market economy or a centrally planned organization. For it is quite usual to see a wholesale supplier acting as a trader between the producer and the retailer. In former centrally planned economies, wholesale suppliers were centralizing the delivery of many products and inputs and they had the last say over their planned clients. In market economies, on the contrary, a decentralized network of wholesale traders tries to adjust to the demand expressed by retailers. Wholesale organizations can therefore convey two information flows. In a centrally planned economy, it was an information transferred from the top to the retailer which pertained to the current state of shortage. In a market economy, it is an information transmitted from below to the producer about the needs of the retailers - and in last resort of consumers. A first issue is thus to know how could it be envisaged to introduce wholesale trade - of such great importance in the misdoings of the former centralized planning - in Michael Keren's model of transformation, together with retail trade?

2. In Michael Keren's model, input suppliers remain in the background. They are implicitly assumed to adjust to the producer's demand of inputs. The producer is supposed to adjust to market needs as expressed by means of information transmitted to him by the retailer. There is no doubt that such a sequence is at work in a fully-fledged market economy, though with a number of agents higher than just one producer and one retailer (both of them can admittedly be regarded as representative agents in the model). But it is obvious that the same sequence did not work in former centrally planned economies where short supply was the hardest constraint on the producer's behavior. Therefore the producer of the planned economy used to adjust to supply shortages and to transfer the shortage backward to wholesale and retail shops, and then to consumers, whatever the information he happened to receive from all of them. In the transition period, something still remains of this legacy of the former economic system. Put

otherwise, we may wonder whether it is realistic or not to build a model of a transitional economy in which all supply constraints and seller market behavior are assumed to have already disappeared.

3. Let us now assume that the producer is not able to adjust to the information provided by the retailer because of tight supply constraints or due to an outdated and inflexible technology or by lack of skilled manpower, all assumptions which can easily prevail right after the breakdown of the planned economy. Introducing this assumption in the discussed model, the producer (and hence the economy) will not be able to increase production and the retailer will have to allocate a steady output. As a consequence, the transformation process will have turned a production economy without market (i.e. the former centrally planned economy) into a market economy without (increased) production. Such a picture corresponds to several real transitional economies which suffer from a steady or even a decreased level of output today. A market economy allocating a steady output thanks to the role of retailers sounds like a kind of static Walrasian equilibrium. In a transitional economy as this one, how could retailers incite producers to overcome their supply or technological constraints in order to pave the way for a growing production? Our guess is that the discussed model as such cannot provide an answer.

4. Now, extending the lessons drawn from Michael Keren's model, we would go as far as to say that the transformation of Eastern European countries into market economies not only requires a developing network of retailers; the transformation process also demands some kind of trading companies - more or less designed as Japanese "sogo shosha" or German "Handelsgesellschaften" - capable of gathering information for producers on a wide scale covering both domestic and world (import-export) markets. This should probably be a next step in the transformation process.

5. Finally, a very marginal comment points at the concluding remark in Michael Keren's paper concerning productive and non-productive sectors. Since the eighties the so-called services have become a sector thanks to which productivity has increased in the whole area of developed market economies and in transnational corporations. This sector obviously includes retail trade. Therefore, if we want to increase productivity in transitional economies, a prerequisite is to develop services, namely retail trade. Speculation is unavoidable on an emerging retail trade market when all supply shortages of inputs have not yet disappeared. In post-socialist economies, speculation is a question of either swift revenues yielded from existing misallocation of resources or criminal economic activity, both being legacies of the former system. We have to recall however that speculation is also a means for achieving a rapid primary accumulation of capital which is needed in the first stage of capitalist development. Willy nilly, a primary accumulation process is necessary in transitional economies nowadays.

PART 2

EVOLUTION OF MARKETS: EXPERIENCES
AND PROSPECTS FROM THE WEST

5 On the historical development of stock markets

Larry Neal

1. Features of contemporary emerging stock markets

Stock markets represent the purest form of market activity. As Alfred Marshall (1938, 326f.) put it, "Any one share or bond of a public company, or any bond of a government is of exactly the same value as any other of the same issue: it can make no difference to any purchaser which of the two he buys." Consequently, the ideal features of a perfectly competitive market with fully informed agents, numerous buyers and sellers willing to deal with any counterparty, and a homogeneous commodity are most nearly, and most often, approached in a stock market. Moreover, emerging stock markets are clearly the salient feature of the current thrust toward marketization in the transition and developing economies of the world. They are of central importance for these economies to mobilize capital for reconstruction of their infrastructure and for exploiting opportunities in other markets as they emerge.

A quick look at the 1994 *GT Guide to World Equity Markets* helps to focus our historical account of stock market developments upon the aspects most relevant to today's emerging markets. In 1993, a world-wide fall in interest rates led investors to move from cash and fixed interest securities into equities, especially in emerging markets.

> In the second half of 1993 alone, Mexican equities rose by 57 percent, the Philippine market by 104 percent; Malaysia was up by just under 70 percent and Indonesia by 63 percent. Nor was the euphoria restricted to the now popular emerging markets of Latin American and the Far East. Previously obscure markets such as Poland and Zimbabwe accelerated to record levels.
> …Scandinavian equity markets lifted restrictions on foreign investment; Switzerland improved its accounting standards and entered a new phase of "investor-friendliness". The French government offered new fiscal incentives to attract equity investment, while the Italian market announced long-awaited measures to improve shareholder protection. The Netherlands finally relaxed some outdated restrictions on equity investment by the world's largest pension fund, the ABP. (GT-Management, 1994, 2).

Examining more closely those emerging markets that are relevant to this conference, several interesting features show up in common, despite the presence of national idiosyncrasies. First, the capitalization on the markets is relatively high, both with respect to gross domestic product and to bank deposits. The Czech capitalization is 58 percent of GDP and shares held by individuals amounted to about one-third of their holdings of bank deposits; Hungarian capitalization of $ 820 million at the end of 1993 has since increased substantially, while the Polish market had reached $ 4 billion by April

1994 and is expected to rise to more than 30 percent of GDP. Second, brokerage fees are very high and the volume of trading is relatively low, with very limited times available for trading. Brokerage fees were 0.5 percent to 1.5 percent in the Czech Republic, between 1 percent and 2 percent in Hungary, and ranged from 0.8 percent to 1.2 percent in Poland. These were very high, even by historical standards. Third, the trading that does occur is disproportionate concentrated on the shares of the companies with the largest capitalization. This, however, is perfectly normal and characterizes not only modern exchanges in the US and UK but historical exchanges as well. Fourth, the largest stockholders are a mix of financial intermediaries - investment funds, commercial banks, insurance companies, and pension funds - rather than individuals or other non-financial companies. This is normal in the initial phase of a developing market, but the future pattern of participants will be determined by the rules that are developed for joint-stock firms, traders, and purchasers to participate in the market. Fifth, despite wide differences in the regulations governing the participation of foreign investors, they made up from 20 percent (Poland) to 70 percent (Hungary) of the holdings in the organized equity markets (GT-Management, 1994, 5-6, 15, 20-21 for the Czech Republic, Hungary and Poland, respectively). This is encouraging and very consistent with the historical pattern of developments; foreigners and politically marginal groups were the most active participants initially in those markets that prospered.

By contrast, the stock market looks much different in united Germany, the largest, most advanced industrial economy with the strongest historical ties to these transition economies. Despite a resurgence of activity after the collapse of the Berlin Wall and the re-unification with East Germany, the capitalization of domestic equities amounted to only 26 percent of German GDP, compared to 62 percent and 120 percent for the US and the UK. Only 10 of the nearly 800 stocks listed in Germany accounted for 63 percent of the trading volume in 1993. Only a bit over 5 percent of the German population actually held any stocks, compared to over 16 percent in France, 21 percent in the US and UK, and 35 percent in Sweden (GT-Management, 1994, 12). A far greater proportion of the external equity of German firms is simply held by other non-financial firms (42.4 percent) than in either the transition economies or in the other advanced industrial countries. While the stunted development of the Germany equity markets relative to other advanced nations has existed throughout the twentieth century, reforms in the regulation of German stock exchanges have occurred only recently. These have come only in response to the realization that the leading German firms have been turning to other marketplaces to issue new equity in the 1990s, especially London and even New York. The latest development to encourage the growth of the German equity market has been to regulate against insider trading, imitating the practice of the US Securities and Exchange Commission. But attempts to create a unified securities market in Germany under the aegis of the holding company, Deutsche Börse, have been repeatedly stymied by opposition from the eight regional exchanges. Needless to say, the German exchanges have not been open to listing of foreign securities, least of all from the transition economies of Central and East Europe, although the Deutsche Börse has been open to participation by foreign traders - 66 of the 232 stock exchange members are overseas credit institutions (GT-Management, 1994, 13).

The alternative mode of financing that German firms have followed for nearly two centuries - bank lending - is also the preferred mode for German investment in the transition economies. This raises the question of which mode of financial intermediation is most desirable for the transition economies, one that is most congenial to the investors from the largest economy in the vicinity or one that will mobilize capital from the widest possible sources of funds? And that raises the deeper questions of how intermediaries and markets develop in the financial sector, how they complement or compete with each other, and ultimately how they mobilize and allocate capital in the economy.

2. How stock markets and banks emerged historically

What are the implications of these contrasts and comparisons, particularly for the relative efficacy of credit intermediaries versus capital markets? An examination of the historical development of capital markets over the course of several centuries and in a variety of cultural contexts will help focus our attention on the key issues.

Markets for credit seem to be part of the human legacy as far back as the written records will allow us to observe. And the written records themselves are typically the expression of government regulation, so that one may infer markets existed even earlier. Evidence of firms recognizable as banks, the *trapezai* of Athens, has recently been adduced from the extensive classical literature of ancient Greece (Cohen, 1992) and transferable shares in joint-stock ventures were a standard feature of maritime business in classical Rome.[1] But there is no evidence that an organized secondary market existed in the shares that merchants had invested in, for example, particular voyages of individual ships. Indeed, the business affairs of the *trapezai* in ancient Greece appear to have been focused on efforts of well-to-do Athenians to keep their wealth less visible to the rest of the community - one of the reasons that evidence of their operation is indirect and circumstantial. The *agora*, by contrast, was a public market place, where transactions could be observed by all concerned, including the tax authorities. It was the site for subscriptions to public funds raised for financing festivals or wars, but not for private business ventures. Transfer of shares in ships or voyages implies not only a transfer of financial claims upon the future profits of the venture but also a transfer of control over the management of the venture. This was something best handled in private, among fellow merchants that one could trust. The basic division of labor between banks and markets as suppliers of capital was already evident in antiquity. If owners of equity in an enterprise are primarily concerned about control, they will prefer confidential access to credit from credit institutions; but if they are primarily concerned about liquidity, they will turn to the impersonal market where shares can be transferred readily at a price transparent to all.

Some of the city states of early modern Europe did issue debt to the public. The city of Florence in the mid-14th century created long-term municipal debt - the Monte Comune. It was traded on a secondary market and 15th century direct taxes were based

---

1 The *societas maris* as described in de Roover, 1971, 49-53.

on its market, rather than book, value implying that an active secondary market existed (de Roover, 1966, 22, 25). But the relationship of banks to this market appears to have been incidental. For example, the Medici bank in Florence reported a total of 122 670 florins in assets for the catasto of 1457, but of this total only 8 569 were holdings of the public debt. In 1407, however, the city of Genoa founded the *Casa de San Giorgio*, the first known public clearing bank, which also funded into long-term debt the accumulated debts of the city. Even though it failed in 1444, it served as the model for public clearing banks of the late 16th century throughout northern Italy and Europe, including the *Banco della Piazza di Rialto* of Venice in 1587, the *Amsterdamsche Wisselbank* in 1609, and the Bank of England in 1694 (see Neal, 1992). It was these public banks that served as the interface between banks (or less formally constituted financial intermediaries such as notary publics, attorneys, or goldsmiths) and stock markets. Once founded, they served to facilitate the development of both organizational forms - financial intermediaries and capital markets - for providing capital to business firms.

3. The Amsterdam stock exchange in the 17th century

The first organized stock market arose in Amsterdam and is described in Josseph de la Vega's *Confusion de Confusiones*, published in 1688 and probably intended as a guide to the Portuguese Jews of Amsterdam who were being called into the service of William of Orange for purposes of financing his war against France. According to de la Vega, it was the nature of the Dutch East India Company (*Verenigde Oostindische Compagnie*, hereafter VOC) that created the opportunities for a stock market in Amsterdam.

The VOC was formed in 1609 to create a permanent capital fund that could be used to build up fortified ports in monsoon Asia. These were necessary so that sufficient stocks of Asian goods could be accumulated at the ports to allow the annual convoys of ships from the Netherlands to turn around quickly with full cargoes. Shareholders in the first three voyages of the convoys saw their investments converted into a permanent fund from which they could not withdraw. They could claim annual dividends, however, and transfer their shares to other investors. To broaden the resale market for the initial investors, shareholders were not allowed to vote on any matters. Instead, operating control of the company was vested in 17 Directors, the *Heeren XVII*, appointed in set proportions by the six cities of the Netherlands, who also had a fixed proportion of the total capital stock of nearly 6.5 million florins, divided into transferable shares of 3000 florins each.

Transfer and ledger books were maintained at each of the six chambers of the company, but as the Amsterdam chamber had just under half the stock, that was where most of the transfers, and nearly all the trade, of the stock occurred. The transfer books were available four or five days a week and recorded the locations of the ledger entries for both the seller and buyer, the amount of stock transferred, and the names of two witnesses and the clerk. A very small transfer fee was charged per share. Delays did occur due to the sloppiness of the clerks in recording entries and the necessity of checking to make sure the seller had at least the number of shares being sold to his or her credit in the main ledger. Dissatisfaction with the speed of transfers meant that most trading in VOC shares was done on the basis of forward, or *termijn*, contracts. These were settled at regular *rescontre* dates established every three months. Moreover, given the fixed capital stock of the immensely profitable company (over the nearly two centuries of its existence the VOC *averaged* an annual payout of 18 percent on its original capital (De Korte, 1983, 93), the market value of each share became so large that trade was more conveniently done in artificial fractions, called *ducatons*, of the shares. The combination of time deals and ducatons led to the emergence of specialized traders, who could make a living from the combination of commissions and trading gains made speculating against the occasional investors in VOC shares. Nevertheless, at the time de la Vega wrote, the number of specialized traders was small and they confined their market making to a small corner of the Amsterdam Exchange. While the stock of transferable municipal debt issued by the Dutch cities and provinces had expanded enormously over the century since declaring their independence from Spain, it does not seem to have been traded actively in the secondary market for securities described by de la Vega in 1688. This may be because each city issued its own debt and successive issues were guaranteed against specific taxes enacted for that purpose. Hence, no one debt issue provided much incentive or opportunity for trading after it had been placed.

In terms of the issues we identified with respect to today's emerging stock markets, this first stock market had only one security issued in large enough quantity and dispersed among enough different investors to support a group of specialized traders, namely the share capital of the VOC. Their transfer charges were low and their brokerage commissions were the same as those set for brokers in the commodity trades that dominated the Amsterdam Beurs. Despite trading in securities of direct concern to the state, they were not formally regulated in any way. Freedom from regulation was prized sufficiently, it has been argued, that no printed price list was produced for the benefit of their clients despite the obvious advantages this innovation gave to stockbrokers in London as early as 1697. To date, it appears that the stock exchange of Amsterdam did not print a price list in any form until the restrictions of the printing guild in Amsterdam were abolished by the Batavian Republic in 1795 (see Neal, 1990).

The number of stock traders in the Amsterdam Beurs in 1688 was sufficiently limited enough for them to prefer to deal only with other members of a close-knit group already dealing in other affairs with them. In this way, any breach of contract in stock-trading could be compensated by an offsetting breach of contract in some other transaction unrelated to the stock market, but very much part of the group's activities. The group that emerged by the end of the 17th century in the Amsterdam Beurs was comprised of members of the Sephardic Jewish community that had migrated from Antwerp when Spain forced them to convert to Christianity or be expelled. Excluded from the merchant and craft guilds in Amsterdam as well, they were forced to deal in the diamond and coral trades, pawnbroking, and coin-changing. Their role in mobilizing funds and supplies for armies throughout Europe emerged during the Thirty Years War and reached its zenith under William III, Stadhouder of the United Provinces from 1672 to 1702 and King of

England from the end of 1688 to his death[2]. The role of immensely wealthy "Court Jews" who emerged in this period must have provided a similarly close-knit clientele for Jewish stock-brokers in Amsterdam. There were, however, similar networks of co-religionists among the Huguenot populations dispersed in all directions from France by Louis XIV and among the Catholic supporters of Charles VI and the Habsburg monarchy, not to mention the exiled James II in France. All of these participated in the mobilization of the huge funds required to finance the European wars of the 17th and early 18th centuries, and therefore in the development of Europe's early stock markets.

It is likely that trading in the stock markets was done largely among individuals in these separate groups rather than between the groups. But it is interesting that a large number of such distinct groups could persist simultaneously in the cosmopolitan environments of Amsterdam, London, and Paris at the end of the 17th century. Moreover, their memberships were disrupted often enough by dynastic disputes and religious quarrels or wars so that no stable set of mutually exclusive credit institutions could be established anywhere. Rather, recourse to some form of capital market had to be devised from time to time for any group, say the exiled Jacobites in France or the Irish "Wild Geese" scattered throughout Catholic Europe, if they were to sustain their vitality. Driven from positions of power and uprooted from their ancestral communities, these displaced elites were unable to sustain formal credit institutions and so were forced to go to the largely informal capital markets that existed at the time if they were to preserve or regain at least some of their wealth.

4. Goldsmith bankers and the creation of a stock market in London

A classic example of the way turmoil could replace credit institutions with credit markets occurred in England in the year 1672. In that year Charles II of England issued his Stop of the Exchequer, when he ordered the Exchequer to stop repaying the debt he currently owed, mainly to goldsmith-bankers in London. His motive was to reclaim access to the current stream of tax revenues coming into the Exchequer in order to direct them toward equipping troops and ships to begin the Third Anglo-Dutch War. His hope was that a quick victory would be as profitable in terms of captured cargoes and ships as the First and Second Anglo-Dutch Wars had been for England in the previous 20 years. Then, presumably, he could either repay the goldsmiths or replace them. Half the goldsmith-bankers of London are supposed to have failed as a consequence and the much larger number of bourgeoisie and aristocracy who had deposited funds with them were left without access to their funds as well.

There was as yet no organized stock market in London. However, there were shares in the English East India Company to be traded, as well as in the Royal African Company, the Hudson's Bay Company, and the Mines Royal, and such price quotes as we have tended to move up when trade was expanding and to fall when it was disrupted

---

2 The high point of "Court Jews" in Europe at this time is brilliantly described and analyzed in Israel (1989, 123-45).

(see Scott, 1912; chs. 14 and 15 chronicle these developments). We cannot get direct evidence now on the exact course of events that ensued as the Third Anglo-Dutch War turned against Charles II, but it is clear that activity in the trading of shares of existing companies increased and that Londoners began to propose more joint-stock companies. It also appears that the lesser goldsmith-bankers who had not loaned large sums to the Crown and who survived the Stop of the Exchequer began a period of growth based on the renewed confidence depositors had in them (see the discussion in Quinn, 1994). An unanticipated, but instructive, consequence of the Stop of the Exchequer was therefore an impulse both toward the development of a stock market and for a re-direction in the business of the goldsmith-bankers.

It clearly was the Glorious Revolution of 1688 and the arrival of William III from Holland with his cortège of Dutch advisors and financiers that completed the creation of a London stock market. With William, there arose a formal stock market with a body of active traders subject to licensing by the City of London, regularly-produced price lists, and an identifiable location of its own - the coffee houses of Exchange Alley located next to the Royal Exchange, the Bank of England and the post office. Scott records an explosion of joint-stock companies engaged in a wide variety of domestic projects. He attributes this to a diversion of merchant capital from foreign trade into profit opportunities at home as a result of the disturbances to foreign trade caused by the war from 1689 to 1697. The new government, more concerned about battles abroad than regulation of business at home, was sufficiently distracted that it allowed these novel departures from the normal routines for financing business ventures to take place. But it also appears that the London stock exchange had imported foreign financial expertise as well as foreign capital and this must have had some additional effect in showing British investors the possibilities of organizing capital on an impersonal market.

For one thing, the bookkeeping procedures of the first joint-stock company formally chartered by the new regime, the Bank of England, was identical to that described above for the Dutch East India Company. The difference was that the transfer clerks had the ledgers immediately behind them in the main hall of the Bank so they could record the transfers very quickly and their signature alone was sufficient to witness the transfer. In short, the transplanted innovation was more efficient than the original because only the operational part was imported while the environmental constraints were left behind in the Netherlands.

True, the stockholders in England were accorded voting privileges unlike those in Holland, but £ 500 of the £ 1 200 000 of capital stock was required to have one vote, and no one person could have more than one vote in the elections of the Directors. To stand for election, a stock of £ 2 000 was required and while foreigners could hold stock and vote if present at the General Court, they could not be Directors (Scott, 1912, 339-340). As far as control of the management of the Bank was concerned, the Bank was clearly a Whig-dominated institution and responsive to Whig political goals as formulated in the House of Commons by that party's leaders. There was little chance that this would change in response to the relatively minor alterations in the distribution of shares that could arise from normal trading on the stock exchange. (When it appeared possible during the South Sea Bubble in 1720, the Bank directors promptly mortgaged enough of the stock to ensure no takeover could possibly occur.) In short, the Bank's organizational structure and distribution of initial shares effectively stymied hostile takeovers - consequently there was no hesitation in making the shares freely transferable so that an active market in them could develop.

The Whigs also managed to undercut the previously chartered East India Company by forming their own New East India Company in 1698. Trading in shares of both companies reflected more a struggle for political control of the monopoly of trade with Asia than a search for profitable investment by the rentier class, until the merger of the two companies in 1708. From then on, however, trading in East India shares reflected more the search for profit than the seizure of power until the Regulatory Act of 1772 began to change the relationship of the government and the Company. After 1772, the pattern of price movements in its shares became more erratic and the threat of further interventions by the government, which kept increasing its annual tax on the company to support the standing army maintained in India, lowered the market price of India stock compared to what would have been justified on the dividends alone (Neal, 1990). The vicissitudes of the East India Company stock demonstrate the importance of creating a viable market in shares by divorcing the profit motive of purchasers from the power motives of opponents to the current management.

The rise and fall of the South Sea Company underscores the necessity of stripping the possibility of managerial control from outside equity in order to make it marketable. In 1711, the Tories had their opportunity to fund the accumulated war debt from the War of the Spanish Succession by forming the South Sea Company. Its initial capital stock of £ 10 million made it larger than the Bank of England and the East India Company combined. But its initial subscribers were primarily a new breed of goldsmith-bankers, the leading members of which had also made fortunes dealing in the stock of the Bank and the EIC. George Caswall was the leading dealer in large transactions of Bank stock and Elias Turner was by far the largest dealer in India stock. They clearly saw themselves as viable competitors to both the Bank and the United EIC. They made their goals clear in 1720 when they tried to emulate John Law's *Compagnie des Indes* in France by having the South Sea Company fund all the remaining debt of the government. I have explained elsewhere the rationale behind the explosion in price and volume of South Sea stock that occurred in 1720, but it clearly built upon the confidence in the stock market that had arisen in the public over the previous decade and initially had a reasonable, if very innovative, basis. The denouement of that episode was to re-organize the South Sea Company to the benefit of mainly the Bank of England and convert the bulk of its voting stock into non-voting perpetual annuities bearing an annual interest of 3 percent. The resulting stock of standardized, interest-bearing, liquid financial assets formed a reliable, permanent basis for active traders. True, no additions were ever made to the stock of annuities administered by the disgraced South Sea Company, but first the Bank of England in 1726, and then the government directly during the War of the Austrian Succession, issued their own identical versions of the South Sea 3 percent annuities in increasing amounts. And trade in these formed the overwhelming bulk of activity on the London Stock Market for the century from 1723 until the massive repayments of war debt that began in 1820.

By 1712, only 40 years after the Stop of the Exchequer had effectively stymied the rise of goldsmith bankers in England to a status comparable to Court Jews on the Continent or to the Augsburg and Genoese bankers of the Spanish monarchs in earlier years, a financial revolution had occurred in which the constitutional monarchy of England and Scotland could raise previously undreamed amounts of capital through access to a formal capital market. The key was to provide liquid, income-earning assets - financial claims that earned steady interest and could increase in capital value and in any case could be cashed in readily whenever desired. It appeared to contemporaries and to most subsequent historians of this financial revolution that the capital market had eclipsed the banks as providers of credit to the most voracious demander of credit - the fiscal-military state of 18th century England. As a corollary, fluctuations in the price of the government's debt or in the price of shares of its major creditors - the Bank of England, the East India Company, and the South Sea Company - determined ultimately the price at which credit could be extended by merchants to each other and to their customers (Neal, 1994). But a closer look at the composition of the traders actually responsible for the continued vitality of the market forces a re-evaluation of the relative roles of markets and banks. According to Dickson's study of the financial revolution (Dickson, 1967):

> The first available [stock ledger] for the former [East India Company] is dated 1706-8. The number of accounts in it identifiable from their turnover as those of dealers is over eighty, twenty-seven of which were in Jewish names. The majority of the dealers were London merchants and goldsmith bankers. For example, Peter Delme and John Hopkins were later among the richest men of the day. Peter Henriquez jun. was a merchant, a lender to government and agent for correspondents in Amsterdam. George Caswall, Stephen Child, William Hamond, Richard Hoare, John Marke, Thomas Martin, John Mead, John Narbonne and Benjamin Tudman were goldsmith bankers. Both bankers and merchants dealt in short-dated securities too: thus Caswall, Hoare, Martin and Tudman, together with the merchants and East India stock dealers James Colebrooke, Edward Gibbon, John Lambert and Thomas Le Heup, were among the subscribers of Navy and other bills to the South Sea Company in 1711... (p. 495)
>
> In the ledger [of East India Company stock] for 1715-19 there are over sixty dealers, fourteen of whom are Jews; twenty-three had also been dealers in 1706-8. As at the earlier period, several were bankers, Edward Bowman, Nathaniel Brassey, Sir George Caswall, Thomas Greene, John Humphreys, William King, John Marke, Thomas Martin, Richard Nicholls, Thomas Snow, Elias Turner, George Wanley and Matthew Wymondesold... The remaining Bank stock dealers were substantial merchants, like the Anglo-Dutch Sir Justus Beck (who went bankrupt during the Bubble to the tune of £ 347 000), Anthony da Costa, Sir Matthew Decker, Sir Theodore Jannssen the great South Sea director whose fortune was largely confiscated after the Bubble, Sir Randolph Knipe, and Francis Pereira. Beck, Decker and Pereira were also East India dealers....the other dealers [in government stock] were surpassed in turnover by the professional brokers and jobbers Edward Crull and John Nodes... (p. 498)

Several points are worth highlighting from these remarks by Dickson. First, there were a large number of specialized dealers, individuals whose transactions in just the main government stocks were probably sufficient in volume to earn them a living, and this had occurred by 1708, within 20 years of the transplanting of Dutch expertise. Second, the dealers were drawn from the ranks of goldsmith and merchant bankers primarily, albeit with a very strong representation from Dutch origins, whether Jewish, Huguenot or Dissenter. We know from other evidence that the goldsmith-bankers had not forsaken their banking functions for participation in the business of stock-trading at this time; rather they saw it as a useful complement to their banking functions. Third, within the group of traders, the function of broker and dealer was often mixed, despite the formal regulations governing the functions of licensed brokers, which forbade them to act as principals in the transactions they arranged for their customers.

One consequence of this rapid development in the numbers and diversity of the traders may have been to exacerbate price volatility in the overall market. Figure 5.1 reproduces the movements of the overall price index of the London stock market that I created for the 11 year periods 1698-1708, 1709-1719, and 1724-1734. Figure 5.2 shows that the rapid growth of the prices in the first period, cut short by the outbreak of the War of the Spanish Succession, generated volatile holding period rates of return that fell during the war. From the resolution of the war in 1712 until the outbreak of the turmoil associated with the South Sea Bubble in 1720 the price of stocks grew steadily with positive and sustained holding period rates of return. After 1724, the price index stagnated, the volatility of the holding period rates of return disappeared, although it remained positive. A recent study by a sociologist of the American bond futures market, the epitome of a sophisticated modern financial market, indicates that price volatility even there increased in trades outside normal trading groups.

He attributes the growth of overall volatility to the development of an increasing number of trading groups (Baker, 1984, 775-811). We can think of many other reasons for the change in price volatility for this early stock market, of course, but it is an anomaly to economists, at least, that price volatility in experimental markets seems to increase with the expertise and number of traders. A logical explanation for this phenomenon is the rising importance of "price discovery" for traders seeking to stimulate turnover in a market in order to maintain their incomes from commissions. And the best way to discover the depth of a given market at a given time is to experiment with a range of different prices.

After the trauma of the South Sea Bubble, funded government debt was re-organized in the form of perpetual annuities issued initially both by the South Sea Company and the Bank of England and then directly by the government during the War of the Austrian Succession, eventually becoming consolidated in the Three Percent Consols. This greatly increased the amount of the national debt, but also increased the availability of a liquid, easily transferable, interest-earning financial asset. The volume of trading on the London Stock Exchange probably increased despite the disappearance of nearly all the so-called "bubble companies" that had appeared, some for only a few days, during the year 1720. Certainly the volume of transfers of the various forms of government stock increased enormously over the course of the 18th century (for a contrasting, and erroneous, view, see Mirowski, 1981, 559-577).

Figure 5.1 Price index for the London stock exchange

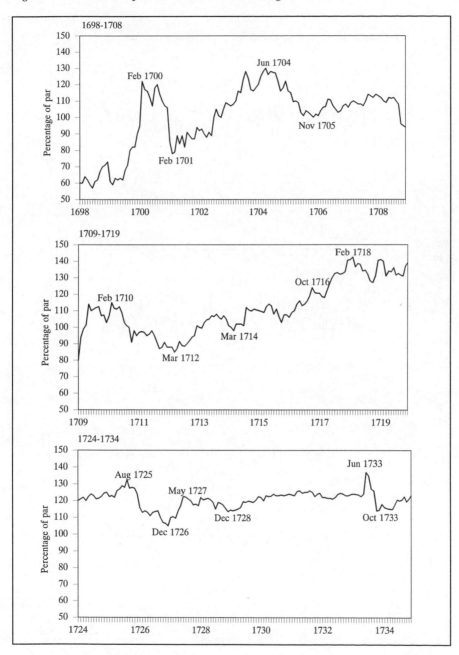

Figure 5.2 Volatility indicators for the London stock exchange

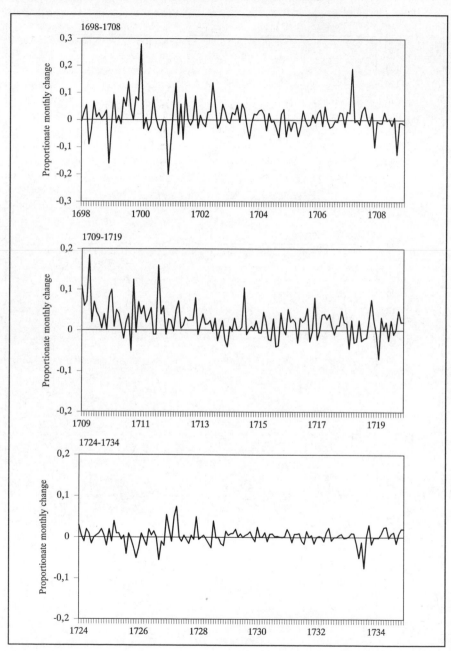

The restrictions on forming new joint-stock companies posed by the Bubble Act of 1720 may have limited the potential for enterprises to raise capital by issuing external equity, but the existence of a large, liquid stock of government debt available for adjusting quickly the portfolios of financial intermediaries led to the rise of a number of financial intermediaries specializing in providing capital to particular industries and/or regions in Britain. These included attorneys in the industrial northwest, scriveners in the agricultural southeast, and export merchants in London, Bristol, and Liverpool for the manufacturing Midlands. By the middle of the 18th century, a growing number of country banks began to appear, although they would not really proliferate until the huge expansion of government debt in the London stock market during the Napoleonic wars.

The complex web of credit relationships spun out by these financial intermediaries across England, Wales, Ireland and Scotland over the rest of the 18th century responded faithfully to disturbances originating at the center - the capital market in London dominated by the extensive trading in government debt. Figure 5.3 shows how the disruptions in trade credit, indicated by the incidence of bankruptcies, were correlated with the fluctuations in the price of government debt in the London capital market.

These fluctuations, in turn, were dominated by the effects of war finance, which required a substantial increase in the volume of funded debt at the conclusion of each war. The supply shock thus created always led to a fall in the price of Consols or their equivalent and created a rise in the rate of interest that financial intermediaries would have to pay to their depositors to maintain their business. A relationship between the financial intermediaries and the capital market was created by 1726 that persisted through the increasing shocks of ever larger-scale wars until the changes in legislation that followed the stock market boom and bust of 1825.

5.   The formal London stock exchange

In the intervening century, the London Stock Exchange gradually acquired more formal characteristics that were to be unique to it. The member brokers clearly had formed a co-partnership in 1773 when they re-named The New Jonathan's to The Stock Exchange (Morgan and Thomas, 1962, 68), and they asserted their cohesion when they consolidated their listing of stock prices in 1786 in Edward Wetenhall's *Course of the Exchange* (Neal, 1988, 163-178), and finally formed a joint stock corporation in 1801 (Morgan and Thomas, 1962, 70-71). The changes of 1773 and 1801 corresponded with the construction of new buildings for the use of jobbers and brokers when the volume of business in securities trading outgrew the physical limits of the existing facilities. The use of coffee houses located along Exchange Alley when the stock traders were excluded from the Royal Exchange dates from the end of the 17th century, during the creation of the national debt with the wars of William III. In 1762, as financing of the Seven Years War was reaching its peak, 150 of the most substantial brokers tried to obtain exclusive use of Jonathan's by paying a rent of £ 1 200 a year, each of them subscribing £ 8 annual dues toward this. But this attempt to limit access was thwarted by an excluded broker who brought suit against Jonathan's and won right of access on grounds that "Jonathan's had been a place of resort for dealers in stocks and shares from time immemorial." (Morgan and Thomas, 1962, 68.)

Figure 5.3 Consol yields and bankruptcies in England, 1700-1826

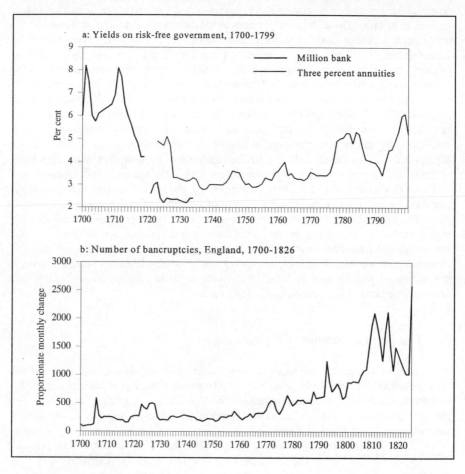

The formal naming of *The Stock Exchange* and the building of a new facility in Threadneedle Street followed the crisis of 1772, which had originated in Scotland in ill-timed speculation on the fall of East India stock and had culminated in Amsterdam with similarly ill-timed speculation on the rise of East India stock (Wilson, 1941, 169-182). The construction of the Capel Court facility began in 1801 at the height of dealings in the vastly increased sums of government debt supplied during the war with Napoleonic France. The initiative appears to have been taken by a dissident group of stockbrokers who had not been included in the close circle of subscribers around Walter Boyd, whose firm had taken the lead in contracting for the first large loan issues authorized by Pitt to provide subsidies to the allies in the First Coalition.

From the animosities between the two (or more) groups came the odd institutional structure of the London Stock Exchange, formally constituted in 1801. The inscription on the cornerstone of the original building explains its motivation:

"On the 18th of May in the year 1801, and forty-one of George III, the first stone of this building, erected by private subscription for transaction of business in the public funds, was laid ... At this era, the first of the union between Great Britain and Ireland, the public funded debt had accumulated in five successive reigns to £ 552 730 924. The inviolate faith of the British nation, and the principles of the constitution, sanction and ensure the property embarked in this undertaking. May the blessing of the constitution be secured to the latest posterity." (Morgan and Thomas, 1962, 71)

The Exchange itself was owned by a joint-stock corporation with closely held shares by the Proprietors, who set the terms for use of the building by subscribing Members. These, in turn, were the active traders, divided by then into the distinct categories of Jobbers and Brokers. When the Royal Commission examined its operation in 1878, it split almost evenly over whether the Members themselves should not form a joint-stock corporation to have equal legal standing with Proprietors and to give permanence to whatever changes in procedures were implemented in response to their inquiries. Given that the rulings of the Committee on General Purposes, elected annually by and from the Members of the Stock Exchange, appeared effective and prompt and were recognized as enforceable by strictly internal sanctions under British law, four of the twelve commissioners felt little was to be gained from such a change.

The more problematic institutional arrangement was the division of the Members into Brokers and Jobbers. The reliance of the British government upon contractors for placement of each new issue of debt doubtless led to the emergence of jobbers as specialized dealers after the Napoleonic Wars. The contractors often continued to hold large amounts of the new issues after their initial placement in order to keep up their price and cooperated with each other to "make a market" for the government stock. The distinction between brokers and jobbers seemed to hold up after the war primarily in government stocks. The government's procedures also validated the practice of trading in subscription receipts for private joint-stock companies that were applying for a charter from Parliament. Promoters could induce major price swings in subscription receipts only partly paid up on the anticipation that the charter would finally be granted under the terms of the Bubble Act of 1720. The political vicissitudes of the approval process in Parliament were often reflected in wild price swings in the receipts; only the wiliest of professional traders in the London market would be willing to act as counterparties to the trade opportunities that arose.

During the stock market mania of 1825 when hundreds of new firms were being promoted, the delay between advertisement of a new venture and news of its charter being granted lengthened and the uncertainty over the value of subscription receipts increased as a result. The abolition of the Bubble Act in late 1825 was likely an attempt to reduce the uncertainty in the market, and the price swings in subscription receipts, by speeding up the disposition of applications pending. In the Joint Stock Companies Act of 1844, dealing before allotment was formally outlawed and "every contract for, or sale or disposal of, such share or interest shall be void, and every person entering into such contract shall forfeit a sum not exceeding £ 10." This legislation, cited approvingly by the Royal Commission, was repealed, however, by the Joint Stock Companies Act of 1856. The difficulty was that such contracts would continue to be enforced by the Committee on General Purposes, provided they were accepted as common practice by the membership. And they were good business for the traders of the London Stock Exchange, as long as the possibility of fraudulent dealings did not discourage trading in the established securities.

While experimentation showed that regulation of contracts among the active traders in the London Stock Exchange was best left to the traders themselves, it was not so clear that they could be trusted to convey accurately information on prices of the securities they were trading. The hallmark of a capital market is the conveyance of information to all participants in the form of price postings, and to be efficient the prices at which trades are made must be reported accurately and quickly to all concerned. By contrast, financial intermediaries are most effective when they maintain confidentiality with respect to the terms on which they are lending to their clients. The confusion between the role of Brokers and Jobbers, which was endemic to the operation of the London Stock Exchange, created concern about the accuracy of prices reported in the regularly published price lists made available to the public.

The *Daily Official List* referred to by the Committee had been formed in 1866, consolidating three daily lists that had arisen by then - one each for British and foreign government stocks, non-railway companies and railway companies. Wetenhall's twice-weekly *Course of the Exchange* continued as well, presumably for the benefit of less active investors, although by this time it listed an extensive sample of all varieties of the stocks traded on the London Stock Exchange. The origin of the three distinct daily lists, presumably for three distinct groups of investors interested in three different categories of securities, regardless of whether they were British or foreign - governments, railways, and non-railway corporations - goes back at least as far as 1824. James Wetenhall began publishing the *British and Foreign Share List* on a daily basis in late 1824, while continuing publication of his twice-weekly *Course of the Exchange* (1825).[3] The *British and Foreign Share List* consisted mainly of quotes on shares in the mines being promoted in Spanish America (22) and in minor metals in the British Isles (12), and a large array of "Miscellaneous" promotions (56), with a few (5) new insurance company stocks, as well as some gas, light, and coke companies (7) and a selection of "Iron Railways" (8). It left out entirely the "Canals", "Docks", and major insurance companies that were the staple of the twice-weekly *Course of the Exchange*.

---

3 To date, I have only located one issue of this publication, No. 171 for Friday, July 8, 1825. It gives the afternoon price from the previous day, "July 7, 1 to 4 o'clock," and the morning price of the publication day, "July 8, 10 to 1 o'clock." Assuming it was published six days a week, the "No. 171" indicates it began publication on December 21, 1824.

Table 5.1 Volatility of various stocks in 1824-26 (Coefficient of variation of monthly average price)

	Average
Canals	115
Docks	149
Insurance	115
Waterworks	121
Gas & Light	214
Mines	681
Railways	643

Comparing the listings of the two stock price lists on July 8, 1825, one notes first that this was No. 11, 131 of *The Course of the Exchange* and only No. 171 of the *British and Foreign Share List*. Second, *The Course of the Exchange* included only 27 mine stocks and only 7 of them were British. By contrast, fully 36 insurance company shares were listed as well as 40 gas, light, and coke companies. Fifteen railway stocks were listed although only three of them had actual prices quoted for their shares, reflecting the fact the others were still in the process of obtaining Parliamentary approval. The "Miscellaneous" category in *The Course of the Exchange* included 61 stocks, so there was a nearly complete overlap of the coverage of the two printed price lists in that catchall section. It is striking that foreign government, as well as British government, securities were missing from the daily list and the number of railways were fewer in the daily list. If Wetenhall was gauging his market correctly for the two distinct versions of his price-list, it appears that the notorious speculators active in the London stock market in 1825 were focusing on the mines and miscellaneous categories of bubble companies rather than railways and insurance companies. The volatility of prices in these categories as compared to the others in Table 5.1 was also much greater, which lends some credibility to this conjecture.

6. The spread of stock markets in the 19th century

It is clear that the London Stock Exchange evolved in the 19th century along a path that was dependent upon the initial allocation of property rights. It was owned by a subset of the traders who increased the value of their property by variously increasing members, and raising their fees. Membership was enlarged sporadically whenever new trading opportunities arose. Examples are the mines and new governments which arose in the remains of Spanish America in the 1820s, the provincial railways occurring in the 1830s and 1840s, and overseas railways or public utilities which spread around the globe starting in the 1850s and continuing to World War I. Incomes of members, and consequently their fee base, were increased by providing them with a monopoly position in the process of "making a market" for new ventures before allotments were made.

Reciprocally, they were limited from participating in complementary or substitute forms of intermediation. Eventually the distinction between brokers and jobbers and the conflicting responses of each to the new opportunities for trading activity that arose over time led to an internal political conflict resolved in favor of the more numerous brokers by 1909.

By contrast, the New York Stock Exchange, formed in 1792 to trade in bonds issued by the new Federal Government, limited the number of members, which made membership very expensive, but gave free rein to their activities outside the Exchange. Members consequently would use their banking, insurance, or mercantile activities to increase the volume of trading they did on the exchange. Due to regulation of banks by the individual states, no nationwide banking system could develop in the United States comparable to that in the United Kingdom and Germany. However, the brokerage firms in New York did establish nationwide agencies, stimulated by the success of Jay Cook in marketing Union government bonds nationwide during the Civil War. This may have stimulated the rise of complementary exchanges in New York to deal in securities with low volume, usually by new companies such as land companies in new frontier areas or mining companies wherever minerals had been discovered.

It also led to the rise of regional exchanges, which usually concentrated on trade in issues of stock by locally known and operated firms. But it appears that New York and London brokerage firms were often involved in the trading activities of such regional exchanges. It can be conjectured that they were using contacts with the regional exchanges as a substitute method of monitoring the performance of the local firms for the benefit of distant investors located in New York or London. Satellite markets rather than affiliated banks were used by both the New York and London stock traders for purposes of long-distance monitoring of the performance of their companies. For New York, this was due to the prohibitions against nationwide branch banking for the New York banks affiliated with brokerage firms; for London, this was due to the prohibition of banking affiliations for the brokers and jobbers.

An interesting outcome was that while American railway stocks and bonds became major items on both the New York and London exchanges after the American Civil War, there was very little overlap in the railroads whose securities were placed on these two markets. The New York market focused on East Coast and mid-Atlantic railroads while the London market took up Southern and Western railroads. And this regional division of placements persisted until the beginning of the 20th century (Davis and Cull, 1994, ch. IV). The explanation lies, perhaps, in the relative strength of affiliations with local monitors in the various regions of the United States that had been established by brokerage houses in New York or London.

A similar story may be told about the proliferation of local and national exchanges that arose in Europe after the Napoleonic Wars. The Berlin Börse arose in 1817 to trade in bonds of the Prussian state, although the much older and more active exchanges in Hamburg and Frankfurt dominated the German secondary market for securities, until 1871, when Berlin became the premier market place. Nevertheless, regional exchanges continued to play an important role in such places as Stuttgart, Düsseldorf, Cologne, and Essen (Michie, 1992). In each case, the local markets concentrated on securities issued by local joint-stock companies, whether mining, textile, or shipping enterprises. Again, the monitoring function they played for the investors located in Berlin, Frankfurt or Hamburg may have been important, but more likely was the importance of affiliations with brokerage firms in either London, Amsterdam, or Paris.

Paris and Amsterdam became important centers for foreign listings in the later 19th century. Paris concentrated on joint-stock firms, typically mines and railroads, in Europe and the Mediterranean, while Amsterdam was much more global in its coverage, (although probably much smaller in trading volume). A global network of stock exchanges had clearly emerged at the eve of World War I, interconnected by telegraph and telephone communication links, with a system of hubs located in New York, London, , Berlin, and Paris. Each of these in turn had branches radiating into a network of local, regional, or national exchanges with which their brokerage houses had established some form of reliable affiliation.

7. Lessons from history

It is obvious from this background that the emerging stock markets of the developing and transition economies today have a great deal to learn from the history of the secondary markets for securities. We are now seeing the re-emergence of a system of inter-related exchanges around the globe, which is merely resuming an evolutionary path that was brutally blocked by World War I, the Great Depression, World War II and the regulatory responses of national authorities to these traumas. If pre-World War I history is a guide to successful policies, the emerging markets have to provide at least one large-scale, widely held security in which trading can be actively pursued without interfering with managerial control of the enterprise, whether it is a government or a large public utility. Railroads and democratic governments were the enterprises of choice in the late 19th century; established democratic governments with independent central banks and telecommunications and electric power utilities appear appropriate for the late 20th century. Once a tradable product has been created, the operation of the markets can be regulated in a variety of ways. But it seems important to allow private, as opposed to public, ownership of the market facility, to uphold the methods devised by the traders for resolving their contractual disputes, and to allow entrepreneurs to form enterprises mimicking in legal form, as well as in organizational structure, those available for investors in the industrialized parts of the world. They also have to allow them to affiliate with brokerage firms in the central markets where foreign funds are most readily mobilized. The cautionary note is that initial decisions taken in the regulation of a market, whether made by the government or by the traders, will determine the kinds of enterprises that will have access to the market and the wider markets to which the enterprises will be able to gain access.

References

Baker, Wayne E. (1984); The Social Structure of a National Securities Market; *American Journal of Sociology*, 89, 775-811.

Cohen, Edward E. (1992) *Athenian Economy & Society: A Banking Perspective,* Princeton: Princeton University Press.

Davis, Lance E. and Robert Cull (1994) *International Capital Markets and American Economic Growth 1820-1914,* Cambridge: Cambridge University Press, ch. IV.

De Korte, J.P. (1983) *De Jaarlijkse Financiele Verantwoording in de Verenigde Oostindische Compagnie,* The Hague: Nijhoff, 93.

De Roover, Raymond (1966) *The Rise and Decline of the Medici Bank, 1397-1494,* New York: W. W. Norton & Co., 22 and 25.

De Roover, Raymond (1971) The Organisation of Trade, in Postan, Michael M., E. E. Rich and Edward Miller (eds) *Cambridge Economic History of Europe,* Cambridge: Cambridge University Press, 49-53.

Dickson, Peter G. (1967) *The Financial Revolution in England,* London: Macmillan.

GT-Management (1994) *The GT Guide to World Equity Markets*, London: Euromoney Publications.

Israel, Jonathan I. (1989) *European Jewry in the Age of Mercantilism 1550-1750,* Oxford: Clarendon Press, 123-45.

Marshall, Alfred (1938) *Principles of Economics,* London: Macmillan, 326-7.

Michie, Ranald C. (1992) The development of stock markets, in Newman, Peter K., Murray Milgate and John Eatwell (eds) *The New Palgrave Dictionary of Money and Finance,* London: Macmillan.

Mirowski, Philip (1981); The Rise (and Retreat) of a Market: English Joint Stock Shares in the Eighteenth Century; *Journal of Economic History,* 41 (September), 559-77.

Morgan, E. Victor and William A. Thomas (1962) *The Stock Exchange, Its History and Functions,* London: Elek Books, 68.

Neal, Larry (1988); The Rise of a Financial Press: London and Amsterdam, 1681-1810; *Business History*, 30 (April), 163-78.

Neal, Larry (1992) Development of Financial Institutions, in Newman, Peter K., Murray Milgate and John Eatwell (eds) *The New Palgrave Dictionary of Money and Finance,* London: Macmillan.

Neal, Larry (1994), The Finance of Business during the Industrial Revolution, in Floud, Roderick and Donald N. McCloskey (eds) *The Economic History of Britain*, vol. I, Cambridge: Cambridge University Press.

Neal, Larry (1990) *The Rise of Financial Capitalism,* Cambridge: Cambridge University Press.

Quinn, Stephen (1994) *Banking Before the Bank of England: The Unregulated Goldsmith-Bankers of London, 1660-1694*, unpublished PhD Dissertation, University of Illinois.

Scott, William R. (1912) *The Constitution and Finance of English, Scottish and Irish Joint-Stock Companies to 1720*, vol. I, Bristol: Thoemmes Press.

Vega Passarino, Josseph Penso de la (1688, 1939) *Confusion de Confusiones*, The Hague: Nijhoff.

Wilson, Charles (1941, repr. 1966) *Anglo-Dutch Commerce and Finance in the Eighteenth Century,* Cambridge: Cambridge University Press, 169-82.

Comment on Larry Neal

Karl Lohmann

The very interesting study by Professor Neal reassesses the development of stock exchanges in 17th century Amsterdam and London. There is still hope that history teaches lessons. Financial institutions are badly needed to allocate and manage capital rationally in post-communist economies of Central and Eastern Europe. Due to the link between stock exchanges and other financial institutions, the study of performances of such successful enterprises is crucial to the understanding of the economy as a whole.

The research in economic history shows that, given a diversity of cultural and institutional conditions, very different financial systems have evolved to produce efficient solutions (Timmermann, 1989; 14).

1. I would like to add some facts to the history of the famous Amsterdam Stock Exchange concerning its financial surroundings. In my opinion the workability of the financial institutions is of central importance to the success of stock exchanges in transitional economies with particular emphasis on the existence of a clear and credible general legal framework as a necessary prerequisite, cf. the often cited 'embedding of social institutions'.

The safest place in 17th century Amsterdam was its 'Wisselbank'. "The magistrates of Amsterdam", wrote the English commentator Onslow Burrish, "all those concerned in the government of the Bank and in general the whole body of the Seven Provinces, take pains to propagate this opinion and appear, at least, to be of the same mind themselves." (Burrish, 1728; 288.)

The contemporary American historian Simon Schama describes the reciprocity of the 'Wisselbank' and the Amsterdam Bourse: "The bank was the watchdog of capitalism in Amsterdam … The Amsterdam Bourse was the moral antithesis to the bank. It was as hazardous as the bank was secure. If the bank was the bastion of prudent conservatism, the bourse was a playground for unrestrained passion and reckless enthusiasm. The bank was the church of Dutch capitalism; the bourse was its circus." (Schama, 1988; 346-347.)

Whereas Schama underestimates the influence of the Flemish refugees on the development of Amsterdam, Neal stresses the importance of the Jews "that had migrated from Antwerp when Spain forced them to convert to Christianity" and of the "Portuguese Jews of Amsterdam who were being called in the service of William of Orange for purpose of financing his war against France". Moreover, it supports Neal's thesis concerning the historical patterns of development that "foreigners and political marginal groups were the most active participants initially in those markets that prospered."

2. Not only was there a know-how transfer from Antwerp to Amsterdam, but also from Amsterdam to London when William III from Holland became King of England. The transplantation of Dutch expertise created a more efficient stock exchange than the original one in Amsterdam "because only the operational part was imported while the environmental constraints were left behind in the Netherlands", as, for instance, the restrictions of the printing guild in Amsterdam.

The empirical results concerning the Price Index (Figure 1) and the Volatility Indicator (Figure 2) for the London Stock Exchange 1698-1734 are of special interest for this paper. The Volatility Indicator in particular enables us to test modern theories (for example: efficient-market theories or GARCH-theories) with a broader historical background. Further research should be conducted in order to identify patterns of volatility as those predicted by modern theories (Economist (1993), 9), Volatility is not only affected by the number of traders but also by the heterogeneity of trading groups with various investment objectives, different time frames and different attitudes towards risk. Indeed, it is an anomaly to economists that price volatility seems to increase with the heterogeneity of traders. The more evenly various assessments are distributed, the greater the market's buying and selling capacity should be. As a result, high price volatility can be avoided. In my opinion, however, the explanation of increasing price fluctuations with "price discovery" needs some more investigations.

As far as Figure 3 is concerned, a more formal correlation analysis would be more convincing. Furthermore, equal units of time should be applied to both drawings.

3. Since our conference takes place in Germany, I would like to make some remarks concerning stock markets in Germany. In fact, the market capitalization of domestic equities in relation to Germany's GNP continues to be very low in comparison to other industrialized countries - especially the United Kingdom and the United States. An important explanation for these figures can be found in the minor role of shares in Germany's pension system. The low importance of shares for private retirement savings in this country stands in such contrast to the English-speaking countries that it cannot be ignored. However, one should note that the proportion of shareholders in Germany shows significant differences between Western Germany (6,65 per cent) and Eastern Germany (0,51 per cent) (Deutsche Börsen, 1993; 80).

At the end of 1993, 1 473 shares were listed on Germany's stock exchanges, 796 were issued by domestic and 677 by foreign corporations (Deutsche Börsen, 1993; 22).

In the same paragraph Neal raises the important question which mode of financial intermediation was the most desirable for transition economies: bank lending, that has been successful for nearly two centuries in Germany or an intermediation that would mobilize capital from the widest possible sources of funds.

Banks in Germany became an important source of capital and entrepreneurial expertise - at least in the early stage of industrialization (Timmermann, 1989; 7). According to Gerschenkron (1962; 14), the private banks had to act as substitutes for entrepreneurs and private capital.

I would like to conclude this discourse with a short comment on a citation given by Neal in his paper. With reference to the *New Palgrave Dictionary of Money and Finance* the author states: "Nevertheless, regional exchanges continued to play an

important role in such places as Stuttgart, Dusseldorf, Cologne, Bochum and Essen."
(Michie, 1992; 668.) However, the stock exchanges referred to are not representative;
important stock exchanges such as the ones in Munich (Bavarian Stock Exchange,
founded in 1830), Hanover and Bremen were obviously omitted. And interestingly,
the stock exchanges in Cologne and Essen were closed at the end of 1934.

References

Burrish, Onslow (1728) *Batavia illustrata or a view of the policy and commerce of the
    United Provinces*, London.
Deutsche Börsen (1993) *Annual Report*, Frankfurt am Main.
The Economist (1993) *A Survey of the Frontiers of Finance*, 9-15 October.
Gerschenkron, Alexander (1962) *Economic Backwardness in Historical Perspective*,
    Cambridge, Mass.: Belknapp Press.
Michie, Ranald C. (1992) The development of stock markets, in Newman, Peter K.,
    Murray Milgate and John Eatwell (eds) *The New Dictionary of Money and
    Finance*, London: Macmillan Press.
Schama, Simon (1988) *The Embarassment of Riches. An Interpretation of Dutch
    Culture in the Golden Age*, Berkeley and Los Angeles: University of California
    Press.
Timmermann, Vincenz (1989) Universal Banks-Experiences and Possible Lessons for
    Socialist Countries, Discussion Paper No. 69, December, Sozialökonomisches
    Seminar University of Hamburg.

6 The pattern of evolution, emergence of markets, and institutional change in telecommunications - a very special or a more general phenomenon?

Karl-Ernst Schenk

1. Introduction

For decades telecommunications has been a sector of national monopolies, massive state intervention and international cartelization of national carriers. What has happened in this sector during the past ten to fifteen years, truly is a miracle. There is deregulation and dissolution of national monopolies, internationalization of competition on the basis of new "mobile" networks and the opening up of existing networks. This transition is a challenge to those who are familiar with monopolized industries. How this change came about and how it might be interpreted in the light of the existing wisdom about institutions and institutional evolution is, indeed, a challenging question. A deeper insight into the related processes in this sector and into its interaction with administrative and the political superstructures tightly interwoven with it, may help to clarify some aspects of our inherited concepts of evolution and lend itself to broader generalization. Most certainly some technological developments harboring a dynamic demand, in particular cellular mobile technology, have been in at the onset of this miracle.

It is an open question whether a very specific constellation or a more general one gave rise to the evolutionary process in this sector. In order to provide more evidence on critical factors I will put forward a number of propositions which, hopefully, may be valid for a broad range of phenomena or sectors. We will first explain why the sensational development occurred after a long period of stable economic development which, judged in terms of institutional change, does not qualify as evolutionary. Secondly, we will analyze the question of sequencing the evolutionary process. This may provide hints to the leading and lagging parts of the system observed. Are there typical sequences and can these be explained by taking recourse to common economic knowledge?

The principal propositions advanced in this paper are,

- that the expectations of a larger number of players in this field about future economic benefits of new technologies will have to be built up in order to trigger an evolutionary process in a stable industry;
- that starting from new technologies in hitherto non-monopolized segments some wave-effects on adjacent market segments in telecommunications and on their institutional arrangements play a major role in this process, and
- that it is wishful thinking to rely on economic competition alone as a motor of evolutionary processes. Such competition depends on a number of conditions among

which the building-up of expectations necessary to initiate changes in the superstructure of the monopolized sector is a crucial one.

The main point to be made is that of the nature of the evolutionary process. Whereas successful moves by progressive individuals or groups and imitative or adaptive behavior of a majority of others lie at the heart of von Hayek's (1963) concept of evolution, they do not play a major role here. It is more an adaptive homogenizing of the expectations of the various groups of players that, in my judgement, seems to play the central role in this process. If the expectations are sufficiently changed for a majority of players in the decision-making and lobbying superstructure such a development may induce action. However, this can only happen in a time-consuming process and provoke a sequence of changes which will be discussed more in detail.

2.   Patterns of the evolutionary processes in mobile telecommunications

According to von Hayek (1963) our orders in human civilization emerge from innovative moves of people or groups and from the imitating or adaptive behavior of others.   In Hayek's view evolution is a process which starts as a microeconomic phenomenon. Imitators, first in small and later in larger numbers, add momentum to the process of dissemination until it becomes a mass phenomenon. But, this holds true only if the innovation in this process, be it technical, organizational, or other is proved to be successful. An innovation is considered to be successful if others, after a certain time after its launching, believe that it is to be so. In order to bring about supplementary action, innovation, or adaption sufficient to cause changes it needs an individual's or group's apprehension. Since new knowledge will have to be acquired and the learning of new facts will have to take place, this building-up takes time.

Consequently, a pre-condition for evolutionary change is the modification of knowledge sufficiently broad to generate a mass phenomenon. Due to the fact that knowledge is specific to the initiator and not simply available to others a period of dissemination of knowledge in some way or another is indispensable. My contention is that this general pattern of cause and effect is distinctly different in present telecommunications and perhaps also in other monopolized and government-patronized sectors. However, knowledge about new technological developments in digital switching and radio transmission of voice and data was not monopolized but widespread. It was not a bottleneck to further developments but played a major role by affecting the expectations of players in this sector about the sustainability of the existing institutional structure.

In view of the characteristics of the new technologies, especially of radio transmission and the economies of cellular radio transmission it was clear to most players in the field of telecommunications that the institutional setting could not sustain this new development. If these technologies were applied, a major redistribution of profits and rents had to take place. Thus, it seems necessary to clarify the reasons for this change of expectations among the players in the market.

3. Characteristics of the new technologies in radio transmission

The development of the technological foundation of wireless transmission and the first steps to transmit and receive voice by transportable equipment have taken a long time. Prior to the 1980s or 1990s, the equipment was too heavy and voluminous and the finding and identification of users in their actual location was too difficult. But the subsequent development of small electric batteries, of efficient switching devices as well as the use of a range of cellular microwaves allowing to economize on this scarce resource, made mobile technology attractive and raised expectations about its diffusion within a relatively short time. From the economic point of view there are a number of characteristics which contributed to making mobile telecommunications attractive and responsible for the building-up of expectations:

* There are, first and foremost, *economies of mobile use*; i.e. the possibility to use the same phone (or other mobile equipment) and call a number wherever appropriate. This implies, inter alia, a more efficient time management and a greater readiness to make and to receive telephone calls.
* *Economies of investment* in equipment for users and network operators. Savings are accomplished specifically by the fact that not only mobile co-users but also users of fixed connections may be called and that the equipment of the fixed network may be used on a larger scale with decreasing costs.
* *Economies of scale* for suppliers of equipment (user and operator facilities) which give rise to the expectation of lower prices for operators and users in the near future.
* *Economies of standardization* (harmonization) of signaling devices on an international scale generating expectations of profiting from the economies mentioned not only nationally, but also internationally.
* Last, but not least, the *economic effects of using wireless signals in a cellular fashion*. This means that the same frequency can be used repeatedly by a wireless network operator as long as the distances between the locations of these manifold uses are large enough not to interfere with each other. If this prerequisite is observed, it is possible to establish a network of many cells, each of them served by a base station for transmitting and receiving signals to telephone or other stationary or mobile end user equipment in this cell. The neighboring cells use different frequencies in order to observe the principle of non-interference with the signals of the first cell. If such a structure is established it is, of course, necessary to hand over users who want to move from one cell to another from one base station to the other, and to coordinate the necessary change of frequency at some point. In effect, this technique leads to an economy in the use of frequencies. The natural scarcity of frequencies no longer is a problem.

It is evident that the advantages mentioned above do not only affect the operators of the new networks but that these new techniques imply advantages for a larger set of groups, for some groups more than for others. Nevertheless, a sufficiently broad set of those groups is addressed by them. And this has reinforcing effects on the expectations of each of them. This meets important conditions for generating changes of expectations and subsequent changes necessary for evolutionary processes. One of the most pervasive consequences is the economizing effect of the cellular technique. These consequences concern the costs of establishing a cellular network and the conditions of market entry by cellular network operators. The network may be constructed easier and quicker than a wired network. No digging up of streets is required to connect a single user to the network; all that has to be done for a large number of users is the installation of one antenna. Equipment can be manufactured in large batches achieving economies of scale.

These cost advantages of mobile networks make it easy for operators to enter the market. It is obvious that the entrant may start in areas of high volume demand and skim customers with a relatively high willingness to pay for the new service. Furthermore, the network can be cautiously expanded step by step into other lower paying areas. But, of course, the customers already acquired will expect the coverage of the whole country or license area within some reasonable time.

In the assessment of the characteristics of the evolutionary process the role of specific knowledge, an issue that generally features most prominently as a stylized fact in concepts on evolution, has not been mentioned yet. Is this coincidence or rather a fact that should raise more questions? It appears interesting enough to think about an answer. This answer supposedly will have to do with the specific institutional conditions in the telecommunications sector. What happens if the critical condition important to release an evolutionary process does not depend upon knowledge but on institutions which resist change? The idea we will pursue here is that knowledge may be generally available as a precondition for the dissemination of a new technology but that this development is retarded or prevented by institutional barriers. Is there a process comparable to the dissemination of knowledge which is critical for overcoming those barriers and for releasing an evolution?

As an institutionalist one should, of course, be aware that institutions can be and have been impediments to change in a large variety of cases and on different decision making levels. Thus, my course of inquiry into institutional barriers and processes to surmount or to remove these barriers may have a somewhat broader bearing than the subject of my inquiry might suggest at first sight.

Summarizing our observations on the major characteristics of the evolution in telecommunications makes clear that expectations about economic advantages play a role in this process. But after this technology had matured, the institutional conditions did not point into a direction favorable for the advantages to be realized. Thus, some sets of conditions related to our argument have to be assessed in more depth, some of them propelling, others slowing down this process. Institutional conditions will be discussed first, followed by technological conditions, observations on the administrative and political superstructure of the sector, and on how they have affected change in varying environments in the USA and Europe.

4. Institutional conditions for change

Are there impediments which wind down expectations and keep some or all groups from adopting a new course of action? If so, what are the general regularities leading to this institutional disfunction? In domestic voice telephony and transmission facilities the decision-making structures in most industrial countries have traditionally been marked by a monopoly of state or private companies. Thus, the state or its agencies have been heavily involved in decision making on network structures, prices, and other parameters of the supply of telecommunication services as peripheral equipment. This involvement took the form of three regimes:

- directly state-administered monopoly with a postal or telecom ministry at the top;
- as long as only AT&T was in the market, monopoly regulation by specialized agencies like the Federal Communications Commission (FCC) in the United States ;
- regulation of competitive carriers as in the USA in the seventies and later.

Among these regimes used for the coordination of actors there is only one which constitutes a combination of hierarchy (regulation) and markets (competitive carriers). The other two do not rely on market coordination or any other kind of competitive element.[1] A look at the comparative performance of the monopolistic carriers under these regimes, directly administered or regulated, and at parameters of their efficiency in providing services to the customers is revealing. The directly state-administered monopoly which prevails in European countries typically performs poorly as far as the application of new technologies for increased customers' utility and tariffs are concerned. This does, however, not automatically apply to the technological standard of the transmission and switching facilities of these carriers. The latter are no worse than those of the competition. But, generally, they are luxuriously over-engineered and mostly heavily overstaffed. A similar picture is presented by countries with monopoly regulation. For these reasons, it is fair to conclude that these hierarchical forms of monitoring, evaluating, and coordinating the performance of an industry like telecommunications have some severe disadvantages. Worse performance under these regimes at the customers' interface indicates that

- in these organizations either less attention is paid to the coordination between subsystems or between the organization and its environment;
- or the attention of the top management in these organizations has shifted from there to another interface, namely to the one where monitoring takes place by a ministry or an agency[2].

---

1 In Germany the monopoly is explicitly aiming at a nationwide supply of services with uniform conditions and at generating a financial basis for the infrastructural obligations of the German Telekom and the other two DBP-services. It is not argued that a natural monopoly is the reason of the legal monopoly. See Weinkopf (1992) 4.

2 This proposition was elaborated on in a more general context in Schenk (1988).

Summarizing, it may be said that the behavior of organizations under those regimes reflects distinct characteristics which can be traced to incentive and sanctionary structures. Both regimes exhibit a lack of monetary sanctions to pay attention to and to coordinate behavior at interfaces critical to the public (users). On the other hand, the top management of the organization has ample motivation and inducement to pay much attention to the relationship with its supervisors. Its own welfare depends very much on how it meets the general and individual expectations of the people in the supervisory organ and how it presents the partisan interests of the organization to them.

As long as complaints of customers about poor and expensive services do not exceed a certain limit, the politicians and/or administrators in charge will have no reason to monitor more than in a loose and routine fashion. There are no incentives to do more than that. And such a monitoring behavior will clearly also be very insensitive to changes of the environment of the service organization. Even if its monopoly position will be undermined by foreign competitors as for instance (as this has only recently been the case) that of German Telekom by arbitrage opportunities offered by British Telecom and other international companies, the relationship between supervisors and top management will remain nearly untouched. As empirical evidence suggests reactions will take time and are not brought forward by deliberate initiatives of these parties but rather by pressure from outside.

Changes of this kind will, after a lapse of time, be answered, firstly, by increases of monopoly tariffs which ensure profits at an accustomed level. The same effect will be reached if cost reductions which are due to improved technologies do not lead to reduced prices. In a second phase it is in the interest of the management to change the structure of tariffs in such a way as to lower those in the contested segments of the market and to raise or keep them constant or insufficiently reduced in the uncontested ones. As evidence clearly suggests this has been the strategy of the German Telekom during the past couple of years. This strategy helps to conceal the deeply lying deficiencies of the organization and appease the supervisors for another couple of years.[3] However, it also hurts the interests of enterprises and private customers which have to compete with foreign companies and are able to compare tariffs internationally.

As a consequence, opposition will develop towards the way things are handled by politicians, supervising agencies, and the monopoly carrier under their supervision. Such a superstructure does not exist in the USA: by far the largest carrier, AT&T, had been submitted to a regime of regulated competition more than ten years ago. This industry structure comes close to a quasi-monopoly. But market entry was possible and indeed took place a long time before AT&T had to abandon the local Bell companies in 1984. Thus, one might say that a more disciplined behavior of the quasi-monopolist was to be expected. Inefficiencies were not of the magnitude of a political issue, but rather a concern of the anti-trust authority, the Federal Trade Commission. The differences and the changes of the political environment in the USA and Europe will be elaborated in due course. It is very important to be aware that the building-up of attitudes towards

---

3 In Germany this strategy continued until February 1994 when the Minister of Post and Telecommunications succeeded in imposing tariff reductions for a number of calls (starting in 1996).

existing institutions as observed in Europe neither leads to instantaneous reactions by bureaucrats and politicians in charge of this sector nor to reactions by the monopoly carrier itself. Apparently, the building-up has to exceed a certain threshold in order to trigger active opposition or lobbying.

In terms of benefits and costs the opposing groups seem to act quite rationally. It makes sense not to act as long as the expectations about the benefits of change are small. In appraising this calculus it should be kept in mind that the groups of users are divided in terms of their attitude towards the carrier (and its administrative superstructure). Due to a low density of business locations and relatively poor public transportation services, some groups, especially in rural areas, may value a telephone much higher than urban groups since it may save them much more time to arrange business or private matters than by a personal visit. On the other hand these groups may benefit from the tariff and investment policy of the monopoly carrier more than urban users, particularly if a uniform tariff policy is practiced irrespective of the higher costs of establishing a rural network. Hence, the group criticizing the monopolistic practices may be too small and may be countervailed by groups of profiteers and, therefore, not willing to act effectively or to bear the cost of actions or lobbying activities.

But factors to change the position of groups are at work. And this is all the more so if patterns of cross-subsidization come under outside pressure. This pressure originated in the USA in 1984. A growing number of users can no longer be heavily cross-subsidized by a small group of business-users who strongly depend on high-priced trunk calls and international calls. Thus, changes in this direction are imposed from outside, i.e. by competitive international carriers offering billing arbitrage opportunities to this more price-sensitive group of users. Other forces working in the same direction will help to change the balance of attitudes and, therewith, the balance of benefits and costs of action or lobbying. Some of these forces will be addressed subsequently.

5.   Technological conditions for change

One of these forces is a technological development opening up new contested market segments. Indeed it is very important to underline that the change of attitudes addressed above is strongly reinforced by expectations about new technologies, particularly when new market segments are opened up in which the carrier incumbent in the fixed network has no established position.

The new wireless transmission technologies - among them, first of all, mobile technology - are striking examples for the emergence of new markets. They will be and are indeed able to partly substitute or supplement existing monopoly services. Basically, they offer not only the same facilities for the user, but more than that. The satellite technology differs from the traditional cable transmission only in that it is more flexible in installation and adaption to the demands of specific groups of users. It is especially advantageous when used very intensely (or interactively) for business purposes within the same group. Mobile technology, on the other hand, has a number of new technological features which make it attractive to a much broader range and very large number of users and, for this reason, to potential new operators and providers of equipment. Mobile network technology appears especially attractive to users since it is linked to the fixed network. It allows calls from the mobile to the fixed network and vice versa. Moreover, it is possible to take advantage of the established transmission and switching facilities of the fixed network, thus saving double investments.

Cellular technology is of course particularly important. It allows for market entrance of cellular carriers step by step without investment in very large and indivisible volumes. As a consequence the new network can be extended successively in accordance with the location of dense demand clusters. More base stations of an identical technical design can be supplied if the density of demand grows within these clusters. All this is possible without large scale investment but rather adaptively in relatively small portions. This is of utmost importance since it keeps down the barriers for market access, and simultaneously, the natural monopoly argument as the most powerful objection to admitting two or more competitors in network-based services. But this holds only true if the leasing arrangements for fixed lines from the incumbent telecommunications organization by the mobile operator are enforceable at fair conditions for both parties. Thus, in order to take advantage of the existing fixed infrastructure and yet to establish a competitive situation between the two operators, it is necessary to take care over (1) access to the fixed network and (2) fair leased-line tariffs and undiscriminating treatment of calls to and from the mobile network. This is a typical case for a change of regime, i.e. from monopoly regulation to the regulation of competition.

Expectations for the future are about a completely independent mobile network based on the same properties of the present technology and usage but with an even finer cellular structure, making the most expensive local part of the fixed network superfluous. Apparently, with these technological properties, there will be no reason for regulation because market entrance becomes even easier and less costly. Wireless connections can be established at lower costs than wired ones. Competitive bidding for and licensing of the frequency band will be the appropriate regime (see Huber, Kellog and Thorne, 1992, 4.115, 4.132 and 4.7; Calhoun, 1992, 49).

These remarks were necessary to corroborate the argument that the technological development in radio transmission in long distance and local networks points clearly in the direction of institutional change towards regulation of competition and licensed competition. Furthermore, there is no reason to believe that a network necessarily will have to be operated on a national scale in order to be efficient. And this is so as long as the above mentioned access is provided for local and regional operators. Consequently, the attitudes of groups opposed to a national monopoly in both networks, long distance and local, were reinforced by the expected economic and institutional consequences of this technological development. In the United States of America it was the independent Federal Trade Commission which in 1984 enforced this development and succeeded in splitting up the network into the long distance network of AT&T and several independent regional companies. Competition by other carriers in long distance transmission had taken place even before this step but now it was officially protected and has since deeply changed the institutional superstructure and the structure of the telecommunications sector (see Section 7).

Thus, it was not merely a coincidence that the liberalization of the telecommunications market and the development of a new and more promising generation of mobile equipment took place at the same time. The liberalization of this market was driven by the expectation of most players that market entry of mobile network carriers would be possible and that, due to the bright market prospects in this segment, they would have a real chance of competing even if they had to do so against AT&T and its mighty inheritors.[4] As a consequence, a second market for equipment in the mobile segment was sparked by this regulatory change. This happened already before the final arrangement between the Federal Trade Commission and AT&T about the divestiture of its regional carriers was agreed upon. Thus, it is only natural that the US producers of equipment were able to achieve a relative advantage in the command of new technologies and new markets especially vis à vis their European competitors, most of whom at that time still operated in a traditional environment of state-administered monopoly and protected national equipment markets.

6. Evolution and consequences of new interest coalitions

Due to these changes in the international role of equipment providers and the expected attractiveness of the European market for the rapidly expanding new networks, the old political coalition structures were shaken up. The Post and Telecommunications Ministries in continental Europe can no longer neglect the interests of these new groups which are driven by expectations about future profits. They can no longer act solely as a partisan of the traditional telecommunications administrations and incumbent monopolies. The majority of voters - and at the same time of telephone customers - can no longer be persuaded to subsidize the investments of the newly established mobile telecommunications branches of apparently inefficient Post and Telecommunications Organizations (PTOs) by their telephone charges. The US experience indicated clearly that, with private network operators in mobile telecommunications, it would no longer be possible to leave it to the monopoly operators of the wired network to fix tariffs for the use of their lines by mobile carriers. Thus, interests have undergone a deep change with the introduction of these services.

It had become evident that all parties to the operation of new mobile networks would benefit from its advantages. But these parties have unequal power in bargaining for these advantages. The strongest party which will have to open its fixed network to the mobile service operators is the traditional PTO. As a monopolist, PTO would be in the position to dictate the prices for telephone calls and data transmission which originate in the fixed net and end in the mobile one (or vice versa) and for transmitting signals between terminals or base stations for mobile use. Even as a mobile network operator -

---

4 It was these prospects which in 1982 led the Federal Trade Commission to take up its case against AT&T, the owner of most local and long distance networks in the USA. The divestiture of the local networks by AT&T followed logically from this belief that competition by wireless operators was viable. See Huber, Kellog and Thorne (1992); Calhoun (1992).

which PTO is at the same time in most countries - it could discriminate against private operators by its pricing policy and use the charges of private operators to subsidize its activities.[5] Indeed, there is a clear motivation to do so, because this method seems to be the easiest way to participate in the division of the advantages from the new technology.

In Germany, for example, under the traditional regime of directly state-administered monopoly, the private operator was in a weak position to prevent German Telekom from adopting such discriminatory practices. The only way was to start a public campaign in order to solicit support of other groups of users who were discontent with the monopolist policy. As a matter of fact in Germany administered monopoly prices have been changed.   During this process even the German Ministry of Post and Telecommunications has completely revised its traditional position towards German Telekom.

7.   The stable institutional setting and its shake-up

At the beginning of the Eighties, the telecommunications sector in most industrial countries (except the USA) was still in its traditional and stable condition (see Schnöring, 1992):

- monopolistic network operators and monopolistic structures in the final users equipment and services segments;
- strong political influence of the telecommunications providers;
- low network innovation rates;
- operation of the networks within the national borders; international traffic was conducted according to cooperatively developed and stable rules;
- no competition between Public Telecommunications Operators, no transgression of national borders by service exports or direct investment;
- national market orientation of the equipment industry even of some major suppliers (like ITT, Philips) that formally were multinational;
- international competition of these suppliers only in the markets of foreign countries without endogenous supply bases, but also with stable long-term relationships with the foreign PTOs.

For the sake of a proper account of the shake-up, a few remarks appear in order about the political setting which facilitated and supported this decision-making structure and stabilized it for generations in most industrial countries. Traditionally, the coalitions of groups favoring direct state involvement and administration in telecommunications were strong in most countries and dominated the political decision-making process for telecommunication legislation:

---

5 This was exactly the case when the first private carrier in Germany, the Mannesmann D-2 operator, started business and approached the German Telekom, operator of the competing D-1 network.

- Typically the supporting coalition consisted of the bureaucrats of the ministries in charge, the administrators, and the trade unions of the postal and telecommunication services. Both groups profit from the monopoly and have a special interest in it. Their benefits were job security, organizational large-scale slack, and a comfortable job environment, unhampered by competition.
- A much larger group, the majority of voters, was lobbied into supporting the company and to accept the monopoly solution. In exchange, the lobbies promised availability of supply and equality of tariffs in all national regions, the argument being that only the persistence of the monopoly could guarantee the distributional goals.

Both groups formed a kind of silent coalition against all elements of competition. On the other hand, being the main users and revenue contributors, the proponents of competition in the telecommunications sector were industry and trade. But since a large proportion of the industry acts as an equipment supplier to the monopoly and since other sectors profit from a monopolistic price differentiation in the postal services, coalition of the industry and trade was divided, weakened, and not effective enough to dominate the decision-making process. As the monopoly administration and its supervisors were able to generate the support of political interest groups and vice versa this state of affairs persisted over decades.

The shake-up of these long-standing and stable structures started at two fronts:

- Discontent with the monopolistic behavior of the monopolists in their customers' environment.
- Expectations about new technologies; in terms of market growth and large scale effects in the equipment producing industry mobile telecommunications was the most promising one.

There is ample evidence that the two factors were interrelated. They first gained momentum in the USA, the leading country in terms of low entrance barriers, technological development, and market size. Due to the obvious increase of technological potentials open for use expectations rose but apparently remained unused. The widening of this virtual gap contributed to increased discontent with the market structure which was, rightly or wrongly, held responsible. The separation of the private American Telephone & Telegraph Company into eight divisions, i.e. into the long distance company (AT&T) and seven regional carriers, the so-called Baby Bells, contributed to enhance this discontent, also in Europe.[6] As a consequence of an increased competition under the regulatory regime of the USA, with the

---

6 Another company, General Telecom Electric (GTE) Corp., also participated in the regional markets. Since then, the quasi-monopoly of AT&T, with a market share of 85 percent, became an oligopoly with only 60.4 percent of the market. The rest fell to MCI and US Sprint.

Federal Communications Commission (FCC) in charge, spurred technological innovation by digital switching, improved quality, better services, and lower prices.[7]

To complete this assessment of demonopolization and institutional change it should be mentioned that in 1985 two other large companies in industrialized countries reflected a similar trend: Nippon Telegraph and Telephone Corporation (NTT) in Japan and the British Telecom (BT) in Britain. In both countries, this institutional change was facilitated by the political climate and accompanied by steps towards privatization which had not been necessary in the United States.

8. Internationalization of competition: Europe at the crossroads

This first shake-up of the traditional market structure was followed by a considerable quality improvement in the telecommunications. The de-monopolized and private carriers, particularly AT&T as a long standing private corporation with enormous research resources and an own equipment supply base, were in a favorable position. From now on they were free to tap profit sources of unprecedented magnitude at home and abroad. They had difficulties in finding investment opportunities for their growing profits. Nevertheless, they could afford to invest large sums into very problematic acquisition transactions. This development enhanced those advantages private companies like AT&T have always had when compared to state-owned PTOs in other countries, particularly in Europe. These advantages were strengthened by R&D in technical equipment which allowed the companies to circumvent monopolies and to 'profit skim' abroad and at home. Examples of facilities developed for such purposes again were wireless satellite transmission and mobile telecommunications. In order to prevent the profits made in foreign markets from being noticed by the regulators it was convenient to found separate companies abroad. From now on competition was international, players became global. Institutional change was accompanied by deep-cutting changes in the structure of markets.

Particularly mobile telecommunications markets then were and now are expected to yield the largest growth and profit potentials.[8] All players were convinced that these

---

7 The leading carriers manage to make big profits. In the case of AT&T this was also possible mainly by reducing staff (in the AT&T telephone division from 373 000 in 1984 to 230 000). For old shareholders the increase of the share value since then is about 600 percent. In the meantime AT&T has acquired a number of other companies, a strategy which did not prove to be as successful as expected. The success of the largest deal in 1991, the Computer Company NCR for $ US 7 billion, is not yet clear. But another deal, the acquisition of the mobile telecommunications operator McCaw Cellular in 1993 has aroused much controversy. By this move AT&T breaks up its agreement with the antitrust authority to keep its hands off the local networks.

8 A recent study by Arthur D. Little Inc. indicates that within three to five years in the USA consumers in 42.5 million households will consider buying cordless phones, and that 12 million will actually buy them. In Japan the number of portable telephones is expected to rise from 550 000 in 1990 to eight million in 2000 (ibid.) According to other sources, the number of mobile phone users could reach 20 million in USA by 1995 and 50 million worldwide by the end of decade (cf. Huber, Kellog and Thorne, 1992).

markets in the future would be the stage for a great showdown by which the division of markets and profits would be decided for decades to come (Hayek, 1963). The most interesting changes took place in Europe, the largest economic battle field. In Europe, the various groups of players were distinctly affected by the new development:

(a) PTOs expected expanding markets and profit opportunities
  • from the introduction of mobile facilities;
  • by converting from endogenous supply partners to more advanced and (thanks to competition) less costly suppliers from abroad.[9]
On the other hand, there was a number of reasons to secure a supply base at home which was not dominated by US and Japanese manufacturers. As a consequence heavy political pressure for a home-based buying strategy was expected.
(b) European equipment suppliers were already under pressure:
  • by losing more and more competence in the new markets for mobile communications facilities;
  • by their increased vulnerability in relatively small and divided home markets (Müller, 1989, 268f.);
  • by a probable change of the long-standing dual government policy of combining the goal of infrastructural development of telecommunications with the goal of patronizing national equipment resources by heavily subsidizing the R&D of home manufacturers;
(c) European governments and the Commission of the European Community encountered strategic crossroads:
  • with a not yet functioning common market for equipment;
  • with non-standardized and incompatible mobile networks being introduced in various countries and parts of Europe;[10]
  • with higher future risks implied by continuing the long-standing dual national policy in the telecommunications sector. For, given the distinct disadvantages of the national home manufacturers, it was by no means certain that future R&D subsidies would be successful in closing the gap (see Müller, 1987, for evidence from Great Britain).

In this tense situation it was not easy to find a strategy appropriate to covering the diverging interests of the players. As things stood, there was no hope to implement monopoly deregulation and privatization within a reasonably short time (Müller, 1989, 268-272), i.e. to emulate the way on which the other global players fared so well. On the other hand, for the European players a unified European market was obviously a *sine qua non* condition in any new strategy.

---

9 It is estimated by insiders that German Telekom until today, years after this change has begun, still pays between 10 to 15 percent higher prices to its endogenous suppliers.

10 The success of the Nordic Mobile Telephone standard NMT of the Scandinavian countries which has led to the adoption of the NMT system in 29 countries illustrates the problem. The larger European countries developed their own standards and analogue systems (cf. Hultén and Mölleryd, 1995).

The answer by the EU-Commission and national governments was a dual approach:

- In the so-called Green Paper of the EU-Commission (EU-Commission, 1987), a recommendation for a unified end-user equipment market was agreed upon in order to bring down prices by 15 to 25 percent (on the basis of 1985). This implied savings of approximately 0,7 billion ECUs (Müller, 1989, 270).
- The opening up of government procurement markets in the member countries with the expectation of considerable price reductions (Müller, 1989, 271).
- The establishment of a Groupe Spéciale Mobile (GSM) at the European Telecommunications and Standards Institute (ETSI) in which all major players take part but in which the PTT administrations are the finally responsible signers of an agreement on a common European (GSM) standard for digital transmission.
- A European Community program (RACE) to subsidize international cooperation in the field of telecommunications R&D.

Adding up the various effects on the equipment side from varying sources (European standardization, increased price competition by opening up the procurement markets), the cost incurred by the network operators were estimated to drop by 2 percent to 8 percent (Müller, 1989, 271). Assuming that these cost reductions will be passed on to the users, telephone traffic could increase due to the favorable price elasticity of demand.[11] Given high fixed costs and large-scale advantages this should result in lower handling costs for this additional traffic. Also, other proposals by the EU Commission, namely to decrease cross-subsidization of tariffs, would - if put into practice - lead to lower cost and an expanded service volume, particularly in the more price-elastic trunk calls service.

The EU Commission proposal was supplemented in 1989 by an "Open Network Provision" to stimulate entry to the public networks by private suppliers in competition with incumbent network operators. But the proposal was highly controversial since - if put into practice - it might lead to profit skimming by the resale of leased lines by private service providers (re-sellers). Thus, the so-called voice monopoly of the fixed network operators has not been touched yet. But, in mobile and satellite communications the monopoly has given way to regulated competition, in Germany with three competitors in the mobile and satellite sector. It is expected that in a couple of years (1998) this regime will also replace the monopoly in the fixed network including not only the EU members but also the present or former EFTA countries.

9. Conclusions

In order to learn more about the patterns of evolutionary development we suggest it as particularly rewarding not to review a sector with competition but one in which stable

---

11 Estimates are between - 0.4 for trunk calls, - 0.6 for international, and around - 1 for transatlantic calls. For local calls only - 0.1 to - 0.3. (Müller, 1989, 272, with reference to Winders, 1987.)

monopolistic markets and internationally operating cartels co-exist with strong government influence on short-and long-term decision making backed by political interest coalitions. Our original contention was that a sector containing these properties together within a noticeable technological progress with a certain period of time operating in specific market segments would exhibit a very distinct pattern of evolution.

It could be demonstrated first of all that this pattern can be described by making use of a process of changing expectations. Various factors contributed to these changes:

- Technological change which generates expectations about advantages for a number of major players in the market, groups of new and old users and last but not least governments.
- Competition originating in one country emulated by other countries exerts a mounting pressure on third countries (and on groups resisting change) and reinforces the vigor of the originally weak coalition of interests which opposes the traditional institutional setting. A change of position of some groups across the dividing line between the pro and contra coalitions may be observed.
- Last, but not least this competition which pertains not only to market shares of an increasing number of internationally oriented network operators affects not only the equipment producing industry (and other adjacent sectors), but also the governments and their traditionally practiced telecommunications regime.

With expectations growing about the emergence of internationally operating competitors and the threat implied in their market power, first the EU Commission and later most European governments revised their attitude towards national operators and equipment producers. In particular, they initiated steps towards privatization and a regulated competitive network pattern. This building-up of expectations is a necessary element prior to the shake-up which can be observed in the institutional setting, even in those European countries of a very conservative institutional structure. And clearly, the administrative and political superstructure will have to undergo pervasive changes before competitive markets can emerge.

The way by which this institutional change takes place is a remarkable phenomenon. The institutions of leading countries such as the USA, Great Britain and Japan are not simply copied. The competitive advantage is narrowed in a more sophisticated way by establishing a common standard in one of the most expectation-driven sectors of the economy. To the European mobile telecommunication operators and equipment providers this move even seems to be promising because it will give them a competitive edge in a worldwide contest which comprises all segments of the sector. Together with other measures the common European standard has contributed much to change the structure in this sector by:

- converting members of the international cartel of (state administered) telecommunication operators to contestants in a vigorous international competition;
- changing the role of equipment providers from government-patronized national suppliers ("Hoflieferanten") to competitors on national, European, and world markets.

The European governments are in the process of changing their attitude towards "their" equipment suppliers by increasingly giving up their dual-objective policy in telecommunications of building up and developing the national infrastructure and of at the same time patronizing and promoting the national supply industry. It seems that in the future the national markets will be open to competition even where this is not yet the case.

References

Calhoun, George (1992) *Wireless Access and the Local Telephone Network*, Boston, London: Artech House.

EU-Commission (1987) *Towards a Dynamic European Economy*, Green Paper on the Development of the Common Market for Telecom Services and Equipment, COM (87) 29 final, Brussels.

Hayek, Friedrich A. von (1963) *The constitution of liberty*, London: Routledge & Kegan Paul.

Huber, Peter W., Michael K. Kellog and John Thorne (1992) *The Geodesic Network II*, Washington, DC: Geodesic Co.

Hultén, Staffan and Bengt G. Mölleryd (1995) Sweden, in Schenk, K.-E., J. Müller and Thomas Schnöring (eds) *Mobile Telecommunications: Emerging European Markets*, Boston: Artech House.

Müller, Jürgen (1987); Zur Neuordnung der Fernmeldemärkte; *DIW-Wochenbericht*, Berlin, 10 September 1987, 489-498.

Müller, Jürgen (1989); Telecommunications in the European International Market; *Intereconomics*, Hamburg, Nov/Dec, 268-272.

Schenk, Karl-Ernst (1988); Comment on the Theory of Hierarchies and Why it is Relatively Underdeveloped for Comparative Purposes; *Journal of Institutional and Theoretical Economics*, 144, 849-856.

Schnöring, Thomas (1992); Entwicklungstrends auf den europäischen Telekommunikationsmärkten; *Wissenschaftliches Institut für Kommunikationsdienste*, no. 102, Bad Honnef.

Weinkopf, M. (1992); Bypass and Tariff Arbitrage in German Telecommunications: A Case for Regulatory Intervention?; *Wissenschaftliches Institut für Kommunikationsdienste*, no. 95, Bad Honnef.

Winders, J. (1987) *The Economics of Telecommunications*, Ballinger.

7 Why do some markets die so slowly? - The case of CFCs

Ellen C. Krupa

1. Introduction

Environmental legislation can force firms to leave certain markets. This paper deals with the question of how companies leave markets and under which conditions new markets for alternative products can be created. In the case of chlorofluorocarbons (CFCs) an international agreement requires the CFC producing and consuming industries to respond to a well-defined phase out plan for these chemicals. Further production, consumption and trade of the regulated chemicals is scheduled to be banned by January 1st, 1997. National regulations go even further. In Germany, a complete ban on CFCs will take effect on January 1st, 1995.

Private consumers usually do not have contact with the raw chemical but with the products that are manufactured with CFCs or contain CFCs. Common examples are CFCs used as propellants in spraying cans or as blowing agents to produce soft and rigid foam materials used in car seats or dashboards. The common refrigerant used in mobile air conditioning units is also CFC. Household refrigerators, likewise, require CFC in order to cool down stored food. As soon as the ban becomes effective all markets for CFC-containing products will vanish.

Customers in the affected markets are not interested in the production technology or the materials needed to produce the goods. They have a demand instead for the properties of the goods, e.g. they demand a cooling mechanism. It is not likely that their demand for end products will change dramatically. New, CFC-free products will be required to serve their demand once the ban takes effect. New markets for CFC-free goods will be very closely related to the old markets that the companies have been forced to leave. Hence, exit and entry conditions are closely tied together.

The close connection between exit and entry conditions makes the CFC case a unique and interesting addition to the existing literature on market exit. Companies normally leave markets in response to a major economic shock. Substantial changes may have occurred in patterns of demand[1] or technology[2] and may have made existing production techniques no longer viable. In the present case, neither of these conditions hold.

We are dealing with firms that are forced to leave product markets that are still economically viable. A politically motivated ban has presented organizations with a stark choice: adopt or experience an end of their business operations in affected market

---

1 See for example Schmookler (1966), Mowery and Rosenberg (1979) and Kleinknecht and Verspagen (1990).

2 See for example Solow (1957), Arrow (1962) and Albach (1994).

segments. As the new markets are so closely tied to the old ones it is assumed that the companies with long market experience might wish to stay in their old market segments but with new and this time environmentally friendly products.

The subsequent discussion aims to identify the main characteristics of a market decline brought on by regulation and to outline the factors that are conducive to or hinder the development of substitute products. To examine these factors in greater detail, this paper presents an analysis of the German refrigeration industry as it responds to the scheduled phase out of CFCs.

The following Section describes a conceptual framework suitable for the analysis of the household refrigerator market and other regulated markets in which a switch to a similar but environmentally sustainable product is an available choice. Elements included in the framework are:

- the Montreal Protocol and its implications
- the unexploited scientific and technical opportunities in the refrigeration industry
- an explanation of how firms exited CFC-utilizing production and switched to CFC-free production.

The framework will be discussed in the order outlined above.

2.   The Montreal Protocol and its implications

The ozone-destroying potential of CFCs first became a subject of public awareness in 1974 with the publication of the Rowland/Molina CFC hypothesis (Molina and Rowland, 1974). By 1978, with a ban on CFCs in propellants put in place in the US, Canada, Norway and Sweden, public attention quickly faded from the subject. When the ozone hole over the Antarctic was discovered in 1986 CFCs again became the subject of widespread public concern, and this time even stronger than before.

For the first time the formerly vague hypothesis of the ozone-destroying character of CFCs could be proved scientifically. The release of CFCs had been conclusively shown to lead to the destruction of the ozone layer. By reducing the amount of ozone in the stratosphere, and thus contributing to an increase in the amount of UV-B radiation reaching the Earth's surface, ozone emissions posed a serious health. A report conducted by EPA/UNEP concluded that ultraviolet radiation induced skin cancer, cataracts, suppression of the human immune system and the development of some cutaneous infections. Plants and aquatic organisms also were shown to be harmed by exposure to higher than normal levels of UV-B radiation. Tests carried out on some 300 crops and other plant species have indicated that two thirds were sensitive to ultraviolet radiation. This suggested that significant increases in the amount of radiation reaching the Earth's surface could significantly decrease food production.

A ban was suggested as one possible way of reducing the risk of unforeseen but long-term damage that might not be included in conventional cost-benefit analyses. Given the uncertainty about the substances' pathways and effects, many favored strong measures to curtail CFC production (see for example Opschoor and Pearce, 1991).

Economists have analyzed the problems of non-market interdependencies for some time - applying the concept of externalities since Pigou (Pigou, 1931). Externalities are social interdependencies not taken into account by formal markets or by arrangements between the affected individuals or nations. All affected party's preferences cannot adequately be considered when a decision is made. The classical solution in economics to externalities has been to internalize them by either developing well-defined markets for the 'spillovers' or controlling them through collective provision for regulation. Given the known damages induced by increased UV-radiation it can be assumed that the consumption of CFC-containing products leads to a decrease in social welfare, making a ban seems to be justified (see for example Foran, 1990).

On September 16th, 1987, just one year after the discovery of the huge hole over the Antarctic, 25 nations signed the Montreal Protocol on Substances that Deplete the Ozone Layer (UNEP, 1993). As of May 1994, 134 nations had become parties to the Montreal Protocol (UNEP IE/PAC, 1994, 8). The Montreal Protocol achieved the first international agreement that dealt with a global environmental problem on a global scale. However, even in its early stage, the Protocol contained a passage that established the notion of a permanent review process and possible re-negotiations in case that new scientific evidence was found. Therefore, the loose phase-out dates could be tightened any time. Up until now there have been four amendments to the original Protocol with the phase out schedule being tightened each time. In addition to the international regulation many nations have introduced even stronger national regulations on CFCs. Given these circumstances firms will be driven out of the CFC producing and using business within a couple of years.

Since the Montreal Protocol of 1987, it has been clear to CFC producing and consuming industries that the market for chlorofluorocarbons and hence the markets for CFC-containing products will be phased out. Yet, instead of exiting these markets and developing CFC-free products, firms in many affected industries have shown themselves reluctant to act. The market for household refrigerators is no exception. Rather than actively investigating CFC-free coolants, producers of household refrigerators waited for the chemical industry to supply a new refrigerant. When an outsider, an East German company, began to actively market a substitute technology that had been known to the industry since the turn of the century, the dominant firms in the domestic refrigerator market again showed themselves to be unresponsive. Instead of conducting research on the feasibility of this product as a substitute for the industry standard, they waged a publicity campaign designed to question its reliability. Only when it became clear that there is a considerable demand for CFC-free products did they finally switch to the new technology. The transition to the new production lines was completed in a matter of months.

We expect that private profit maximizing enterprises will appropriately allocate resources to the exploration and development of new products and new production techniques to respond to potential market demand. Theory predicts that companies will act if they expect some economic benefit net of the incurred costs. But how can we explain a behavior that obviously did not take advantage of available market opportunities. Why might companies let prospects of future profit simply elapse without capitalizing on them?

It can be assumed that the affected industries were aware of the Montreal Protocol and its implications. CFC-producers are usually multinational chemical companies that are very well informed about national and international legislation concerning their business. In the mid-eighties 17 of the world's chemical companies joined together to form the Alternative Fluorocarbons Environmental Acceptability Study (AFEAS) and the Programme for Alternative Fluorocarbon Toxicity Testing (PAFT) (see Harris, 1992). PAFT is a cooperative research effort sponsored by 15 of the leading CFC producers. The first of the PAFT program sectors was launched at the end of 1987 to address the toxicology of substances like HCFC-123[3] and HFC-134a.[4] Twelve chemical producers have also jointly funded a research program to determine the potential environmental effects of alternative fluorocarbons and their degradation products. The Alternative Fluorocarbons Environmental Acceptability Study (AFEAS) was initiated in December 1988 to assess the potential impact of CFC alternatives on the environment and to identify gaps in knowledge.

All German domestic refrigerator producers knew of the Montreal Protocol from its inception and were aware of its implications for their business. In 1991 an informal group of major manufacturers, AEG, Bauknecht, Bosch-Siemens, Electrolux and Liebherr agreed to use HFC-134a as the new refrigerant.[5] Holding 47 percent of the German refrigerator market in 1989 they had enough economic power to impose agreed general technical systems on the market. As their engineers also work as consultants to the DIN (German Institute for Standardization) and the TÜV (Technical Control Association) they could use their technical expertise to influence standardization and certification processes.

3.   Unexploited scientific and technical opportunities in the refrigeration industry

Before CFCs were invented as safe coolants, the refrigeration industry depended upon refrigerants such as ammonia, sulfur dioxide and methyl chloride with their attendant problems of toxicity or flammability. The shortcomings of these chemical compounds were acceptable in industrial applications but the trend towards household and retail shop

---

3 HCFC is the abbreviation for hydrochlorofluorocarbons. They are partially halogenated hydrocarbons. Not all of the hydrogen atoms in the molecule have been replaced by chlorine or fluorine, so that one or more hydrogen atoms remain in the molecule. These chemicals are more easily decomposed in the troposphere and as such their ozone depletion potentials are less than those for CFCs. They still have a considerable global warming potential.

4 HFCs is the abbreviation for hydrofluorocarbons. They are hydrocarbons in which some of the hydrogen atoms in the molecule have been replaced by fluorine atoms. These molecules do not have an ozone depletion potential anymore but still contribute to some extent to global warming.

5 On the 15th of July 1992 the above mentioned companies announced a voluntary self-commitment to start CFC-free production of refrigerators at the end of 1993. The switch-over should be completed by the end of 1994. As refrigerant they wanted to use HFC-134a. This announcement was released by the ZVEI (Zentralverband Elektrotechnik und Elektronikindustrie e.V.), the German electrical manufacturers' association. Interestingly, dkk Scharfenstein (later Foron) was not included.

refrigeration in the 1920s presented the need for a range of non-toxic, non-flammable refrigeration compounds.

With the introduction of CFCs as safe refrigerants, research on other potential coolants stopped. In the eighties the refrigeration industry faced a situation where no easy alternatives to CFC-12 existed. Substitutes for use within domestic refrigeration were either not commercially available or still under development. All alternatives would require some re-design of components or equipment. Some of the most promising alternatives include:

- Ammonia: Ammonia has been, and still is used in industrial refrigeration applications. Although it has in the past been used in domestic refrigerators, it is not used anymore for this purpose because it is toxic and forms explosive mixtures when exposed to air. The small quantities of ammonia used could be contained within hermetically sealed units which would minimize the above concerns. As such, there is no technical reason why ammonia cannot be used again in domestic refrigeration equipment. Ammonia is extensively used in industrial refrigeration.
- HFC-134a: HFC-134a was thought first by the chemical industry and later by the domestic refrigeration industry as the best long-term alternative to CFC-12. Its boiling point and temperature/pressure characteristics are very similar to CFC-12. It is not, however, a 'drop-in' alternative as the following difficulties had to be considered:
  - its lower thermodynamic efficiency results in 8-15 percent higher energy consumption; with good system redesign this loss in efficiency can be reduced to 5-10 percent;
  - it has a lower volumetric capacity, therefore, more refrigerant has to be used to obtain an equivalent system capacity;
  - it is immiscible with the compressor lubricating mineral oils used with CFC-12; new oils would have to be developed prior to its use within refrigeration units;
  - there is a possible associated problem of electrodeposition of copper in the compressor which could reduce the technical product life of the refrigeration appliance;
  - it has a strong solvent action and attacks the currently-used refrigerant seals and the desiccant;
  - in the eighties there were no long-term toxicity results available; the product would be commercially unavailable before 1991;
  - it will have a higher cost when it is available, about 3-7 times the current cost of CFC-12, as a result of a comparatively lower yield and a more complex manufacturing process; additional costs will occur with the use of the necessary new lubricants and modified components (e.g., new valves have to be constructed);
  - it contributes to global warming;
  - it is unlikely to be able to be practicable handled under existing socio-economic conditions in developing countries (they have the highest demand for refrigeration).
- Hydrocarbons: Hydrocarbons like propane and isobutane are efficient refrigerants being used in industrial refrigeration but as hydrocarbons are flammable they are a less natural fit for household applications. This coolant is technically a fully substitutable alternative which is commercially available at low cost. In some countries like Britain

legislation (British Standard BS 4434) prevented the use of hydrocarbons as refrigerants within the occupancy categories of industrial, public assembly and residential. Such regulation does not apply to Germany.

Problems with all potential CFC substitutes made it difficult for firms producing and consuming coolants to leave a known and familiar path. As a first step, the industry tried to produce refrigerators that could be operated on a reduced CFC-12 quantity. Manufacturers then moved towards HFC-134a. This chemical is a derivative of CFCs. But very quickly it proved impossible to use this substance as a 'drop-in'. If refrigerators were to be operated with HFC-134a as the refrigerant, the final product had to be changed considerably.

Additionally, an environmentally friendly refrigerant should neither add to ozone depletion nor to global warming. As HFC-134a has a substantial global warming potential it cannot be considered a suitable alternative in the long run. Ammonia and hydrocarbons do not have this serious shortcoming and they had been used as refrigerants before CFC-12 was introduced to the market.

Assuming that engineers prefer to stick to technical standards, the next step should be to examine the already known substances. Interestingly, this did not happen thoroughly in the R&D laboratories of the refrigeration industry. The re-use of hydrocarbons as coolants was explored at the Institute for Medical Microbiology at the University of Duesseldorf. Bowing to necessity, lacking research funds for an urgently needed refrigerator, the temporary head of the department Professor Rosin and his staff decided to build the equipment themselves. With the help of Dr Helga Krumschmidt of the Institute for Physical Chemistry at the University of Duesseldorf they experimented with mixtures of propane, butane and isobutane and developed the so-called Dortmund mixture as a simple and effective refrigerant. In 1990, after their move to the Dortmund Institute for Hygiene, they successfully installed the mixture in a refrigerator (see for example Bresgott, 1992).

However, presenting this technology did not lead to its adoption by West German refrigerator manufacturers. Household refrigerator producers persisted in their concerns about flammability and energy consumption, despite the fact that hydrocarbons like pentane and butane have been successfully used as refrigerants in large industrial refrigeration facilities for decades.

As in many other instances, it also seems to be the case that environmentally friendly production seems to be related to a quest for 'new' technical standards. Abernathy and Utterback (1975) introduced the concept of a dominant product design and suggested that the occurrence of a dominant design may alter the character of innovation and competition in a firm and an industry.[6] Although hydrocarbons are not a new technology in refrigeration it seems to be worthwhile to explore the effects of that switch-over. But the question remains, why was the refrigeration industry so reluctant to adopting a new technology? The case study seems to point to technological standards. Once established,

---

6   See for example Utterback and Suárez (1993), Tushman and Anderson (1986), Abernathy and Clark (1985) and Abernathy and Utterback (1975).

a successful technology creates a substantial reduction of uncertainty (Dosi, 1988; and Arthur, 1989). Sticking to their previous production processes, refrigerator companies maintained technological and market expectations more securely than they could by going to the HFC-134a alternative. The CFC-technology path was not only the mode of action with respect to an ex post description but also determined future decisions as it was the basis from which companies tried to find an answer to the question of where to go from where they were. However, this case indicates that the level of uncertainty associated with innovations is much stronger than that which traditional economic models deal with. This includes the lack of knowledge of the precise cost and outcomes of different alternatives. The hypothesis that engineers typically try to improve the desirable characteristics that are specific to a certain product seems correct in this context. This observation challenges partially the traditional concept of technology which assumes that information is generally applicable and easy to reproduce and re-use (see for example Arrow, 1962). According to this concept firms can produce and use innovations by accessing freely a general stock or pool of technological knowledge.

A different approach to path dependencies takes Mokyr (1994). He points out that modeling the competition between old and new technologies is difficult because it takes place outside the marketplace. When a new idea - by some predetermined selection criterion - turns out to have a higher fitness than the existent technology, the competitive market alone should eventually turn it into a success story. Yet, there is no guarantee that even an innovation of superior fitness will in fact be 'selected' for survival and reproduction. A good example is an innovation that is part of a greater technological system; here an innovation might be rejected because of its incompatibility with other components, as often happens with network technologies. Profitability is the most intuitively attractive selection criterion, but in the past surely other selection criteria were important. Non-market selection criteria fall into two broad categories: legal measures taken through the social control and economic regulation on the part of official and quasi-official institutions (e.g., such as producer associations or institutes for standardization).

Behavioral approaches suggest that within each society there are powerful forces that tend to resist change because they have a vested interest in the status quo. In this context technological change involves substantial losses sustained by those who own specific assets dedicated to the existing technology. These assets could be formal skills, reputation, tacit knowledge, specialized equipment (investment), certain natural resources, and barriers to entry that secured monopoly or monopoly-like positions. When the new techniques arrive, it is optimal for those groups that stand to lose from technological change to resist them.[7]

4. Is there a market for an environmentally friendly refrigerator?

Before we can look at the strategies undertaken by firms to create, reconstruct and redefine their competitive environment, we have to go back to one of the key problems

---

7 Mokyr (1992; 1994) provides examples of how these groups use non-market mechanisms.

in dealing with market theory. We have to approach the question of the market itself. To talk about market delineation is a somewhat old-fashioned issue because the theoretical debate slowed in the early seventies. Nevertheless, the problem of market definition in the applied literature has not been solved yet.

In the CFC case, it is not very helpful to use a demand driven definition of a market - that is to question whether there is sufficient consumer demand for a certain product. Consumers ask in the case of refrigeration for specified services[8] that can be provided by a product. It seems reasonable to assume that consumers are not interested in the CFC-containing product itself but the properties that go with it. This assumption is crucial when we consider the switch to environmentally friendly products. We do not have to deal with the notion of declining demand, but have markets with stable demand structures.

For consumers the utility value of a refrigerator is not determined by its refrigerant or insulating materials but only by its capability of keeping food and beverages fresh and cold. Consumers perceive different types and brands of refrigerators as more or less identical products. The typical consumer does not know much about the technical details of a refrigerator. Their purchase is influenced by price, first of all, and then by external appearance and equipment. Increasingly customers have also made their buying decision also dependent on energy consumption and the environmental friendliness of products.

Looking at the specific case of refrigerators it seems to be appropriate to assume a supply driven market definition. It makes a big difference if manufacturers choose to produce a refrigerator with or without CFC being the refrigerant. For producers of refrigerators, a ban on CFC would lead to a substantial change in the production techniques.

Goods experience a product life cycle. At the outset, development and testing are required to conceptualize and design a product. For this reason, the early stages of production are very likely to be undertaken by an innovative firm. Over time, however, a successful product tends to become standardized and many manufacturers can produce it. The mature product may be produced by firms that do little or no research and development, specializing instead in copying successful products invented and developed by others.[9]

The history of refrigerator production shows how production patterns can shift over time. Household refrigerators were invented in the United States. Marketing of the product became possible after Th. Midgley invented chlorofluorocarbons (CFCs) in 1928. Not having the serious disadvantages of the former refrigerants CFCs were very efficient coolants. CFC-based household refrigerator production, in turn, quickly turned out to be a great market success in the United States. After the Second World War with restructuring of industries, demand for household refrigeration increased substantially in

---

8 "The basic economic magnitude (value or utility) is service, not good. It is inherently a stream or flow in time ..." Knight (1921, 92). He brought up the issue of services instead of goods. Standard economic allocation theory is in truth concerned with services. Material objects are merely the vehicles which carry some of these services, and they are exchanged because of consumer preferences for the services associated with their use or because they can help to add value in the manufacturing process.

9 See for example Klepper and Graddy (1990) and Javanovic and MacDonald (1994).

all industrialized countries. The technology of refrigerator manufacturing became well known and companies in the US, Europe and Japan started the production, each with slightly modified products to better serve the consumer taste in their own countries.

In the industrialized countries the market for household refrigerators had by the mid-1980s reached near saturation. A British study on the UK market for domestic refrigeration shows that this market is dominated by replacement sales, accounting for 80 percent of total sales of refrigerators. Almost all households have some form of refrigeration unit, which they generally replace after 8 to 12 years of use, although technically each refrigerator has an average product life of 15 to 20 years (Department of Trade and Industry, 1990, 100). Data so far collected on the German market points into the same direction.

Figure 7.1 Refrigerator sales in Germany (1975-1991)

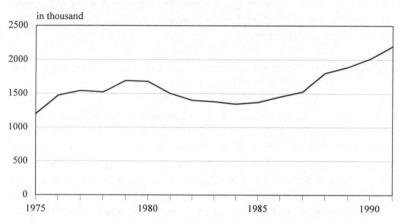

Source: Statistisches Bundesamt: Fachserie 4, Reihe 3.1 (Produzierendes Gewerbe), various years.

Unit sales in the German market remained practically stable over the period of the mid-70s to the mid-80s. From the mid-80s the market has grown steadily. This is mainly due to two causes. The number of single households increased considerably as the baby boom generation entered the housing market with its preference for living alone. With German unification the East German consumers entered the West German domestic refrigeration market and added to the demand. Unit sales in 1991 reached a total of almost 2.2 million per annum.

Nevertheless, demand for new refrigeration units is expected to remain relatively static. Replacement sales will continue to grow and dominate the market. This is mainly due to the trend towards fitted kitchens, meaning replacement might take place a little bit earlier than usual.

Responding to static demand for new units, refrigerator producers have tried to stimulate demand. This is being done by offering new equipment with added features in an effort to shorten product life. Before HFC-134a and propane/isobutane became an alternative these features included:

- integrated units for fitted kitchens which will present a total color coordinated image of the kitchen;
- zoned refrigerators/freezers, which have three or four different compartments, each of which is maintained at a different temperature, ranging from 'larder' to 'deep freezer' temperatures;
- frost-free refrigerators which remove the need for de-frosting;
- 'environmentally friendly' refrigerators which contain a reduced amount of CFC (The first attempt to produce this type of refrigerator led to 50 percent less CFC consumption, including the CFC contained within the insulating foam and was therefore meant to be attractive to the 'green consumer'. However, these refrigerators were 10 percent less energy efficient than their predecessors.);
- less energy consuming refrigerators.

Technicians at the Dortmund Institute of Hygiene published their findings but received no interest from West German manufacturers. Also Greenpeace was approached. They showed interest. Looking for a company to carry out further tests on the propane/isobutane mixture, Greenpeace contacted dkk Scharfenstein (Deutsche Kühl- und Kraftmaschinen Scharfenstein), an East German company that was the leading household appliances manufacturer before German re-unification. They have produced refrigerators for more than 50 years at an rate of up to one million units annually. With German re-unification the company experienced a severe decrease in sales. Between 1990 and 1992 sales turnover dropped by more than 75 percent. On the 6th of July 1992, Greenpeace ordered 10 prototypes of CFC/HFC-free refrigerators from dkk Scharfenstein for a total of 26 000 DM. The first prototype was presented at a press conference in Scharfenstein on the 16th of July 1992. On the 1st of August 1992, Greenpeace started an advertising campaign in order to secure the production start of the CFC/HFC-free refrigerator with advance orders in the future. On the 13th of August 1992, the mail order company Neckermann announced that it had ordered 20 000 units of the new refrigerator and held an option on another 50 000 units. In October 1992, Greenpeace stopped its advertising campaign after having collected almost 70 000 advance orders. In February 1993, during the German domestic appliances fair Domotechnica, Bosch-Siemens, Foron (the former dkk Scharfenstein) and Liebherr introduced refrigerators not only operating on a CFC/HFC-free coolant but also using pentane blown foam as insulating material (Greenpeace, 1994). Foron started production of the CFC/HFC-free refrigerators on the 15th of March 1993.

The CFC-containing refrigerator market is to be phased out, but at this point of time it is difficult to assess which impact the introduction of a new technology has had on industry structure. At the outset of the market transition, it is assumed that the old manufacturers will be the ones that enter the newly emerging market for CFC/HFC-free refrigerators. Developments at the present time, indeed, tend in that direction. But what actually will happen to those companies like AEG and Electrolux which placed their hopes in HFC-134a in the medium run is not yet clear. Having made heavy investments in HFC-134a, which they will not be able to recoup, they are now being forced to invest in the new technology - this time a CFC/HFC-free technology.

One of the main problems associated with change remains. The commercial potential of new or existing technology is not immediately obvious. It takes time for companies to understand the market potential of new technologies. The benefit to overcoming this obstacle quickly is that it allows a company to be the first mover in a newly emerging market. The advantage of being the first in a new market is the promise of attaining a larger market share as the market develops (see for example Robinson, Kalyanaram and Urban, 1994). The definition of a first entrant seems to point to the problem. Lieberman and Montgomery (1988) have used the following definition: the market pioneer is the market's first entrant, and a firm must have reached a competitive scale of commercialization to be recognized as an entrant. This points into the direction of the problem to actually accumulate the necessary initial scale of commercialization - in other words the necessary first stock of output to be sold to customers. As soon as that has happened the process of competition begins.

The creation of the CFC/HFC-free refrigerator market was the result of a number of fairly unique circumstances. Among the most important was the willingness of individual companies to pursue an innovation path that did not display advanced technical sophistication but was rather a simplistic and efficient approach. Due to the very special situation in Germany at that time it was possible to find an outsider to the West German refrigerator market that had the technical potential of producing refrigerators in sufficient quantities with the new technology. To start production it was necessary to secure a minimum scale. This became possible when Greenpeace collected advanced orders for a product where consumers normally do not allow additional time for delivery.

By reviewing the strategy of the main players on the West German refrigerator market it seems reasonable to assume that the oligopolistic structure of that market would have effectively hindered this development. At the first glance it seems to be true that the old companies in the refrigerator market are no longer very innovative. The competitive challenge instead came from a company (dkk Scharfenstein/Foron), which faced the threat of being closed down by the Treuhand. The competitive challenge from the small East German first was met by the large West German companies within months. Once, spurred to action, the western refrigeration companies began to compete amongst themselves over who could be the first to gain a large share of the newly emerging market for CFC/HFC-free refrigerators.

5. Outlook

A change in a technical paradigm does not take place just because a superior technology or product has been invented. Only by securing the success on the market can a technological break-through be realized.

For future research it would be worthwhile to look at the processes that determine the selection of particular innovations and explore their effects on industrial structure. To obtain useful results it seems necessary to determine how the socially optimal outcome should look like and how this result can be resolved by the market. On the company side it might be worthwhile to find out whether there are organizational routines that make firms good at exploring technical opportunities and translating them into specific marketable products.

In the case of the refrigeration industry we have an oligopolistic market structure and companies who are also engaged in other European markets for household refrigeration. It seems obvious to ask to what extent these companies facilitate the cross-border diffusion of commercializeable technological knowledge. Will they introduce the butane/propane refrigerator in the other European markets, as regulatory restrictions in these countries are brought to the same level as in Germany? It seems worthwhile to explore to what extent firms assist or inhibit the geographical dispersion of newly implemented technological knowledge.

References

Abernathy, William J. and Kim B. Clark (1985); Innovation: Mapping the Winds of Creative Destruction; *Research Policy*, 14, 3-22.

Abernathy, William J. and James M. Utterback (1975); A Dynamic Model of Product and Process Innovation; *Omega*, 3 (6), 639-656.

Albach, Horst (1994) *Culture and Technical Innovation. A Cross-Cultural Analysis and Policy Recommendations*, Berlin: Walter de Gruyter.

Arrow, Kenneth J. (1962) Economic Welfare and the Allocation of Resources for Invention, NBER, in Nelson, Richard N. (ed.) *The Rate and Direction of Inventive Activity*, Princton, NJ: Princton University Press, 609-625.

Arthur, W. Brian (1989); Competing technologies, increasing returns, and lock-in by historical events; *Economic Journal*, 99, 116-131.

Bresgott, Michael (1992); Dortmunder Ärzte gaben nicht auf: Öko-Kühlschrank surrt im Revier; *Westdeutsche Allgemeine Zeitung*, 7 August 1992.

Department of Trade and Industry (1990) *CFCs and Halons: Alternatives and the Scope for Recovery for Recycling and Destruction*, a Report by Coopers & Lybrand Deloitte in association with Mott MacDonald and C S Todd & Associates, London, UK: HMSO.

Dosi, Giovanni (1988); Sources, Procedures, and Microeconomic Effects of Innovation; *Journal of Economic Literature*, 26, 1120-1171.

Foran, Jeffrey A. (1990); The Sunset Chemicals Proposal; *International Environmental Affairs*, 2, 303-308.

Greenpeace (1994) *Greenfreeze weltweit: Die Chronologie einer umwelttechnischen Revolution*, Hamburg: Greenpeace.

Javanovic, Boyan and Glenn M. MacDonald (1994); The Life Cycle of a Competitive Industry; *Journal of Political Economy*, 102 (2), 322-347.

Harris, Michael R. (1992) PAFT: Programme for Alternative Fluorocarbon Toxicology Testing, paper presented at the 'Alternatives to CFCs and Halons - Technologies and Substances' conference in Berlin, 24-26 February.

Kleinknecht, Alfred and Bart Verspagen (1990); Demand and innovation: Schmookler re-examined; *Research Policy*, 19, 387-394.

Klepper, Steven and Elizabeth Graddy (1990); The Evolution of New Industries and the Determinants of Market Structure; *Rand Journal of Economics*, 21 (1), 24-44.

Knight, Frank H. (1921) *Risk, Uncertainty and Profit*, Boston: Houghton Mifflin Company.

Lieberman, Marvin B. and David B. Montgomery (1988); First Mover Advantages; *Strategic Management Journal*, 9, 41-58.

Mokyr, Joel (1992); Technological inertia in economic history; *Journal of Economic History*, 52 (2), 325-338.

Mokyr, Joel (1994); Cardwell's Law and the political economy of technical progress; *Research Policy*, 23, 561-574.

Molina, Mario J. and F. S. Rowland (1974); Stratospheric Sink for Chlorofluorocarbons: Chlorine Atome catalysed Destruction of Ozone; *Nature* 249, 810-812.

Mowery, David and Nathan Rosenberg (1979); The influence of market demand upon innovation: a critical review of some recent empirical studies; *Research Policy*, 8, 102-153.

Opschoor, Johannes B. and David W. Pearce (1991) *Persistent Pollutants: Economics and Policy*, Norwell MA: Kluwer Academic Publishers.

Pigou, Arthur C. (1931) *The Economics of Welfare*, London: Macmillan.

Robinson, William T., Gurumurthy Kalyanaram and Glen L. Urban (1994); First-Mover Advantages from Pioneering New Markets; *Review of Industrial Organization*, 9 (1), 1-23.

Schmookler, Jacob (1966) *Invention and Economic Growth*, Cambridge Mass.: Harvard University Press.

Solow, Robert M. (1957); Technical Change and the aggregate production function; *Review of Economics and Statistics*, 39, 312-320.

Statistisches Bundesamt, Fachserie 4, Reihe 3.1 (Produzierendes Gewerbe), various years.

Tushman, Michael L. and Philip Anderson (1986); Technological Discontinuities and Organizational Environments; *Administrative Science Quarterly*, 31, 439-465.

UNEP (United Nations Environment Programme) (1993) *Handbook for the Montreal Protocol on Substances that Deplete the Ozone Layer*, 3rd edn, August.

UNEP IE/PAC (UNEP Industry and Environment Programme Activity Centre) (1994), *OzonAction*, no. 11.

Utterback, James M. and Fernando F. Suárez (1993); Innovation, Competition, and Industry Structure; *Research Policy*, 22, 1-21.

ZVEI (Zentralverband Elektrotechnik und Elektronikindustrie e.V.) (1992) *Freiwillige Selbstverpflichtung der deutschen Haushalt-Kältegeräte-Industrie zum Ausstieg aus der FCKW-Anwendung als Kältemittel und Isolierdämmgas*, Frankfurt: ZVEI.

PART 3

FROM HIERARCHIES TO MARKETS: THE POST-SOCIALIST EXPERIENCE

8 Knowledge, transaction costs and the creation of markets in post-socialist economies*

Wim Swaan

1. Introduction

The first years of the transition to a market economy in Eastern Europe have shown a sharp decline in output in all countries concerned, even if the initial conditions and the policy pursued differed considerably. This transformation crisis can be related to a complex of macroeconomic, microeconomic and institutional factors (Kornai, 1993; Schmieding, 1993). Particularly disquieting is that liberalization and removal of barriers to entry have not led to a growth of economic activity: for the first couple of years at least, the transformation has been characterized by an L-curve, rather than the expected J-curve (Nuti and Portes, 1993, 8-9).

The present study focusses on the transformation costs at the level of enterprises and markets as one of the factors contributing to the fall in output. Three levels are considered: the costs of reorganization of firms (Sections 3 and 4), the impact of dynamic transactions costs, that is, the cost of establishing transactions (Section 6), and the role of competence in the effectiveness of inter-firm and intra-firm coordination (Section 7). Differences in transformation costs among firms and branches may imply that market creation will proceed at a different pace throughout the economy and that the establishment of effective governance structures, including ownership, would be partly an endogenous process (Section 8).

A central argument to this study is that in the short run behavior is not in the first place determined by the degree of economic liberalization, but rather by the sudden disintegration of the party-state hierarchy (Section 2). This implies, among other things, that the process of entry and exit is initially much more troublesome than in developed market economies (Section 5).

While actual developments taking place in post-socialist economies have provided the major impetus and inspiration for writing this study, no explicit empirical analysis or description is provided. Only for the purpose of illustration scattered reference will be made to particular developments. The aim of this study was first of all to provide a foundation for empirical work, thereby providing an understanding for a set of

* This study is part of an ongoing research project. Much of the argument is open to further development. The current version is a partial revision of a paper that was earlier presented at the Fourth Trento-EACES Workshop "Centralization and Decentralization of Economic Institutions: Their Role in the Transformation of Economic Systems", at the University of Trento, Italy (Swaan, 1995). The research for this study was financed by the Research Fund of the Institute of Economics of the Hungarian Academy of Sciences. The paper benefitted from remarks from Katalin Balázs, Egon Franck, Yevgeny Kuznetsov, Klaus Nielsen and Pekka Sutela. The usual disclaimer applies.

phenomena that are common to post-socialist economies. By taking the theoretical behavioral literature as a frame of reference, it may become clear to what extent special aspects of behavior in the post-socialist transition are rooted in general characteristics of human economic behavior.

The argument strongly relies on the work of Nelson and Winter (1982), building on the concepts of bounded rationality (cf. Simon, 1945) and tacit knowledge (cf. Polanyi, 1958). Bounded rationality implies a huge potential for behavioral change, but also indicates that the effectuation of potential change may be a complicated, slow process. The tacit character of a large part of human knowledge limits the transfer of knowledge and the speed of learning, in particular in large organizations. Another notion this study builds upon is that the behavior of firms cannot be considered to be directly determined by the market environment and the state of technology - rather, markets and technology are themselves created by individual firms and their organizational capabilities (Schumpeter, 1934, 1939; and recently Teece, 1993; following the study of Chandler, 1990 on the United States, Britain and Germany).

2.   The disintegration of the party-state hierarchy and transaction costs

The literature on post-socialist transformation might give the impression that behavior is mainly influenced by economic liberalization and stabilization policy. In the short run, however, behavior is much more influenced by the collapse of the institutional structures in which individuals and organizations used to operate. Whereas liberalization and stabilization policies can be seen as (partly) intended processes, the collapse of the socialist system is largely an unintended process. Stabilization policies, if implemented at all, have indeed been harshest in countries were the process of disintegration was most chaotic, such as in Poland and Russia. Apart from a number of very desirable changes, the sudden disintegration of the party-state hierarchy also had negative consequences. Here I will focus on the impact on economic transactions.

Given the central role of the party-state hierarchy in coordinating economic activities, it needs little explanation that its disappearance caused major disruption in transactions (Kornai, 1993). Ábel and Bonin (1993) have pointed to the problem of 'state desertion', as a result of which regulation of state enterprises has become ineffective. However, if the role of organs of the party-state hierarchy would have been restricted to regulating enterprises, its disintegration would have caused much less disruption.

In the U-form hierarchy of Soviet-type economies (Qian and Xu, 1993), all transactions used to be arranged through the channels of the hierarchy. This does not only lead to extreme coordination costs, it also implies that enterprises entirely lack the experience and skills to initiate and effectuate transactions on their own once the hierarchy has disintegrated.

This problem is particularly serious in trade and distribution, as this mostly requires multi-stage transactions. Producers in centrally planned economies operated in almost total isolation of retail and wholesale, both in domestic and foreign trade. Distribution entirely depended on intervention from countless party and state organs, as neither producers, nor wholesale companies, nor retailers had any interest in active marketing. Producers were mostly even not allowed to engage in direct relations. The disintegration of the party-state hierarchy accordingly implies a serious blow to very feeble distribution networks.

The lack of appropriate supporting institutions imply high transaction costs for firms, in addition to their lack of transaction skills. One example, which has been widely discussed in the literature, is the absence of a well-functioning banking system, leading to misallocation and underallocation of credits (Calvo and Coricelli, 1993; Kornai, 1993). Let me here discuss another example: the absence of satisfactory mechanisms of contract enforcement.

In discussing contract enforcement in market economies, Williamson (1985, 70-71) has pointed to the major role of third party assistance in resolving disputes. Third party assistance may take many forms: from ad hoc arbitration by professionals to institutionalized boards of branch organizations. In the context of centrally planned economies the term third party enforcement is to be understood almost literally: it was the party, in particular its local organs that were continuously involved in resolving disputes that arose in the execution of transactions planned by state organs (Hough, 1969; Grossman, 1983; Csanádi, 1990). As a consequence, the disintegration of the party-state hierarchy does not only imply that enterprises suddenly have to conclude transactions on their own, they also lack institutions to settle their conflicts. In the former Soviet Union, Gorbachev's measure to remove the party from the economy had a disastrous impact on output (Ellman and Kontorovich, 1992, 22, 26). As court ordering is just one form of third party assistance, legal change is in itself not sufficient to solve these problems of contract enforcement. Indeed, most forms of third party enforcement do not arise by design but organically.

3. The initial response of state enterprises

The lack of transaction skills and the lack of appropriate institutions supporting transactions clearly has a major impact on enterprise behavior. In this Section I will discuss the initial response of state enterprises to the disintegration of the party-state hierarchy. In later Sections the problem of restructuring and the process of entry and exit will be discussed.

In order to focus on the problem of transaction costs and behavioral constraints let me assume that prices and output are liberalized and that the authorities are able to maintain or impose a certain minimum degree of financial stability. In its response to the simultaneous occurrence of liberalization and the disintegration of the party-state hierarchy, a firm faces two problems: how to set its prices, and how to establish transactions with actors that are potentially interested in its products. Consider each in turn.

The major problem enterprises face in setting prices is that they do not even have the faintest knowledge of the shape of the demand curve for their products. Following Estrin and Hare (1992, 12-17) one might say that pre-transition firms do not face a demand curve, but merely a demand point. Accordingly, in setting their prices following liberalization, firms are forced to make wild estimates of demand elasticity. Unfortunately, they are likely to underestimate demand elasticity, as far as they rely on their experiences from the shortage economy. Unsatisfied demand in a shortage economy appears at all firms in a particular branch, and through forced substitution also in other branches. As a result, firms structurally overestimate the residual demand they face, underestimate the elasticity of demand and set their prices too high once they are liberalized, whatever decision criterion they follow. Consequently, the level of inflation following price liberalization depends, among other things, on the degree to which firms underestimate the elasticity of demand for their products.

Even if enterprises would by accident set their prices 'right', that is, estimate the demand elasticity for their products correctly, they will face serious problems in capturing all potential demand at this price level. The more relative prices will change, the stronger output will be affected negatively by the costs of (re-)establishing transactions. Firstly, firms are unlikely to know exactly which purchasers are the ones willing to pay the new price. They may fail to contact some potential purchasers willing to pay higher prices, and superfluously offer the product to purchasers not willing to pay the current price. Secondly, their lack of marketing skills will shift all search costs to purchasers, whose utility (and demand) will decline correspondingly. Thirdly, firms need to reconsider their product mix from a uniform low quality - high quantity supply to more a heterogeneous mix. Even if technology and capacity would allow such a change, firms have to find out which consumers would like what products.

In the foregoing discussion of the firm's output and price decision it was implicitly assumed that firms are searching for the best solution they can reach. Although firms face strong constraints on their knowledge, they would adjust instantaneously to all new information available. Unfortunately, there are strong reasons to doubt whether this is indeed the case. Research on firms' response to adversity in market economies suggest that firms are able to handle limited amounts of adversity, but that strong adversity actually decreases the ability of organizations to change. If undertaken at all, endeavors at change more often than not go in the wrong direction, when adversity is strong. Typically, however, firms choose not to respond at all. They carry on as before, but at a lower level of activity, and eventually may disappear altogether. (Nelson, 1981; Nelson and Winter, 1982; 121-123; Murrell, 1992c, 40-43).

A theoretical explanation for these phenomena is given by Heiner (1983). The decision to change a given repertoire of actions is not only dependent upon the potential gains of new types of actions, but also on the degree of stability of the actor's environment. High instability of the environment leads to low reliability of selecting the right action at the right time and accordingly encourages actors to stick to a previously developed repertoire of actions. Heiner (1983, 562) speaks in this respect of a *C-D gap* between the agent's competence and the difficulty of the decision problem. This manifests itself in magnified forms in post-socialist economies.

4. The costs of reorganizing firms

Having discussed the initial response of state enterprises to economic disintegration, let us now turn to the prospects of behavioral change in the economy. As was already indicated in discussing the initial response of state enterprises to the disintegration of the party-state hierarchy, the abilities of firms to adapt to changing circumstances are limited. While this does not at all exclude change, it incurs costs, in terms of effort and time to be spend on reorganization.

The extent of reorganization costs may be clarified by discussing some of the problems that arise when a firm is taken over by an active owner, who has shown competence in managing firms elsewhere, for instance abroad. This would indeed provide the best conditions for reorganization and behavioral change. I will discuss reorganization costs in general terms; obviously they will be different across branches and firms, depending for instance on the degree of technological complexity and the relative importance of firm-specific knowledge.

Consider first the organizational boundaries of the firm. Under state socialism, the boundaries of the firm were not in the first place influenced by transaction costs considerations at the level of the firm, but rather by transaction costs in hierarchical relations between central organs and firms (Schweitzer, 1981; Ben-Ner and Neuberger, 1988). The costs of redrawing the boundaries of the firm accordingly depend upon the degree to which the two considerations would lead to different organization of firms. Particularly important is the degree to which technology was affected by centralization. The costs of reorganizing megafactories in, for instance, the textile industry, shoe industry or meatprocessing are likely to be prohibitive. In industries where centralization was merely an administrative matter, without affecting plant size and technology, reorganization is less costly.

Secondly, a considerable part of reorganization consists of organizational learning and the absorption of new knowledge. As is argued at length by Nelson and Winter (1982), the knowledge of a firm cannot be reduced to a book of blueprints, or to the knowledge of its engineers and scientists. Instead, the firm's knowledge can be considered to be embodied in the routines that develop as a response to bounded rationality. By implementing activities according to certain regularities, and adapting these only marginally, employees need not to be instructed or to consult with each other on every detail of their work. The costs of coordination in an organization in constant flux would be prohibitive. Similar to individual knowledge, organizational knowledge is partly tacit or personal: it is difficult to articulate and neither the management, nor other participants in the organization may be completely aware of its content (Nelson and Winter, 1982; 99-124; following Polanyi, 1958).

The tacit character of organizational knowledge puts limitations both on the ability of a new owner to transfer knowledge and on the ability of the existing firm to absorb new knowledge. The former aspect is not typical of post-socialist economies. Replication of successful business routines is riddled with difficulties, which are only reinforced by cultural barriers in endeavors of international transfer of knowledge (see for instance Black and Mendenhall, 1990; Hamel, 1991). As routines are the expression of an organizational truce, as Nelson and Winter (1982, 107-112) call it, endeavors at changing routines are likely to be costly. All this does in itself not put a barrier to knowledge transfer - it rather represents a cost in terms of delayed adjustment. Indeed, the limits to the possibilities of transferring firm-specific skills form the very rationale for the existence of multinational firms, as these skills cannot be transferred through arm's length market contracts (Caves, 1982).

As to the ability of existing firms to absorb new knowledge, the existing stock of individual and organizational capabilities in post-socialist economies poses special problems. Since tacit knowledge develops through experience, it is closely related to the institutional structure in which it developed (Murrell, 1992a, 1992b). The capabilities that are lacking most are precisely the ones that in market economies have evolved as part of tacit knowledge. The basis for acquiring marketing and organizational capabilities can be given through standard education, but thorough command of these skills can only be acquired through practice, for instance by following the examples of others.

On the other hand, tacit knowledge as how to operate as a *homo sovieticus* (Dembinski, 1991, 47-49) has lost most of its value. In other words, where a new owner of a firm in developed market economies only faces the problem of transferring its specific knowledge, the new owner of a post-socialist firm is confronted with an organization which lacks the basic capabilities to respond to endeavors at transferring knowledge. According to Nelson and Winter (1982, 130-134), the success of organizational change depends upon the degree to which new routines are built upon reliable subroutines, to which the organization is already familiar. Post-socialist firms will be weak in this respect: as far as they operated according to reliable routines, these have largely lost their value after the disintegration of the socialist system. Virtually a reversal of routines is required: the priority regime within the organization has to shift from the supply department to the sales department and the focus of attention has to shift from quantity to quality (Keren, 1992).

In the more developed post-socialist economies, the low level of appropriate tacit skills is partly compensated for by a relatively high level of technical, easily transferable skills, as is reflected in high levels of education. This combination is indeed rare in economic history, as the social stock of tacit and technical skills mostly have developed in mutual interaction. Unfortunately, the different levels of tacit skills and more easily transferable skills are not always perceived in programs aimed at international transfer of knowledge. Foreign trainers frequently identify the low level of skills with a lack of technical skills and end up in teaching things that are long familiar. Recipients, on the other hand, may be unaware of the importance of tacit aspects of skills. Accordingly, they may either expect success from a further increase of their technical skills, or they may simply deny the importance of learning new skills and see the role of foreign partners mainly as providing capital and equipment (see Dander, 1993 and Vecsenyi, 1992 on Hungary).

In addition to the high level of technical, transferable skills, another relative advantage might be provided by economic reforms under state socialism, like those in Hungary or Poland. Although socialist reforms did not lead to a breakthrough towards market oriented business organization, managerial perception has at least been molded in the direction of market concepts, which may facilitate the absorption of organizational and marketing skills (see for instance Swaan and Lissowska, 1992a, 1992b and Hooley, 1993).

The extent of reorganization costs is illustrated by the findings of empirical research on enterprise behavior in Hungary and Poland. Karsai (1992) and Laki (1992) see increasing endeavors at organizational change in Hungary, yet at the same time note that these are mostly not part of deliberate plans, but rather arise ad hoc. While behavioral change in Hungary is rather a gradual process that already started in the 1980s before the disintegration of the system (Swaan and Lissowska, 1992a), a more sudden change can be noted in Poland. This did not immediately follow the stabilization and liberalization program of 1990, but occurred with a delay of around two years (Pinto, Belka and Krajewski, 1993; Lissowska, 1993). Pinto, Belka and Krajewski (1993, 217-222) identify managers as the driving force between change and point to firm-specific capabilities in behavioral change. Interestingly, behavioral change is not a direct result of changes in ownership and governance structures: the main incentive for successful managers is their anticipation of future rewards once privatization made headway.

5. Creative destruction?

In developed market economies, a much larger degree of change comes from the development of new organizations than from adaptation and reorganization of existing firms. This was emphasized long ago by Schumpeter (1934, 1939, 1942). Innovations, or 'doing things differently in the realm of economic life', implies mostly the creation of a new plant and a new firm by new men (Schumpeter, 1939, 84-96). This leads to creative destruction, 'the essential fact of capitalism' (Schumpeter, 1942, 83).

The destruction of institutional structures in post-socialist countries and the collapse of output has frequently been compared with this Schumpeterian type of creative destruction. Such comparisons might suggest, intendedly or not, that the decline in output due to the destruction of inefficient state enterprises will more or less automatically be compensated for by the creation of new enterprises, albeit with a certain time lag. As will be argued, however, the process of recovery bears more resemblance to the initial development of market economies. This was much less smooth than the type of creative destruction taking place in developed market economies in the second half of the 20th century (see Schumpeter, 1939, in particular

220-448). In a sense, post-socialist economies have to repeat part of the development process they went through before, both during state socialism and prior to that.

Consider first, for the purpose of comparison, the process of creative destruction in developed market economies. Given the importance generally attributed to creative destruction, surprisingly little empirical research is available. Dunne, Roberts and Samuelson (1988) present revealing data on entry and exit in manufacturing industry in the United States in the period 1963-1982. They distinguish three types of entrants: entirely new firms, existing firms constructing new plants, and existing firms altering the product mix of existing plants. Of these, the second group, existing firms constructing new plants, is most successful. Although the entry rate of this group is lowest of the three groups, it ends up with both a lower rate of failure and a much higher average size. The failure rate of the first group (entirely new firms) is slightly lower than that of the third group (existing firms altering the product mix of existing plants), but the latter reaches a considerably larger size. The study also reveals a high level of turnover of firms: of all firms entering in a particular year, 55-65 percent have disappeared within five years.

The vulnerability of new firms has been characterized as being a 'liability of newness': the failure rate of firms decreases with age (Stinchcombe, 1965, 148-150, Hannan and Freeman, 1984, 1989). New firms have not yet built up sufficient levels of reliability and accountability to ensure an uninterrupted flow of resources and sales. They do not yet operate according to established routines: this gives them a lot of flexibility, but also makes them much more vulnerable to unexpected developments.

The process of entry and exit in post-socialist economies shows some marked differences from what can be noted in developed market economies. The destruction of existing firms is only partly related to the entry of new ones, and all the more to the disintegration of the institutional structure in which they used to operate. As a consequence, destruction is not necessarily related to efficiency (Nuti and Portes, 1993, 9).

Schumpeter (1942, 83) characterized creative destruction as '[a] process ... that incessantly revolutionizes ... the economic structure *from within*, incessantly destroying the old one, incessantly creating a new one' (emphasis in original). In post-socialist economies, destruction is neither from within, nor incessant. Rather, it is characterized by an abrupt shock to existing firms, while recovery through the *successful* entry of new firms is likely to be a relatively slow process. There is *a priori* no reason to assume that newness is less of a liability to entrants in post-socialist economies. Existing state firms, on the other hand, are very vulnerable. They lack the support of the institutional environment of the party-state hierarchy, and their endeavors at reorganization may well end in failure.

Moreover, entry by existing firms through building new plants, the most successful type of entry in the United States according to Dunne, Roberts and Samuelson (1988), will initially be restricted mainly to foreign firms. Although entry of this kind is taking place, its effectiveness is constrained by cultural and knowledge barriers, similar to the costs of reorganizing existing firms, as discussed above.

6. The costs of establishing transactions

In discussing the impact of the disintegration of the party-state hierarchy on enterprise behavior, it was already mentioned that firms face high transaction costs due to the absence of supporting institutions. Here the transaction costs argument will be developed further by focussing on the costs of establishing transactions. These are faced both by existing state firms and by new firms.

Following Coase (1937, 1960), much of the transaction costs literature has focussed on comparative static aspects of transactions, in particular on the question whether or not transactions will come about, and what form they will eventually take (see Williamson, 1985, 23-29 for an overview of the various branches of transaction cost economics). In this literature emphasis is laid on costs of ex ante contract negotiation and ex post control and enforcement. However, before contract negotiation can begin, a contact has to be established. In other words, transactions are determined by the triad contact, contract, and control, and not just by the latter two (cf. Nooteboom, 1992a, 7). Coase (1960, 15) indeed briefly mentioned the costs of discovering the person one wants to deal with as one element of transaction costs, without, however, developing this element in his analysis.

Establishing transactions with new partners has a cost of its own. Agents should first of all be aware of each other's existence and of the value of potential transactions. Producers and traders should have some broad perception of the composition of demand. Consumers, on the other hand, should be aware of their preferences for a particular product, and of the existence of particular retail outlets. Search processes are restricted to products and trade partners which are known to exist.

The costs of establishing contact prior to negotiating and effectuating gives transaction cost economics a dynamic aspect. Even if the costs of contract negotiation and enforcement in themselves would not be prohibitive, the set up costs may preclude transactions to take place, at least temporarily. As a consequence, transactions in market economies develop in network patterns (see Beije and Groenewegen, 1992). In the words of Granovetter (1985), economic action is *embedded* in social relations: that is, it is neither determined by social relations (the oversocialized conception of actors in orthodox sociology), nor entirely isolated from social relations (the undersocialized, atomistic view of orthodox neoclassical economics). Structuring of transactions has important information and knowledge advantages, facilitating decision making under bounded rationality. A stable social-economic structure is particularly important for small firms. Both in relations to large firms and in relations among each other, small firms strongly rely on network relations (Romo and Schwartz, 1990; Perrow, 1993). Small firms face relatively higher costs in establishing and maintaining transactions than large firms do and are much more vulnerable to sudden shifts in the environment (Nooteboom, 1992a).

Accordingly, restructuring of a post-socialist economy is not merely a matter of creating a new industrial structure, both in terms of the distribution of firm size and the distribution over sectors. It also requires a new network of transactions to be created and the development of knowledge related to that. As long as prospective buyers and sellers are unaware of potential transactions, these will not come about.

The costs of establishing transactions were a major concern in the work of Schumpeter (1934, 1939) on economic development. Firms do not face a given demand curve, but have to create demand themselves. Each innovation involves a chain of minor events. This chain of events cannot be reduced to one moment, but takes historic time. Resistance from the environment has to be overcome, technical and organizational problems have to be tackled, distribution has to be solved, consumers have to be induced to forget about unfavorable experiences at the initial stage of product development, etc. (see Schumpeter, 1939, for instance 84-86, 226-227, 243-245).

In post-socialist economies, actors need to establish new types of transactions, yet they can hardly rely on the cost reducing devices available in stable social structures. Market networks are almost entirely absent. Transaction patterns will arise in a trial and error fashion. Entrants lack a frame of reference to position their product mix. This gives early entrants a first mover advantage, but in thin markets entry also has a much higher risk of failure. Consumers will be confronted with quickly changing product assortments in retail outlets. This will discourage repeat purchasing, and in turn decrease the prospective benefits of entrants. Davis and Winckler Andersen (1992) refer to these phenomena as the 'problem of fewness'.

In economies where prior to the disintegration some limited scope for the (quasi-) private sector was allowed, like Hungary and Poland, the fate of small private firms in industry entirely depends upon the one or two large state firms to which their transactions were linked: many of them will be irretrievably lost, for instance as a result of the collapse of CMEA-trade.

For the purpose of illustration, the problem of establishing transactions after the disintegration of the party-state hierarchy may be compared with a hypothetical situation in which all consumers from Paris would be replaced by Londoners, while all producers, wholesale and retail companies from Paris would be replaced by companies from the Milano area. For quite some time Paris would be dominated by chaotic conditions and a serious fall in output as actors would lack any frame of reference to base their decisions upon.

In post-socialist economies, one might argue, the continuation of personal contacts and networks from the past could compensate for the disintegration of institutional structures. However, in many cases where contacting costs would be low, this is offset by high costs of contracting and controlling, and vice versa. In a transaction between a state firm and a private subcontractor, for instance, contacting costs may be low if the two partners were already doing business under the previous regime, but due to uncertain property rights of the state firm, contracting costs will increase substantially. In a relation between two new private firms the cost of contract and control may be lower, but here contacting costs may be high initially. Moreover, even if institutional structures function properly (which is clearly not yet the case in post-socialist economies), they too require initial contacting costs for persons who would like to rely upon them. Both legal support and other forms of third party assistance require knowledge of the competent persons (lawyers etc.) to contact in case of problems.

In general, the value of personal contacts strongly deteriorates by a grand reshuffling of functions and institutions as occurred with the disintegration of the socialist system. A contact with the responsible person in a supplying firm, for example, has high value in a shortage economy, but much less in a buyer's market. The contact with a potential purchasing firm loses its value as soon as this firm goes bankrupt. Knowing who to turn to in the party bureaucracy is worthless as soon as this bureaucracy ceases to exit. The example of a collective removal, as given before, may be seen as a metaphor for this process of reshuffling. Contrary to the example of a collective removal, reestablishing contacts and networks in post-socialist economies may be facilitated by relations from the past. The point is that this will incur costs and time.

7. Economic competence and coordination

The problems of establishing transactions are reinforced by the low level of economic competence in post-socialist economies. As was already pointed out in discussing the costs of reorganizing existing firms, marketing and organizational capabilities are for the larger part tacit skills, which are developed through experience and imitating examples from others. The relatively high level of technical skills in the more developed post-socialist economies gives them a high potential of growth: the problem is not that development is excluded, but rather that it takes time to take effect.

Underdeveloped skills do not only limit the actual scope of actions an actor can undertake himself, but at least as much the possibilities of establishing transactions. If potential partners possess only limited ability to communicate the type of transactions they might potentially be willing to demand or supply, actual transactions will be limited accordingly. Foss (1993, 138) speaks in this respect of a potential lack of receiver competence and sender competence. Let me for the moment restrict the discussion to sender competence - in other words, to the ability of delegating tasks to other persons.

Planning and implementation of skills, that is knowing how to get a particular task done by another person or another firm, requires a certain minimum amount of knowledge of the task (cf. Nelson and Winter, 1982, 85-91). First, one should be able to communicate the skill one is looking for. This requires awareness of the skill and awareness of the possibility of contracting out the task related to it. Second, one should be able to select between firms offering the task or skill. Third, one should be able to control performance and communicate about inadequate performance. Shortcomings at any of these levels may prevent transactions to come about. Partly, this can be accommodated by standardization of services, certification arrangements and interpersonal trust. However, without a certain minimum amount of competence prevailing in the economy, such arrangements are unlikely to be effective in the first place, thereby requiring a higher level of individual skills in effecting transactions.

Let me give an example. In a country with high bicycle density and long grown certification arrangements and interpersonal trust, technical illiterates or persons with high opportunity costs of leisure will not face serious problems in having their bicycle repaired at one of the local stores. In countries where these conditions are absent, contracting out bicycle repair may appear to involve serious technical preparation; repeated detailed supervision and discussion during the repair process; and substantial corrective work afterwards as to restore new (minor) failures that arose as a by-effect of the repair process. The repair fee may well be proportionally lower - but willingness to pay more would not make the repair process pass more smoothly.

The problem of planning and implementing skills is especially important in markets for intermediate goods and services. Faced with the costs of selecting and controlling outside contractors or even subordinates, producers may in the end decide to try to perform a task entirely by themselves, even if they are aware that their own skills are not entirely up to the task. The resulting underspecialization will lower the quantity and quality of output and the number of transactions in the economy. The phenomenon that successful entrepreneurs do not contract out work, for instance, might not only be related to endeavors at secrecy, but also to their inability to transfer knowledge to potential suppliers. The reliance on tacit knowledge is particularly large in small innovative firms (Nooteboom, 1992b, 289-290). In order to grow, an entrepreneur should be able to articulate part of his tacit knowledge and transfer it to new personnel.

In post-socialist economies, small entrepreneurs engage in a wide variety of tasks, just exploring the opportunities they find on their way. Local, independent retailers typically sell wide (and weird) product assortments, that strongly vary over time. At least at the initial stage of development, small entrepreneurs are more concerned with striking quick bargains than with offering a stable assortment. Partly, this is related to the origin of firms from the second or informal economy when their behavior (and that of their consumers) was first of all determined by prevailing shortages (Gábor, 1991).

Interestingly, also multinational firms of established reputation appear to be unable to reap the full benefits of specialization in their establishments in post-socialist economies. They either have to set up their own distribution channels, or heavily invest in controlling (and instructing) existing channels. An advice to Western firms entering East European markets tells them to 'control the chain of distribution from factory floor to store shelves' (*Central European Economic Review*, Autumn 1993, 16). Western fast food chains operating in Eastern Europe have difficulties in securing food supply at a quality that satisfies their standards (*Business Central Europe*, November 1993, 30). The number of personnel engaged in securing supply at PepsiCo fast food chains in Poland is three times as large as at their Western branches - but nonetheless its Polish branch continues to rely for the larger part on imports. To avoid supply problems in its Moscow branches, McDonalds set up a farm of its own in Russia, the only farm it owns in the entire world. In a case study conducted by the author at the Hungarian subsidiary of a multinational firm, various arrangements appeared to be taken that deviated from the firm's practice in other countries: the production of inputs was financed and supervised by the firm so as to compensate for insufficient competencies at the suppliers; the transport of inputs was organized by the firm itself, and not by the suppliers, so as to avoid delays; some customers were supplied directly by the firm itself, as existing wholesale firms were unable to do this in an appropriate manner. This led to substantial costs in terms of equipment, personnel and managerial supervision, which were largely unexpected by the time of the initial investment.

The foregoing examples concern firms with well worked out marketing strategies, which have proven to work elsewhere. For new domestic firms the process of developing effective wholesale channels is complicated by a simultaneous search process in organizing the production process and in matching the composition of production with consumer tastes.

As the division of labor is an old subject in economic theory, let me conclude this Section by relating the argument to standard explanations. Following Smith, the degree of specialization has been basically linked to the extent of the market. If demand is small, firms must undertake all activities themselves. The competence approach presented here (cf. Foss, 1993) emphasizes the problem of the transfer of knowledge and the importance of firm-specific knowledge as an additional factor determining the effectiveness of the division of labor.

8. Conclusion

Let me bring together the argument of this study. It was argued that following the disintegration of the party-state hierarchy economic actors face transformation costs that form a barrier to behavioral change. Broadly, these can be divided into the costs of reorganizing existing firms and the costs of establishing transactions. A common element is formed by the limits to transfer and absorb knowledge. This increases reorganization costs, both in terms of time and effort. Apart from investments in plants and equipment, reorganization requires considerable efforts to be invested in organizational learning and the transfer of knowledge, even under optimal governance structures (Section 4). Similarly, barriers to the transfer and delegation of tacit knowledge limit the effectiveness of economic coordination, and put a constraint on the growth of newly founded small firms (Section 7). Independent of knowledge constraints, actors face high costs of establishing transactions (Section 6). The emphasis on constraints to behavioral change does not at all imply that behavioral change at the level of the firm would be precluded. Yet, the success of one firm is offset by the failure of another, and an early successful firm may suddenly face bankruptcy at a later stage.

The discussion in this study did not distinguish between firms or branches. It may be expected, however, that reorganization costs and the costs of establishing transactions will differ widely among firms and branches, depending on, for instance, technology, the possibilities of mass consumer marketing, organizational capabilities, and the degree to which technology and organizational boundaries had been affected by the centralized organization of production in the socialist system.

An interesting consequence of differences in transformation costs, open to further work and testing, would be that market creation will proceed at a different pace throughout the economy and that the establishment of effective governance structures, including ownership, is partly an endogenous process. Firms and branches where reorganization costs and the costs of establishing transactions could be expected to be lower would attract investments more easily, and effective governance structures would arise more quickly here. Hybrid governance structures, like interenterprise ownership, mixed manager-labor ownership, or forced bank ownership resulting from unpaid debts are likely to arise around firms that have difficulties in attracting investment funds (for more details see Swaan, 1995).

A central argument of this study was that much of the phenomena occurring in post-socialist economies can in itself also be noted in developed market economies. New firms for instance, suffer from a liability of newness (Section 5). The problem of communicating firm-specific skills puts a barrier to successful growth of small, innovative firms (Section 7). Firms are mostly unable to respond to strong adversity and any firm engaged in taking over another firm faces the problem of transferring its firm-specific knowledge, in particular in cross-cultural takeovers (Section 4). However, while these phenomena are in themselves not special to post-socialist economies, the extreme scale to which they occur and their particular combination are typical of the post-socialist transformation process. In the short run, behavior is much more influenced by the collapse of the institutional structures in which individuals and organizations used to operate, than by the effectiveness of economic liberalization and stabilization policy (Section 2).

The perspective chosen in this study may be an illustration for the need of extending network analysis to dynamic aspects (cf. Brezinski and Fritsch, 1997). Networks cannot function without institutions and require appropriate capabilities from its participants. In both respects, the heritage of the past puts a constraint on the transformation of post-socialist economies. This may be partly compensated by personal contacts from the past. Yet, contacts from the networks of the party-state hierarchy have lost much of their value due to the grand reshuffling of institutions and functions that occurred. These old networks may be helpful in reestablishing contacts, but not without requiring substantial efforts and time.

References

Ábel, István and John P. Bonin (1993) State desertion and convertibility: the case of Hungary, in Székely, István P. and David M.G. Newbery (eds) *Hungary: an economy in transition*, Cambridge: Cambridge University Press, 329-341.

Beije, Paul R. and John Groenewegen (1992); A Network Analysis of Markets; *Journal of Economic Issues*, 26 (1), 87-114.

Ben-Ner, Avner and Egon Neuberger (1988); Towards an Economic Theory of the Firm in the Centrally Planned Economy - Transaction Costs: Internalization and

Externalization; *Journal of Institutional and Theoretical Economics*, 144 (5), 839-848.

Black, J. Stewart and Mark Mendenhall (1990); Cross-Cultural Training Effectiveness: A Review and a Theoretical Framework for Future Research; *Academy of Management Review*, 15 (1), 113-136.

Brezinski, Horst and Michael Fritsch (1997) *Spot-Markets, Hierarchies, Networks, and the Problem of Economic Transition*, in this volume.

Business Central Europe, November 1993, 30.

Calvo, Guillermo A. and Fabrizio Coricelli (1993); Output Collapse in Eastern Europe; *IMF Staff Papers*, 40 (1), 32-52.

Caves, Richard E. (1982) *Multinational Enterprise and Economic Analysis*, Cambridge: Cambridge University Press.

Central European Economic Review, Autumn 1993, 16.

Chandler, Alfred D. Jr. (1990) *Scale and Scope: The Dynamics of Industrial Capitalism*, Cambridge, Mass.: The Belknap Press of Harvard University.

Coase, Ronald H. (1937); The Nature of the Firm; *Economica*, 4, 386-405.

Coase, Ronald H. (1960); The problem of social cost; *Journal of Law & Economics*, 3 (1), 1-44.

Csanádi, Mária (1990); Beyond the image: the case of Hungary; *Social Research*, 57 (2), 321-346.

Dander, Tobias (1993) Practical aspects of technical assistance to Hungary, Budapest: Institute of Economics, Hungarian Academy of Sciences, Discussion Paper no. 12.

Davis, Jerome D. and Ole Winckler Andersen (1992) 'Market Clearing', The Problem of 'Fewness' and the Eastern European State Enterprise Sector - Continuing Problems?, Paper presented to the 2nd EACES conference, Groningen, September.

Dembinski, Pawel H. (1991) *The logic of the planned economy: the seeds of the collapse*, Oxford: Oxford University Press.

Dunne, Timothy, Mark J. Roberts and Larry Samuelson (1988); Patterns of firm entry and exit in U.S. manufacturing industries; *RAND Journal of Economics*, 19 (4), 495-515

Ellman, Michael and Vladimir Kontorovich (1992) Overview, in Ellman, Michael and Vladimir Kontorovich (eds) *The disintegration of the Soviet economic system*, London: Routledge, 1-39.

Estrin, Saul and Paul G. Hare (1992) Firms in Transition: Modelling enterprise adjustment, London: Centre for Economic Performance, London School of Economics, Discussion Paper no. 89.

Foss, Nicolai Juul (1993); Theories of the firm: contractual and competence perspectives; *Journal of Evolutionary Economics*, 3 (2), 127-144.

Gábor, István R. (1991); Második gazdaság - modernitás - dualitás: tegnapi jövőképeink mai szemmel; (Second economy - modernity - duality: yesterday's pictures of the future as seen today), *Közgazdasági Szemle*, 38 (11), 1041-1057.

Granovetter, Mark (1985); Economic Action and Social Structure: A Theory of Embeddedness; *American Journal of Sociology*, 91 (3), 481-510.

Grossman, Gregory (1983) The Party as Manager and Entrepreneur, in Guroff, Gregory and Fred V. Carstensen (eds) *Entrepreneurship in Imperial Russia and the Soviet Union*, Princeton: Princeton University Press, 284-305.

Hamel, Gary (1991); Competition for competence and inter-partner learning within international strategic alliances; *Strategic Management Journal*, 12, Special Issue, Summer, 83-103.

Hannan, Michael T. and John Freeman (1984); Structural Inertia and Organizational Change; *American Sociological Review*, 49, 149-164.

Hannan, Michael T. and John Freeman (1989) *Organizational Ecology*, Cambridge, Mass.: Harvard University Press.

Heiner, Ronald A. (1983); The Origin of Predictable Behaviour; *American Economic Review*, 73 (4), 560-595.

Hooley, Graham J. (1993); Raising the Iron Curtain: Marketing in a Period of Transition; *European Journal of Marketing*, 27 (11-12), 6-20.

Hough, Jerry F. (1969) *The Soviet prefects: the local party organs in industrial decision-making*, Cambridge, Mass.: Harvard University Press.

Karsai, Judit (1992); "Is There Plenty of Time?" - Internal Enterprise Cutbacks; *Eastern European Economics*, 30 (2), 44-75.

Keren, Michael (1992) The Planned Enterprise Syndrome: Covert Properties, Bureaucratic Allocation and the Agonies of Transition, Jerusalem: The Hebrew University of Jerusalem, Department of Economics, Working Paper 263.

Kornai, János (1993); Transformational Recession: A General Phenomenon Examined through the Example of Hungary's Development; *Economie Appliqué*, 46 (2), 181-227.

Laki, Mihály (1992); A vállalati magatartás változása és a gazdasági válság; (Changes in enterprise behaviour and the economic crisis), *Közgazdasági Szemle*, 39 (6), 565-578.

Lissowska, Maria (1993); La politique économique en Pologne et le comportement des entreprises; *Reflets et Perspectives de la vie économique*, 32 (3/4), 209-222.

Murrell, Peter (1992a); Evolutionary and Radical Approaches to Economic Reform; *Economics of Planning*, 25 (1), 79-95.

Murrell, Peter (1992b); Conservative Political Philosophy and the Strategy of Economic Transition; *East European Politics and Societies*, 6 (1), 3-16.

Murrell, Peter (1992c) Evolution in Economics and in the Economic Reform of the Centrally Planned Economies, in Clague, Christopher and Gordon C. Rausser (eds) *The Emergence of Market Economies in Eastern Europe*, Oxford: Blackwell, 35-53.

Nelson, Philip B. (1981) *Corporations in Crisis: Behavioural Observations for Bankruptcy Policy*, New York: Praeger.

Nelson, Richard R. and Sidney G. Winter (1982) *An Evolutionary Theory of Economic Change*, Cambridge, Mass.: The Belknap Press of Harvard University.

Nooteboom, Bart (1992a) Small Business, Institutions and Economic Systems, Paper presented to the 2nd EACES conference, Groningen.

Nooteboom, Bart (1992b); Towards a dynamic theory of transactions; *Journal of Evolutionary Economics*, 2 (4), 281-299.

Nuti, Domenico Mario and Richard Portes (1993) Central Europe: The Way Forward, in Portes, Richard (ed.) *Economic Transformation in Central Europe: A Progress Report*, Luxembourg: European Communities.

Perrow, Charles (1993) Small Firm Networks, in Sjöstrand, Sven-Erik (ed.) *Institutional Change: Theory and Empirical Findings*, Armonk, New York: M.E. Sharpe, 111-138.

Pinto, Brian, Marek Belka and Stefan Krajewski (1993); Transforming state enterprises in Poland: evidence on adjustment by manufacturing firms; *Brookings Papers on Economic Activity*, 1, 213-270.

Polanyi, Michael (1958) *Personal Knowledge: Towards a Post-Critical Philosophy*, London: Routledge & Kegan Paul.

Qian, Yingyi and Chenggang Xu (1993) Why China's Economic Reforms Differ: The M-form Hierarchy and Entry/Expansion of the Non-state Sector, Discussion Paper no. 154, London: Centre for Economic Performance, London School of Economics.

Romo, Frank P. and Michael Schwartz (1990); Escape from New York; *Challenge*, 33 (1), 45-52.

Schmieding, Holger (1993); From Plan to Market: On the Nature of the Transformation Crisis; *Weltwirtschaftliches Archiv*, 129 (2), 216-253.

Schumpeter, Joseph A. (1934) *The Theory of Economic Development*, Oxford: Oxford University Press.

Schumpeter, Joseph A. (1939) *Business Cycles*, New York: McGraw-Hill.

Schumpeter, Joseph A. (1942) *Capitalism, Socialism and Democracy*, New York: Harper & Row.

Schweitzer, Iván (1981); Some interrelations between enterprise organization and the economic mechanism in Hungary; *Acta Oeconomica*, 27 (3-4), 289-300.

Simon, Herbert A. (1945) *Administrative Behavior*, 3rd edition, 1976, New York: The Free Press.

Stinchcombe, Arthur L. (1965) Social Structure and Organizations, in March, James (ed.) *Handbook of Organizations*, Chicago: Rand McNally, 142-193.

Swaan, Wim (1995) Behavioural constraints and the creation of markets in post-socialist economies, in Dallago, Bruno and Luigi Mittone (eds) *Economic institutions, markets and competition: Centralization and decentralization in the transformation of economic systems*, Aldershot: Edward Elgar, in preparation.

Swaan, Wim and Maria Lissowska (1992a) Economic reforms and the evolution of enterprise behaviour in Hungary and Poland during the 1980s, Working Paper 4, Leuven: Leuven Institute for Central and East European Studies.

Swaan, Wim and Maria Lissowska (1992b) Enterprise behaviour in Hungary and Poland in the transition to a market economy: individual and organizational routines as a barrier to change, in Blaas, Wolfgang and John Foster (eds) *Mixed economies in Europe: an evolutionary perspective on their emergence, transition and regulation*, Aldershot: Edward Elgar, 69-102.

Teece, David J. (1993); The Dynamics of Industrial Capitalism: Perspectives on Alfred Chandler's "Scale and Scope"; *Journal of Economic Literature*, 31 (1), 199-225.

Vecsenyi, János (1992); Management Education for the Hungarian Transition; *Journal of Management Development*, 11 (3), 39-47.

Williamson, Oliver E. (1985) *The Economic Institutions of Capitalism: Firms, Markets, Relational Contracting*, New York, Free Press.

9 From informal to formal markets, what does this really mean? - A case study of the Bulgarian experience in food markets during transition*

Junior R. Davis

1. Introduction

The tension which exists between the microeconomic perspective of many Central and Eastern European countries' (CEECs) ministries of agriculture and the macroeconomic impact of the agricultural sector reflects a paradox within most economic systems. For example, although the agricultural and food sector is one of the most "public" in terms of policy and welfare needs, it is at the same time "private" in terms of the daily decision making process in production, marketing and consumption. The paradox may be explained by the role of markets and the myriad of decisions co-ordinated by those markets. Where markets do not provide goods to an extent that is socially adequate or where markets do not perform efficiently (as in most Soviet type economies) agriculture's "public" dimension is highlighted. The need then arises for government to ensure competitive markets; to undertake public investment in agricultural research and extension; to establish grades and standards; and even price stability. Government policy and public investment come to determine the efficiency and dynamism of a country's agriculture more than almost any other sector. In the context of CEECs, the transition from what may be termed "informal" to "formal" markets, will require the creation and regulation of a number of institutions, arrangements and economic agents in the wider interests of society.

An "informal" market may be defined as one in which the conventional western (free market economy) institutional framework as regards property rights, its legal basis in terms of the regulation and protection of commercial contracts, taxation (providing government revenue for wider social and economic use), norms of business behavior and competition and monopoly policy are ill-defined, subverted or non-existent. "Informal" markets are characterized by high barriers to entry and a lack of transparency. The "informal market" allows the operation of economic agents within the shadows (black economy) of some more "formal" market structure where the above criteria are more strictly defined and effectively regulated. Economic agents within "informal" markets or, using the development economists' terminology, the "informal sector" evade taxation and regulation from the government and also exploit the legislative loopholes existing within the economy. This may take place in either a centrally planned (CPE) or a market economy. Furthermore, in many CEECs where the food and agricultural sectors are

---

* I would like to thank Paul G. Hare (CERT) for his comments on an earlier draft of this paper.

subject to market failure, a tension exists between the desirability and necessity of using markets as a conduit to reach both producers and consumers efficiently and to generate information about the sectors' costs and returns.

In 1950, Schumpeter argued that free market economies would decline in democratic countries, to be replaced by socialism and political controls, because people did not understand the complex mechanisms by which the benefits of market systems were generated. This complexity would cause political support to wane for the contractual property rights essential for market economies to operate efficiently. Special economic groups would then use their political skills to intervene in markets for their own financial advantage, a process that gradually undermines the allocative role of prices. Elements of Schumpeter's argument may find resonance in this paper. However, I am primarily concerned with discussing the potential implications of the policy-mix adopted by the Bulgarian government in food markets to achieve the transition from "informal" to "formal" markets in a wider political-economy context. Ideally, Bulgaria would have opted for: a full price and trade liberalization package, which would allow the creation of competitive (and transparent) markets; the simplification and establishment of private property rights in agriculture and the food chain; the creation of necessary market regulatory institutions; a sustainable finance and credit system; and the stimulation of institutional support for a commercially viable agriculture. However, because some of these issues are particularly complex and involve sensitive trade-offs between maintaining political support, and taking the difficult steps required to successfully complete the reform, the process has been subject to very strong political pressure and constraints.

2. Central planning and mixed economy markets

With regard to food markets there have been two fundamental approaches to resolve the tension between the failure of markets and the need to achieve efficient resource allocation to further food and economic policy objectives: (a) the displacement of markets from their economic function and relying instead on planning allocations, administrative pricing or direct parastatal controls; and (b) the use of government policy to strengthen market efficiency within an overall market-oriented food and economic policy framework. The former approach has largely been followed in centrally planned economies (CPE) and the latter in mixed or free market economies.

The traditional CPE was highly centralized and rigidly organized. It was characterized by an over-emphasis on vertical co-ordination and control channels (and a corresponding neglect of horizontal links among enterprises), which increased the need for centralized information in the formulation and implementation of national plans (for a fuller discussion see Kornai, 1992; Hare, 1991; and Brown and Neuberger, 1978). This, along with discontinuities in planning, led to lags in administrative response, the neglect of special requirements and cumulative shortages, which were rendered particularly acute by taut planning (e.g., efforts to keep reserves as low as possible). Therefore, the planning mechanisms not only created initial bottlenecks but also generated further repercussions. Furthermore, on closer inspection it would seem that the CPE, despite its highly centralized and formal organization, was not a system of rational decision making by a monolithic unit (Kornai, 1980).

"Although vertical command channels are overemphasized officially, the formulation and implementation of plans are pervaded at all levels by bargaining. Results more often reflect the power of individuals than the intrinsic strength of their case, and our attempts to explain or predict the behavior of CPEs may be better served at times by tools of game theory than by traditional economic theories of rational resource allocation." (Brown and Neuberger, 1978).

Under central planning there were non-systematic aberrations of domestic pricing both from prevailing scarcity ratios and from planners preferences. This was primarily due to the system's ability to immobilize the market mechanism. The drive for centralization and the use of centralized policy instruments in the system were probably the most important reasons for the irrationality of the prices. Indeed, in a CPE it would have been difficult to establish a set of economically meaningful prices for even a handful of basic commodities (there was also a real lack of price flexibility). Within the centrally planned economic system, interrelated price adjustments or general price reforms were too costly and could only be undertaken at infrequent intervals. The inability of the planners to formulate economically meaningful and sufficiently flexible prices was also directly attributed to specific planning mechanisms: (a) the emphasis on vertical lines of communication and the corresponding neglect of horizontal connections among operational units slowed down and impeded the transmission and reliability of information; (b) material balancing, with its emphasis on quota fulfillment in physical terms, relegated financial accounting to a subsidiary role in the planning process. Taut planning and its corollary, periodic shortages, inhibited equilibrium pricing (Kornai, 1980, 1992).

Another important factor was the prevalence of generally arbitrary (and often multiple) exchange rates. As many foreign trade decisions were not made on the basis of official exchange rates, the lack of reliable and explicit comparisons between external prices and internal costs tended to interfere with planning and control. Arbitrary exchange rates, like irrational domestic prices, were a contributory cause of macro- and microeconomic inefficiencies and domestic market distortions. This is particularly clear in the case of CEEC food markets, where prices were kept artificially low through high levels of both producer and consumer subsidies. These were delivered as direct state transfers to production units and through the maintenance of administratively determined prices on food markets, regardless of prevailing commodity and input prices on international markets. Even at highly subsidized prices, food still accounted for a large share of consumer expenditure, and changes in prices significantly reduced real incomes (Brooks, 1991). During transition this situation has not changed for most CEECs. Most CPEs suffered declining growth rates, widespread shortages of consumer goods and, by the 1980s, open dissatisfaction among the population. As noted above, the main reason for this has more to do with the complexity of economic systems, the extraordinary amount of information communicated through prices, and the multiple decisions involving the vast information-processing capacities required of modern (globally interdependent) economies. Most of those decisions simply cannot be made efficiently or effectively by a central planning agency.

As quantitative controls have become progressively less efficient, a pro-market approach has gained greater prominence. Mixed economy (or free) markets allow for the free-interplay of market forces, with minimal government intervention to determine the consumption, production and exchange of goods. The free adjustment of prices is central to this process. The pro-market approach incorporates investment in public goods and a commitment to solving the problems of poverty and hunger through targeted interventions that reach the poor without seriously distorting the signals generated in markets. Investments in a (privatized) marketing system can lower marketing costs directly, thus easing the food price dilemma of providing low prices to consumers but sufficiently high prices to producers. These investments could also increase the efficiency and competitiveness of the marketing system by encouraging new entrants into the market. If however, restrictive practices impede this process, vested interests and political considerations become paramount in the creation and regulation of a market and it will be (or rather in the case of most CEECs, will remain to be) distorted and "informal". The transition from informal to formal markets will be retarded, competition and efficiency become secondary considerations and markets may not operate in the interests of society, but rather those of a select group. These ideas will be discussed more deeply with regard to the Bulgarian experience of informal food markets since 1989.

3. Informal food markets in Bulgaria under transition

The economic transformation in Bulgaria commenced in November 1989. As part of a wider economic stabilization program, the transformation caused high levels of unemployment, high levels of inflation and a deep economic recession. Towards the end of 1990, the new government issued Decision no. 8, which stated that as of February 1st 1991, the prices of all domestic consumption goods would be liberalized with the exception of electricity, coal and gas. By the end of 1991 consumer price subsidies accounted for around 12.3 percent of government budget subsidies (general government subsidies comprised 4 percent of GDP in 1991 and 2 percent in 1992 (EBRD, 1993)). However, with the introduction of market prices the subsidies for farm prices and food prices were abolished. The consumer price index[1] grew rapidly over the period May 1990 to December 1992. In February 1991, the liberalization of retail prices led to between two- and five-fold increases in basic food prices. In Bulgaria, retail food price

---

1 The monthly consumer price index has only been available since May 1990, as well as sub-indices for food, clothing, fuel and electricity. It is derived from information collected from 28 separate locations with 120 products identified and six quotations per item and based on the consumer basket of goods and services established by the National Statistics Institute of Bulgaria. The weights for the CPI come from the survey of retail turnover for the overall CPI, and from the household budget survey for cost-of-living indices for sub-groups of the population. The indices show rates of change over the period.

liberalization developed in stages: a slow increase in prices during 1990 changed to a significant increase in 1991.

With an accompanying fall in real incomes these price changes have precipitated significant adjustments in purchasing behavior. Although many public (state and cooperative) sector employees have been made redundant since 1990, the public sector real wage has declined steadily[2]. With the exception of wages in the financial sector, almost all other sectors of the economy experienced a 25 percent decline in the real value of the average wage, during the first half of 1993. This is the result of a government policy of wage growth restraint and the deteriorated financial condition of state-owned enterprises. The growing budget deficit and an inability to cover the demands for adequate payment from some key professions (doctors, teachers, army and police) appear to have exacerbated the situation.

This tough medicine was generally accepted as the price that had to be paid for the opportunity of achieving an improvement in the range and quality of goods and services characteristic of a market economy (Buckwell et al. 1993). As in other CEECs, prices had been maintained at artificially low levels and thus it was necessary to suffer a massive once-and-for-all adjustment in Bulgaria. Some of the expected benefits of price liberalization were soon evident. For example, queues for basic foods disappeared soon . afterwards. This was partly the result of improvements in domestic availability. The increase in the domestic availability of food was not achieved by improvements in production and distribution, but by the loss of CMEA export markets, particularly in the former Soviet Union (FSU). It was also assisted by the contraction in consumption of many foods in response both to relative price changes and the decline in real incomes.

Many of the market institutions prevalent in the agricultural sector of a market economy are missing in Bulgaria. Under central planning it was not considered necessary to develop institutions through which market transactions could take place. In most modern market economies a wide range of institutions has emerged to facilitate buying and selling for spot and future delivery and for reducing the costs of price variability.

In Bulgaria, there are very few first stage (commodity exchange[3]) markets in existence, although a number of initiatives have been taken to create these in the fruit and vegetable market (e.g., there exists a Plovdiv market). Retail markets have played an important role in the Bulgarian economy for many years. Despite the availability of many formal sites, there is a wide range of informal markets appearing in urban areas. Anecdotal evidence suggests that the informal markets often infringe public health regulations.

---

2 Due to lack of information on wages in the private sector, the analyses concerned only wages in the public sector of the economy. However, it is interesting to note that sectors which did not receive any state subsidies, wages were generally below the national average by 1993. For example, during the first half of 1993 the average wage paid in the sewing industry (43.2 percent lower than the national average); agriculture and forestry (33.2 percent), fur, leather and footwear (32.2 percent), and in the public sector (between 17 to 25 percent of the national wage). The highest paid workers were those involved in state subsidized heavy industry, for example coal-mining (92.7 percent higher than the average wage) and ferrous metallurgy (73.7 percent).

3 Commodity "exchanges" were part of the old command system, serving as a location for different parts of the distribution chain to meet to facilitate the organization of supplies through the food supply chain.

These markets need to be formalized and conditions improved. The need for markets depends on the structure of the sector. Given the existing structure of some branches, it is clear that there is little competition for supplies as there are very few buyers. In these circumstanccs, commodity exchanges have no initial role. Currently this applies to all sectors except fruit and vegetables, where an active private production and wholesale trade has already emerged.

There is a lack of market transparency in the Bulgarian agricultural and food chain and a need for more comprehensive market information. Market transparency is a pre-requisite of an efficient market and essential for the allocation of resources within the agricultural sector. Without good market information, decision makers will not have a sound basis for planning either their investment, production or marketing decisions. Whatever the emerging structure of production in Bulgaria, private farmers or cooperatives require information which allows them to make both future and spot decisions. Some relatively crude information systems are emerging, but many of these are of little value because they lack a uniform basis of price reporting. Most western price reporting and market information systems confront the separate tasks of product description (to allow the standardization of quotes and comparisons), price quotation conventions and data dissemination. The absence of an adequate legal framework (e.g., covering contracts, bankruptcy, and the operation of commodity exchanges), commercial law and a food law (to facilitate trade and protect consumers) has further retarded the development of the sector.

The role of market information in promoting efficient markets needs to be distinguished from the view taken by individual organizations. Many individual organizations with market power have an interest in low levels of market transparency because it undermines their privileged position. In Bulgaria (despite some de-monopolization since 1991), the domestic market for food products is not competitive in many sectors. The de-monopolized central organizations hold considerable power despite their financial circumstances. The non-competitive market position of many monopoly processing, distribution and large trading companies, have allowed very high profit margins. This is particularly true in the meat, cereal and dairy sectors (APAU, 1993). Some private investment has taken place in these branches but it is relatively small and there are still large parts of the country in which agricultural producers have only one potential sales outlet or one potential source of some inputs[4]. There are some emerging signs of competition between some state enterprises for supplies but this remains a minor activity and has not strengthened competition substantially. Competition in markets does vary: in some areas it is non-existent, as the factory output supplies local markets. In other cases, where external markets are being served, there is evidence of growing competition with a clear perception that the enterprise can only expand at the expense of others in the sector (APAU, 1993). However, even in the latter there are vestiges of the past which

---

4 For example, the Bulgarian Milk Industry, (which was the sole national organization) has seen limited de-monopolization, e.g., in Stara Zagora there is only one milk production factory, and there are only three for the whole of the Haskovo region (comprising around 1 million inhabitants).

serve to restrict competition (e.g. the development of sectoral associations, the restricted use of old brand names created by the old central organizations).

Market entry is further restricted because of a lack of business confidence in Bulgaria, due to the unstable macroeconomic and political environment; the low levels of investment in potentially competitive enterprises; the relative lack of interest shown by foreign companies to invest in these upstream and downstream industries; and the lack of credit provision (on reasonable terms) to companies seeking to enter the market. A Commission for the Protection of Competition established in 1992, and laws relating to developing market entry and competition, have not been particularly effective in changing the prevailing situation. Most of the limited legislation which exists to regulate markets is often ignored or poorly enforced.

Privatization is seen as a route to improving the efficiency of the industry by encapsulating the incentive system of private ownership. It is of fundamental importance to the development of the Bulgarian agricultural sector, but privatization alone will not necessarily lead to increased competition. For example, a privatized food processing industry may well exploit monopoly power more effectively than a state owned company and the creation of such organizations in the absence of other measures could result in the continuation of oligopoly behavior and disillusionment with the market economy. Thus it is necessary for government to supplement the privatization program with other measures to encourage competition (i.e., providing tax holidays which might encourage new market entry). Without a comprehensive privatization the influence of the state and inter-enterprise oligopoly behavior will remain and the full benefit of private ownership will not be realized[5].

The Bulgarian government's food policy placed great emphasis on maintaining an adequate level of food consumption for urban dwellers. There is a pervasive fear among Bulgarian officials that if prices were fully liberalized, food prices (especially the price of bread) would rise to excessive levels and possibly provoke civil unrest. During the period March 1991 to March 1994 the prices of 14 basic goods and services were monitored and maintained under some degree of control by the Bulgarian Council of Ministers. The reasoning underlying this policy was that the payment of higher prices to producers would result in an unsustainable rise in the price of these 14 basic goods, particularly bread (see Appendix). Two systems of protection from the effects of food price inflation have been in operation:

- a system of indexation of wages, salaries, unemployment payments, pensions and income support measures[6]; and

---

5 There has been very little progress in privatization of the several hundred state-owned farms and service enterprises which are the property of the Ministry of Agriculture. According to preliminary information on the progress of privatization, by 30th April 1994 the Ministry of Agriculture has started procedures for privatization of 46 whole enterprises or technologically separate parts of them. However, only seven transactions for privatization were concluded.

6 In 1990, minimum wages were fully indexed to the level of consumer price inflation. In 1991 this was changed to a system of compensation which involved a flexible adaptation of salaries in different firms as a result of collective bargaining. The level of compensation in 1991 to mid-1992 was around 70-80 percent

- a system of projected prices which has covered basic food accounting for about 45 percent of food expenditure in 1991.

Indexation has not been sufficient to prevent significant price rises, falls in real incomes and switches in consumption behavior. The projected price system and its impact upon food prices and the development of a formal food market in Bulgaria is discussed below. The pre-reform upstream and downstream industries (particularly, food distribution and processing industries) have retained a significant influence on government policy in food markets and indeed benefit from the distortion of such markets. The following discussion will concentrate on the most important feature of informal food markets in Bulgaria, namely the projected price system.

4. The projected price system

The Bulgarian projected price system was introduced in March 1991. The use of a system of projected prices is one of particular policy importance in Bulgaria. In pre-reform Bulgaria consumer prices were controlled and commodity supplies and trade flows were centrally managed through directives to state owned enterprises and collectives. The objective was to ensure low-cost food supplies under a centrally managed trade system. Despite the liberalization in 1991, the government continued to intervene with prices and trade for essential foods. Initially, this was viewed as a temporary measure that would be withdrawn after a social safety net was instituted and as domestic supplies increased. Despite these intentions, the interventions have remained in place. The rationale behind the introduction of the projected price system may be described as follows:

- the political rationale of the system was to contain rises in consumer prices of basic foods to an acceptable level without special budget subsidies. This was to be done by controlling the margins of monopoly processors and big trading companies to prevent them from taking advantage of their non-competitive market position.
- the system was also motivated by a perceived need to protect the economic position of low income groups who may be hurt by the price inflation in basic food commodities.

The projected price system began with an estimated cost of production for agricultural products. Processors and marketing agencies were supposed to pay *minimum guaranteed prices* based on the estimated costs of production. Normative costs of processing and marketing were then added to the minimum guaranteed prices to obtain the projected prices of the covered foods in urban markets.

---

of the prevailing rate of consumer price inflation. However in practice, the indexation of wages to consumer price inflation is much closer. For example, a comparison of the levels of the average wage accrued in the first nine months of 1992 and 1993 indicates that its growth was equal to consumer price inflation for the period (Davis, 1994; The Agency for Economic Co-ordination, 1993).

In order to maintain consumer prices of essential foods below market levels without using explicit subsidies, the government combined the projected price system with export controls. The export controls[7] comprised five measures: (a) export bans, (b) export quotas, (c) export taxes, (d) minimum export prices and (e) export licenses. The export constraints, particularly export bans and quotas, have had a depressing effect on domestic prices, by increasing the supply available to the domestic market. The export controls have been unstable and the export regime for some products changed several times in a year depending upon the domestic market situation. However, some form of export constraint has constantly been in place for the main food products: bread wheat, coarse grain, sunflower oil, live animals, meat and cheese. The combination of the projected price system, a continued lack of efficiency and competition in the food processing and distribution system, and trade restrictions have had a strongly negative effect on agricultural producers. It was the introduction of export constraints that changed a system of guaranteed minimum prices for agricultural producers into a system that tended to repress farm level prices.

In addition to its effects on the level of prices, the projected price system was intended to control monopolistic and monopsonistic power in the processing and marketing activities. Firms processing or marketing the commodities covered by the scheme could only sell above the projected price if their higher prices reflected higher costs and did not result in margins exceeding the norms used in setting the projected prices. This mechanism tended to perpetuate cost-plus pricing behavior throughout the Bulgarian food chain. The government took the responsibility to regularly announce projected prices for monitored goods. Responsibility for control of the system was placed in the hands of the Central Price Commission and local authorities. Initially the system applied to basic food products central to the average Bulgarian diet: white and brown bread, white wheat flour; pasta; sunflower oil; sugar; pork; veal and weaned lamb with bones; some meat products (a variety of sausages); fresh cow's milk and yoghurt; white and yellow cow's cheese (kashkaval); and butter. The list of monitored food products changed in April 1994, the only time since its introduction (see Appendix). The domestic market for these goods is not very competitive, for the reasons discussed above.

The projected price system has changed four times during the period 1991-1994. The system of projected prices of basic food at the consumer level in February 1991 was joined in July 1991 by an identical system at the producer and intermediate product levels, when the government introduced projected prices for some farm level agricultural produce. At this level projected prices were set for: wheat; pig meat; poultry meat; calves; weaned lamb meat; and cow's milk. Projected prices for intermediate products, such as flour, were also introduced.

In April 1992 the government proposed a further package of measures composed of three elements: (a) the partial removal of retail price monitoring of the following food products: meat products; butter; yellow cow's cheese; white wheat flour; sunflower oil; sugar and pasta; (b) substantial increases were authorized for the projected prices at the

---

7 In 1993, 45.3 percent of agricultural and food most favored nation imports were taxed by 40 percent. Import duties in 1994 were increased to 55 percent.

retail level for the remaining monitored foods: white and brown bread; pork; veal and weaned lamb on the bone; fresh cow's milk and yoghurt; and white cow's cheese; finally, (c) minimum guaranteed producer prices for bread wheat; hogs; calves; broilers; weaned lambs; and cow's milk. The minimum prices were politically interpreted by the government as prices below which contracts could not be signed; they were intended as *floor* prices. Initially, there was no intention for these minimum guaranteed prices to be enforced through market intervention by state agencies.

New rules for monitoring the prices of basic food were approved by the Council of Ministers in March 1993. The objective was to change the projected price system into a ceiling price system. The principal change was that the government would no longer determine and publish projected prices. However, the main tenets of the projected price system were unchanged. The central determination of profit margins in the food chain remained in order to subsidize consumers, and attempts to control these normative margins continued. Profit margins for producers were fixed at 12 percent of costs and at 10 percent for traders. The *ceiling* prices were calculated as costs plus these margins. The ceilings are controlled by the National Price Commission, regional governors, mayors and other local authorities. A proportion of the fines collected from organizations pursuing illegal pricing practices was deposited into a fund held by the National Price Commission. These changes were the result of the government's inability to keep retail prices close to the projected prices.

This was evident throughout the first three years of the price liberalization. Since February 1991 the nominal prices for most food products grew quickly. For example, there has been a continued inflation in bread prices at about 4.5 percent per month and of milk prices at 2 percent per month. Cheese and meat prices fell for three months following the initial shock, but since May 1991 have been increasing at a similar rate of about 4.5 percent per month. The consumer price index (henceforth CPI) continued to increase slowly, while real food prices actually fell. There was another hike in food and consumer prices in July and August 1991 because of a government mandated increase in energy prices (Davis, 1994). In April 1994 food prices rose by 25.6 percent, the largest increase amongst all goods and services. Bread prices increased on average 16 percent, meat (total) by 22 percent, milk by 29 percent (including fresh milk by 40 percent), vegetable oils by 25 percent, and sugar by 29 percent (Davidova, 1994). This occurred despite the exemption of basic food from valued added taxation (which was introduced during that month), and the operation of the projected price system designed to limit price rises to the minimum justifiable by cost increases. These developments led to increased pressure on the government from various interest groups for greater market intervention and restrictions on market price setting. Therefore during the same month the Decree of the Council of Ministers on price monitoring was amended. There were two main amendments: (i) the list of products with monitored prices was expanded to 24 products; and (ii) the responsibility to control the prices was transferred to the Tax Administration, with the expectation that the latter has more capacity to carry out the task.

5. The efficacy of the projected price system

The projected price system at the retail level has attempted to monitor the prices of 14 food products for most of the post-communist period. If the retail prices of these goods are fixed below market levels, then retail shortages (of these goods) should be observed in shops and street markets. However, since the price liberalization of February 1991, there has been little clear evidence of this happening. Where prior to March 1991 there were shortages of many goods, food supplies since then have improved greatly. Since March 1991, despite sporadic shortages of monitored foods, it has been possible to buy as many monitored foods as desired. The shortages which remained after liberalization primarily affected urban dwellers, were minor, and probably more the result of supply bottlenecks in the distribution system, rather than a reflection of monitored prices being below market level.

The weighted averages of the non-monitored and monitored food retail price indices immediately after price liberalization and one year after the liberalization show with a few exceptions, that the prices of monitored foods increased more than those which were not monitored. Where February 1991 is compared to February 1992 the prices of monitored foods increased (on average) by 153 percent. This is much less than the 350 percent (on average) increase during the immediate post-liberalization period of January to February 1991. A comparison of the prices of non-monitored foods in February 1991 and February 1992, showed a 78 percent increase. This is a far smaller price rise than that observed for monitored foods during the same period (Davis, 1994).

The price of monitored foods has grown faster than that of non-monitored foods for the following reasons: (a) as previously noted most milk products (e.g., white cheese, butter and yoghurt) were heavily subsidized under central planning. Therefore, the post reform price adjustment for these monitored products should be quite large; (b) unlike "limit" prices which are administratively set (on the basis of the average world market price for oil product (petrol, diesel fuel and gas oil) and carbohydrate liquid gas prices) monitored prices can be exceeded. This accounts for their weaker controlling function. The prices of monitored goods are subject to control in case they outgrow the forecast prices set for the respective goods; (c) due to the increased cost of inputs following the first devaluation of the lev in February 1991. Ivanova (1994) shows that there were small increases in prices of the main (food) crops in 1992. There were more substantial increases in the prices of some livestock products. However, during 1991 and 1992 average prices of fuel, plant protection chemicals and fertilizers rose on average ten-fold. Thus the terms of trade for agriculture deteriorated; (d) the increased costs of imported inputs (machinery, protein feed and pesticides) with subsequent devaluation's, together with the existing export restrictions on grains in particular, have had a negative effect on domestic wheat prices and have effectively isolated the domestic wheat market from the beneficial effect of devaluation[8]. This is also true of live animal, meat and sugar exports; and (e)

---

8   The government has banned all grain exports until September 1994, on the basis of their projections which suggest that Bulgaria would have a grain deficit of 1 million tons. This would be politically unacceptable in the current environment.

another indicator of the efficacy of the projected price system is the extent of the fluctuations of actual prices around projected prices. Overall, it seems that government attempts to monitor retail prices have not had much effect. Therefore, it is unlikely that their removal would result in large price increases.

Successive Bulgarian governments appear to have been primarily concerned with monitoring food prices in nominal rather than real (inflation adjusted) terms. Had the government been more concerned about the latter, it might have reduced some of its consumer support, because real prices for most goods prior to and following price reform were declining. However, the governments seem to have assumed that consumers are only aware of the nominal price increases, and have little conception of real prices and inflation when making purchase decisions. The government appears to have ignored the possibility of price expectations influencing consumer decisions in substituting between products. Therefore, nominal price data have been cited in this paper to describe the movements of retail prices for monitored and non-monitored goods instead of real prices. One of the main reasons for this is that in setting projected prices, the government has estimated future inflation. This data and the procedure for predicting future inflation and prices is not available and therefore it is impossible to calculate real predicted prices using the government's methodology.

It is also possible that the projected price system was not rigorously enforced. The National Price Commission had a small staff of around 30 people. Most of the price monitoring was enforced by local authorities and municipalities. In practice, some authorities enforced the system more rigorously than others. The main effect of the monitoring system has been to place an extra administrative burden on companies who seek to raise their prices, since they must document their costs. However, this does not rule out price increases and provides no incentive to firms to reduce their costs. If the existing consumer price controls were removed, there might be an increase in prices. Processors, traders and retailers might consider this a great opportunity to boost their profits. However, the increase would probably be temporary, because ample supplies of monitored foods exist, incomes are still low and stagnant, and consumer demand would not sustain a great hike in retail prices.

The above discussion of the Bulgarian price projection system and associated trade policies shows that they include some controversial measures: price controls at the retail level and the support of some producer prices; credit subsidies; impediments to export in order to support consumers and import duties up to 55 percent in order to protect producers. Under these conditions it is important to assess the net income transfers induced by these measures and whether consumers and producers were supported or taxed. The quantification of the income transfers for the grain and meat sectors, induced by price, trade and credit policies during the period 1990-1992 show that the main sources of transfer were farmers and food processors (Ivanova, 1994). Transfers from farmers greatly exceeded the transfers to them from the State Budget in 1992. The main recipient of transfers in 1990 were the final consumers, which was a continuation of the pre-reform policy. However, during the period 1991-1992, the recipients were mainly retailers. This suggests that whatever the social objectives of these policies during the recent post reform period, the policy instruments utilized have not been well targeted because they taxed producers without providing substantial support to consumers.

The government appears to have failed to meet a number of the objectives underlying its rationale for introducing the projected price system:

* to protect the economic position of low income groups through the projected price system, by insulating them from the effects of high food price inflation;
* to establish competitive (and transparent) food markets, whilst encouraging new market entrants supported by reliable market regulatory institutions;
* to control (and curtail) monopolistic and monopsonistic power in the upstream and downstream industries; and
* to promote privatization and the establishment of private property rights in agriculture and the food chain.

6. Conclusions

The Bulgarian projected price system has proved to be difficult to enforce and in general does not appear to have prevented *unjustified* price rises (i.e. rises greater than reasonable margins would allow). Anecdotal evidence has suggested that the system has been implemented primarily through the administrative pressure of the local authorities and municipalities over state-owned and private retailers. The projected price system's in-built calculation of profit margin as a share of costs, plus the practice of allowing price increases if justified on the basis of increased costs, has resulted in the following features of the system: (a) a cost-plus approach towards prices and, as a result, (b) an internal disincentive for cost reduction. Ironically, these features of the projected price system are similar to the price control mechanisms implemented during central planning throughout CEECs (see Brown and Neuberger, 1978). Perhaps the two most undesirable characteristics of the current projected price system are that: (a) once such systems have been established they become institutionalized and difficult to dismantle; and (b) as the projected price system has not encouraged the food processing and distribution sectors to decrease production costs or adjust their profit margins to the market conditions, consequently the main pressure to adjust to the changing environment is transmitted to agricultural producers. This leads to the following questions: whose interests do the projected price system promote, and what does the transition from an "informal" to "formal" market really mean?

The transition from an "informal" to a "formal" market is neither clearly defined nor complete. The prevailing food markets in Bulgaria are distorted, but they are neither centrally planned markets, nor free/mixed economy markets. Furthermore, it is not similar to the European Union's (EU) Common Agricultural Policy (CAP) in terms of the logic of the intervention (largely on behalf of producers to preserve rural communities and economies) or the distortionary effect that it has on food markets EU wide (i.e. higher food retail prices and food mountains). The informal markets prevalent in Bulgaria are a curious hybrid; characterized by the continuation of pre-reform links and behavior between enterprise managers/owners and the government machinery, in the interest of self-preservation or the maximization of utility (namely profits) within a distorted, monopsonistic and poorly regulated market structure. Schumpeter's (1950) pessimistic prescription appears to be realized in Bulgaria under transition, but more as result of the economic transition and its resultant social and political uncertainties than a commitment to socialism. The continued existence of pre-reform monopolies, weak governments and political instability (Bulgaria has had four different governments since January 1990) has further hampered the transition process.

The definition of a "formal" market is not sufficiently flexible to encompass the real political-economic situation within most CEECs. The role of individuals, established interests and alliances within both state-owned enterprises and the government in terms of regulating markets and creating the necessary conditions for an economy to function more efficiently remain blurred in most CEECs. Vested interests, whether political (thus encouraging the continued subsidization of food for largely urban consumers in Bulgaria) or economic (i.e., maintaining the position of large state owned food processing and distribution industries) in the development and regulation of markets become paramount in determining the speed of transition from an "informal" to more "formal" market structure. There remains a lack of transparency in food markets, and where some privatization has occurred in upstream and downstream industries, the new managers have retained or established links with the government machinery. Thus, the structure of the sector needs to be radically reformed. There is a lack of economic logic within the current projected price system in terms of its potential benefits to society; but there is a clear logic to its continuation in the interest of certain economic and political interest groups.

On the basis of previous analyses, the removal of the projected price system would affect the consumption of at least five products: white and Dobrudja bread, yoghurt, milk and white cow's cheese (Davis, 1994). If policy considerations such as the consumer welfare implications of full price liberalization are taken into account, policy makers should only concentrate upon these goods. An alternative to using the projected price system might be to devise a method of supporting these goods in favor of consumers, which would have the minimum impact upon the State budget (Davis and Petranov, 1993; APAU, 1993). The other alternative is to allow the market to operate freely, and to find its equilibrium where consumer demand limits further price increases. If the immediate dissolution of the projected price system is infeasible, then perhaps it could be phased out gradually. This may take the following forms: (a) a reduction in the list of commodities covered by the system; or (b) by a progressive removal of restrictions on trade for all these commodities[9].

---

9   Preliminary estimates by Davis and Petranov (1993), show that the negative effects of these interventions on economic efficiency would make it increasingly difficult to sustain these indirect interventions. Their preliminary estimates suggest that if all incomes remained fixed and prevalent (1992) procedures for indexing wages, unemployment insurance, pensions and various welfare payments remained in effect, a 10 percent increase in food prices was estimated to result in a 0.8 billion leva (3 percent) increase in the cost of the social welfare system and a 0.3 billion (0.6 percent) increase in expenditures in the state budget. These estimates were based on the assumption that a 10 percent increase in prices might be in line with the results from a full price and trade liberalization, since an increase in agricultural prices would result in a lower percentage increase in processed food prices if other costs did not rise as rapidly.

The elimination of the projected price system would increase producer incentives and encourage the development of a competitive processing and marketing system. There would be some short-run costs incurred in the adjustments to some indexed government payments for pensions and other support programs, and by consumers. However, a healthy agricultural economy is in the best long-run interests of both the government and consumers. The sequencing of the elimination of the projected price system is an important and complex issue. Although higher farm prices would provide a stronger incentive for owners to actively assert their rights over land and to use their assets efficiently, higher farm prices might also strengthen collectives. This would not be a desirable development, since private ownership or private sector management of farm land in Bulgaria is the government's avowed goal. There are also important political issues involved in completing the liberalization of retail prices, particularly with regard to the activities of influential trade unions and other pressure groups. Retail price liberalization in Bulgaria is a necessary complement to trade liberalization, since the government cannot afford to subsidize all consumers without creating unsustainable public expenditures.

It may be possible to target assistance more directly to those in economic distress as an alternative to using the projected price system to maintain artificially low consumer prices. For example, groups on fixed or low incomes, such as pensioners and the unemployed, appear to be suffering from the effects of price liberalization (because bread is a major part of their diet and bread prices have risen sharply). The experience of most countries is that it is impossible to shield consumers indefinitely from food price increases. Furthermore, if assuring a reasonable level of food consumption remains the government's main food policy objective, then the existing support could be more narrowly targeted to the particular food products discussed above. In the short-term the projected price system will continue in its current form; however, this is clearly unsustainable from a macroeconomic and national budgetary position, into the medium and long term if economic growth remains a prime policy objective. Thus, in the medium term, vested interests in the perpetuation of the system will have to make way for fully liberalized prices, the unrestricted access of all competing food imports and new market entrants.

References

APAU (Agricultural Policy Analysis Unit) PHARE/World Bank (1993) An Agricultural Strategy for Bulgaria; IBRD Technical publication, Washington, USA.

The Agency for Economic Co-ordination and Development (1993); The Bulgarian Economy in 1993, Annual Report; *Business Survey Series*, Juastor, Sofia.

Brooks, Karen M. (1991) Agriculture and the Transition to the Market, World Bank Working Paper, WPS 666.

Brown, Alan A. and Egon Neuberger (1978) Basic Features of a Centrally Planned Economy, in Bornstein, Morris (ed.) *Comparative Economic Systems: Models and Cases,* Homewood, Illinois: Richard D. Irwin Inc.

Buckwell, Allan E., Junior R. Davis, Sofija M. Davidova and Stefan Petranov (1993) Food Consumption During Economic Transformation in Bulgaria, paper submitted to VI. International Conference of EAAE, Stresa, Italy.

Davidova, Sofija M. (1994) *Agricultural Policy and Trade Developments in Bulgaria in 1993-1994*, mimeo.

Davis, Junior R. (1994) Economic Transition and Food Consumption in Bulgaria, Ph.D. dissertation, Wye College, University of London.

Davis, Junior R. and Stefan Petranov (1993) Budgetary implications of food price liberalization in Bulgaria, unpublished working paper, Ministry of Agricultural Development, Agricultural Policy Analysis Unit, Sofia, Bulgaria.

EBRD (European Bank for Reconstruction and Development) (1993); Fiscal Reform and Recent Economic Developments; Quarterly Economic Review, September 1993.

Hare, Paul G. (1991) *Central Planning*, Chur: Harwood Academic Publishers.

Ivanova, N. (1994) Measuring and Analysis of Government Protection to Bulgarian Agriculture during the Transition Period, working paper no. 2, project 92.4 Effects of Agricultural Price and Trade Liberalization on Production and Consumption of Food Products, PHARE: Agricultural Policy Analysis Unit, Sofia.

Kornai, János (1980) *Economics of Shortage*, Amsterdam: North Holland.

Kornai, János (1992) *The Socialist System: The Political Economy of Communism*, Oxford: Clarendon Press.

Schumpeter, Joseph A. (1950) *Capitalism, Socialism and Democracy*, New York: Harper and Row.

Appendix

List of food products with monitored prices
(* Products included in the monitoring system in April 1994)

- At the wholesale level
  - white wheat flour
  - brown wheat flour

- At retail level
  - brown bread 'Dobrudja'
  - white bread 'Stara Zagora'
  - meat with bones (pork, baby beef and veal, lamb and weaned lamb, poultry)
  - fresh pasteurized cow's milk
  - yoghurt from cow's milk
  - white cheese in brine

- sunflower oil, refined*
- butter*
- eggs*
- pasta*
- sausages*
- yellow cheese from cow's milk*
- white sugar*
- small white beans*
- lentils*
- rice*
- potatoes*
- baby food*

10 Towards rational banking in transition economies

*Jozef M. van Brabant**

1. Introduction

From the transition's inception in the eastern part of Europe,[1] commentators have emphasized that something drastic should be undertaken to counter the economic legacies of communism, particularly as far as banking is concerned, and to do so rapidly and credibly.[2] One could group the tasks ahead under three labels:

* Coming to grips with the 'old debts' of state-owned production units, in particular by offsetting in some pragmatic manner assets and liabilities of the state or society as a whole;
* Recapitalizing banks and thus making available the financial resources required to underpin the transformation, and indeed to jump onto the new development path coveted by policy makers; and
* Instilling 'commercial rationality' into the behavior of existing banks through retraining, competition from new banks, joint ventures with foreign partners, and explicit rules enacted by the new 'state,' including on hard budget constraints for all economic agents.

Oddly enough, in spite of these widely shared precepts, invariably policy makers have by design sought to come to grips with these 'most urgent' and 'chronic' issues far more slowly and partially than the sense of urgency and drama they, and most of their chosen as well as self-styled advisers, originally sought to impart. Furthermore, none of the postcommunist economies in transition (PETs), including those with a leadership most committed to real transformation policies[3], has thus far applied a comprehensive, once-

---

* Staff member of the Department for Economic and Social Information and Policy Analysis of the United Nations Secretariat in New York. The views reflected here are mine and do not necessarily concur with my employer's.

1 Comprising the former European planned economies, including Yugoslavia and its as well as Czechoslovakia's and the USSR's successor States. This area is here also denoted as East with a capital *E*. On occasion I add comments based on my 'advisory' experiences in Algeria, Cambodia, and Vietnam more by way of generalizing the points made for the East than of demonstrating erudition.

2 Credibility here signals not solely policies that are credible, but policies that can also be implemented and sustained in a credible manner (UNECE, 1993, 7). This depends on the prevailing disarray, the acceptable adjustment burden, and the successes attained in the course of moving ahead with substantive transition. Without such credibility, transformation will fail.

3 Inasmuch as 'transformation policies' suggests incisiveness of action over a fairly protracted period of time, I much prefer this to 'transition policies.' In what follows, I use the latter notion for the generic events in the East since 1989 and the former to designate policies in selected countries directed at steering

and-for-all strategy on how best to address the knotty issues at hand. This is at least paradoxical. But progress is being made in a gradual, largely *ad hoc*, manner particularly in the PETs that are more advanced with the transition agenda (Brabant, 1994c, d). It could hardly have been otherwise (Long, 1993; Mayer, 1993; Smith and Walter, 1993)!

The main purpose of this paper is to highlight the essential steps to be taken, and when, in order to rationalize the existing system of commercial banking and to elicit effective competition in basic financial operations. I structure the paper in accordance with the cited major generic tasks of banking reform. But first I recall the core issue of intermediation in a market environment and summarize the state of the banking sector on the eve of the transition's inception. The basic intentions of the transition strategy are next. In the following four Sections, I zero in on the fundamental nature of bank intermediation during systemic transformation and then I examine the three principal configurations of the banking sector during the unprecedented overhauling of the socioeconomic and political systems. The paper concludes with some observations on the present state of affairs with banking reform.

2.   The core issue of intermediation and establishing markets

One of the more daunting problems complicating the choice of parameters of the transformation agenda in the PETs is how best to ensure effective intermediation in intertemporal resource allocation as a vital ingredient of the process whereby functioning capital markets may eventually take root.[4] I prefer to do so by dividing the parameters into at least five groups (comprehensiveness, sequencing, intensity, sectoralism and speed) and applying them with a view to selecting how best to come to grips with at least four critical domains of the transition agenda: stabilization, liberalization, privatization and institution building. Policy options are as a rule constrained by issues that, strictly speaking, are not economic in nature. Even so, sociopolitical considerations evidently influence decision making about the five parameters of the four domains of economic policy making whenever managers of the transition have to make a choice - virtually in all important instances.[5]

In this context, it is useful to recall that the heart of the market economy, towards which the PETs aspire, is the exchange of goods or services for money, or *vice versa*. This means, in essence, the transfer of property rights associated with the object of the

---

expeditiously, and with some determination, towards market-based decision making in a pluralistic political setting (see Brabant, 1993c; 1994b, e).

4 I cannot envision an orderly transformation in which well-functioning capital markets would emerge prior to credit markets.

5 That particular choice crucially depends on the ability of a country to pursue credible change, given the nature and strength of its economic, political and legal institutions; on its social cohesiveness and traditions; and on the conditions prevailing at the transition's start. These factors determine the speed at which economic forces and institutions can realistically be transformed.

exchange from one economic agent to another under various contractual arrangements, ranging from simple use (the *ius utendi* in Roman law); through access to the usufruct (the *ius fruendi*, which is generally combined with the first); to the final disposition (the *ius abutendi*, which includes as a rule the two other characteristics of property rights) of the object in question. One of the paramount tasks of the transition is to facilitate this exchange. There are two principal ways of doing so. It is first of all critical to be unambiguous about the nature and assignment of all property rights in law and jurisprudence. Without it, property rights cannot be fairly contested in market transactions with enforceable contract-like properties and it is doubtful that new assets constituted by accumulating 'real' property in exchange for savings can be safeguarded. Of course, settling these legal matters does not necessarily mean that transactions will take place or that they will materialize in the volume and intensity desired to forge ahead with economic modernization. The way to facilitate such exchange in practice encompasses measures to compress the 'transaction costs' for most operations on average (as distinct from the margin) below the difference in utility of the object to the new owner and the net price paid, or to the former owner and the net revenue received, depending on who ultimately bears those costs.

To meet the legal precondition on property rights, one needs commitments worked out in a constitution or another legal act, such as a coherent, modern civil code, and a properly functioning - transparent and predictable - jurisprudence. To engage in more and more complex, commercially viable transactions with steady modernization, intermediation both among economic agents at some point of time and across time becomes critical. This is particularly so in economies, such as the PETs, where regaining some adequate positive growth path that can be sustained for some years constitutes a core element in securing continued sociopolitical support for the transition agenda, hence to blot up in an orderly fashion the unavoidable burdens inflicted on society by incisive transformation. Seen against this backdrop, the key problem of facilitating the transfer of property rights, once its various legal angles are secured, is how best to attain the minimum degree of intermediation required to arrive at affordable transaction costs and reduce that level (in real terms) steadily in the process of moving towards the completion of the first phases of the transformation process. This is easier said than done, as the PETs have been discovering the hard way.

Looking at how modern economies have accommodated such intermediation, it is evident that, once the economy becomes monetized, effective intermediation follows the division of labor according to 'assignment rules', proceeding usually through the essential vestiges of an incipient capital market. These are normally provided by the foundations of commercial banks in their most elementary form: arranging payments, collecting savings (even if only short term), financing credible investment projects (by necessity longer term), and gradually marketing new financial instruments, including to finance government deficits, as well as assisting with the exchange of existing assets. Once the latter materializes in some organizational format, the essential vestiges of an emerging secondary financial market are being built, leading eventually to the elaboration of a fully-fledged capital market, whose intensity and breadth depend on the nature and volume of transactions to be intermediated. Only in this way can the institutions that buttress a modernizing market economy be meaningfully completed. Whether elements of this process, over and beyond the specified elementary banking functions, should already be targeted early on during the transformation process is a controversial issue that I address in Section 4.

3.   Legacies from the past - banks at the transition's eve

At its root, the characteristic problem of the poor degree of intermediation available in the PETs is that on the eve of the transition from plan to market, the 'institutions in place' are quite far removed from those required to buttress and bolster intermediation. More concretely, commercial banks under planning were not really banks. Rather, they were institutions in the chain of central or administrative planning that facilitated the transfer of funds from a hierarchical level of decision making to one class of economic agents. These were the state-owned enterprises (SOE's) in the broad sense[6] entrusted with assets that, under the communist regime, *in fine* belonged to the State or society but whose usufruct was placed in the hands of 'agents' who enjoyed various degrees of control over the proper usage of the partially-relinquished property rights. This led to cumbersome principal-agent problems.

Monetary flows in such an economy were subordinated to physical planning in detail and split into two poorly linked flow circuits. One involved households, who had little monetized wealth and whose current monetary incomes consisted largely of wages paid in cash and some transfers from the government. This revenue was either consumed or put aside. Savings were either deposited in a state financial institution or, through the grey market, exchanged for foreign currency. The other flow circuit was essentially between the State and SOE's. Direct transactions among SOE's tended to emerge only with the crystallization of administrative reforms. The State used the banking network not only as its treasury but also to ensure that mutual payments among SOE's were promptly settled and that mandated investments or regular production tasks, chiefly as stipulated in the physical plan, could be 'financed'. If the State's revenue fell short of its expenditures, it would 'borrow' from banks or resort to money emission.

The banking sector in such an economy consisted mostly of a monobank with various departments assigned to foreign trade, construction, agriculture, household savings, investment, industrial development and related sectors. In the course of tinkering with economic administration, in several economies these 'sectoral banks' were at some point detached from the central bank and endowed with the inherited portfolio of assets and liabilities. Though these sectoral banks eventually became legally separate agents, and were referred to as 'commercial banks', they were neither banks nor did they act on commercial principles, as commonly understood in the market environment. For all practical purposes, they continued to act as coherent parts of the central bank.

In the above system, whether constituted as the omnibank or not, the monobank did not really act as a central bank. Rather, it performed a mixture of duties, including being the

---

6 For simplicity's sake, under the label SOEs I include here all agents - but occasionally, when the context makes it clear, I exempt banks. The reason for treating banks separately will become clear as we proceed.

government's treasurer and the filter through which monetary flows associated with the physical plan of transactions between the 'center' and the 'periphery', and along with administrative decentralization within the 'periphery', were channeled. Rarely was the bank required to assess the intrinsic - that is, commercial - merits of a 'loan request'. In other words, commercial banks simply did not exist.

It is important to recall in this connection that both the State's assets and liabilities were functionally distributed among various economic agents that all nominally reported to the State. They did so, at least formally, in that they were entrusted with society's assets with a view to maximizing society's welfare as per the precepts of communist-style planning. Whether these assets were utilized for the intended purposes depended on the resolution of a quintessential principal-agent problem, the principal being the State, the Government, or Society as such (the latter in particular in the rather elusive form of the Yugoslav-style socialist market economy (Ribnikar, 1993, 1994)), whereas the agent was the SOE as defined. Monitoring of the latter by the former was initially conducted through the system of financial-economic control established within the planning bureaucracy, on the one hand, and ideological-political obedience enforced through the security services and the omnipresent Communist Party with its myriad interest-group tentacles, on the other hand.

The principal-agent problems of communism and of weakening the control of the principal over the agent were measurably exacerbated when it was formally decided, beginning with the 1960s, to pursue administrative, and in some cases elements of genuine economic, decentralization. Admittedly, none ever worked out to full satisfaction and the commitment to decentralization wavered for over two decades in some format that would sustain ultimate central control over key societal variables, however shaky that in the end proved to be. Nonetheless, (nominally) autonomous agents as a result gained on balance broader latitude in contracting obligations against the state's assets, thus in fact ultimately augmenting the state's liabilities, and indeed staking their own claims on these assets, thus further encumbering the principal-agent problems. The gradual institutionalization, if perhaps not outright fossilization, of the communist system; the waning of rigid internal-security enforcement; and the autonomization attempts within the centralized planning framework enormously compounded the task of resolving, what were in effect multiple, principal-agent problems. This manifested itself notably in the case of bank claims on indebted SOE's. This process was associated with the accumulation of implicit or partial rights, which at present cannot simply be ignored or confiscated (Brabant, 1992, 116-23). As a result, any 'renationalization' option for forging ahead with transition tasks is at best theoretical or rhetorical.

On the eve[7] of the big transformation, then, commercial banks, if extant at all, were really not banks in the orthodox sense; they were burdened with poor assets - essentially loans contracted on the basis of nonbank considerations most of which would turn sour as a result of the transformation policies pursued (Čapek, 1994); and neither households nor the so-called banks had much experience either in collecting savings, in adjudicating

---

7 This cannot possibly be a precisely defined date. But having a clear cross-section picture of the broad legacies of central planning for banking helps structure the remainder of the paper.

loan requests, in marketing diverse financial assets, in effectively clearing reciprocal claims, or for that matter in discharging other banking functions that some commentators claim emerging banks in PETs are in need of performing soonest (see Section 4). That is to say, as part and parcel of the transition's agenda, banks must be created *ab ovo* or by drastically restructuring and upgrading the capacities of existing institutions.

One may well ask, in this context, whether a transition program can be credible - and indeed governable (Brabant, 1993a, b; 1994b, e) - without tackling the threefold nature of effective intermediation. The answer obviously depends on the concrete environment for economic restructuring, on the nature of the so-called commercial banks, and on the ability to enforce hard budget constraints. Before looking at these issues, it is useful to recall three critical elements of the transition. First, it is fallacious to assume that with price and market liberalization all economic agents henceforth submit to hard budget constraints or are placed in bankruptcy and liquidated with minimal delays; that state institutions are strong enough to ensure proper restructuring of fiscal revenues (Hussain and Stern, 1993), including from the emerging private sectors, and will be amenable to undertaking the indicated structural changes; and that SOE's begin to shed excess labor and encourage a rapid rise in labor productivity, perhaps in conjunction with new capital investment. Most of these features will remain 'emerging' for some time to come, namely until markets in PET's firm up.

Second, quick privatization is an illusion for many different reasons (Brabant, 1992), but two are paramount. Taking the old-style political powers and their various interest groups, including the *nomenklatura*, out of the resource-allocation process is indeed an urgent task that should be discharged rapidly if the new political leadership has the clout to do so. But as events in the East suggest, the latter's credibility with the electorate is at best temporarily robust. So, even under favorable circumstances, only negotiated progress can be made. Another implicit assumption maintains that upon the assignment of property rights to private agents the latter will foster more efficient use of their resources, thus bolster factor productivity. This is unlikely to be the case for the vast bulk of assets, which are concentrated in operations where owner-management cannot come about without entailing gross inefficiency, where owners' control can be exerted at best very weakly, and where dispersed ownership leaves management in place essentially intact, thus able to continue to mobilize resources mainly in its own interest.

Finally, much of the burden of the transition cannot be offset exogenously, such as through foreign assistance and government resource redistribution. To the extent that foreign assistance falls short of the resources required to offset the transition's burdens, the perimeter for policy choice is determined by the degree to which a sociopolitical consensus - the rock bottom of adjustment pains that can possibly be inflicted[8] - can be mustered and maintained. Unless these limitations over time are clearly reflected in policy, moving ahead with core transformation, including intermediation, remains all but

---

8 The resilience to adjustment shocks and the populations' willingness to bear hardships have thus far exceeded what most observers anticipated when the political events erupted in 1989. Moreover, the pressure at which the consensus web might fracture has itself repeatedly been raised as the true dimensions of the transition have become more apparent. But it would be foolhardy to assume that there are no limits to how much of a burden can be imposed upon the electorate at large.

out of reach, leaving the PETs as only option muddling through their present sociopolitical calamity.

4. Principal aims of the transition strategy

The fundamental objectives of the transformation are very clear: pluralistic political decision making and the rapid construction of an open, modernizing market economy based largely on privately-held property rights. I leave the political tasks aside, even though it would be all but impossible to imagine viable market-based resource allocation without an environment that permits economic agents to air their preferences with regard to production and consumption.

To formulate realistic policy options in full awareness of the implications for the comprehensive transformation course sought, and indeed to fathom the latter's rationale, one must be unambiguous about both the 'nature' and the 'quality' of the markets extant in the PET's for they determine the possible role 'the market' in these countries can conceivably play in the foreseeable future. At the very least, one must recognize that competition, market, and private ownership are not synonyms. In mature market economies, they coexist; indeed one may be necessary for the other(s) to function. But until that occurs, the various aspects are best kept separate, at least conceptually.

A market essentially encompasses a set of manmade institutions (Kregel, 1990, 45). It is not, and cannot be, an immutable part of the natural environment parachuted at some point from the heavens. Any attempt to transplant any existing market lock, stock, and barrel in record time is bound to cause severe, possibly dysfunctional, dislocations (Steinherr and Gilibert, 1994). True, such perturbations *may* in time incite 'the market,' like the phoenix arising from the ashes; but applying that myth to infer about reality requires at the least good governance, including by generating cooperation among all economic agents (Brabant, 1993a, b; 1994b). In some cases, however, the transplant may be rejected altogether. In most instances, the graft will lead to a mutation resulting from the inevitable adjustments and reconciliation pangs. If only for those reasons, various market configurations exist. Each comprises specific institutions that let the forces of competition unfold, including by modifying the market format.

Nonetheless, in the end the market's virtues derive from the coordination of multiple decisions that is generated through competition guided by self-interested behavior of economic agents in such a way as to produce a limited set of acceptable outcomes, which are thus classed as coherent (Kregel, 1990, 47). (These provide a constraint on self-interested behavior, channeling it into a confined range of mutually compatible outcomes.) Where minimal competition cannot now be attained, a proper regulatory framework or the internalization of the decision-making process either through strict state ownership or the owner-manager will be required. Moreover, mechanisms must be put in place to allow dynamic adjustments to take place with minimal obstacles. This too will be a gradual maturation process rather than a wholesale constitutional rearrangement.

In other words, markets function well only when 'good markets' exist. This platitudinous condition cannot be met in economies that are undergoing radical changes from administrative planning. Not only are functioning markets on the transition's eve scarce at best, it is fallacious to assume that even functioning markets are cost-free and that private transaction costs are zero or negligible (Dunning, 1992, 16ff.). The real world is riddled with imperfect and asymmetric information. Moreover, gathering and processing this information is costly. In practice, even to create and sustain reasonably functioning, rather than 'perfect', markets, some burden will have to be borne by society at large over some stretch of time. The transaction costs associated with the creation of a legal framework for the identification, protection and enforcement of contracts on all kinds of market-based transactions, regardless of how they are translated, enforced and adjudicated, provide one poignant example.

Even the basic preconditions for competitive market allocation in goods and services, let alone in production factors, are not (yet?) fulfilled. They are not because endowments over which agents have property rights and the specifics of marketing and production technologies are hardly such that atomistic competition among economic agents bent on maximizing their profit or utility can be presumed to emerge. As a result, market failure in PET's is likely to be endemic. PET's must re-create markets almost from the ground up, in the process remilling their most essential institutional nuts and bolts, including setting private property rights; creating a solid financial infrastructure, perhaps even stock exchanges and other securities markets; establishing private firms and commercializing SOE's, and eventually divesting most of them; erecting the constitutional infrastructure for property rights and for how best to legally protect them; establishing the rule of law and effectively enforcing it; embracing the principle of profit-oriented activities; motivating human attitudes and behavior into accepting income and wealth differentiation; and so on.

In many respects, little progress has since been made with these tasks since the political shocks of 1989-1990. Many of these aspects will not sprout spontaneously. Rather, they require an activist State, particularly during the earlier phases of the transition. This complements the role of the state in tackling the market failures familiar from mature market economies (provided government failure will not exacerbate matters) as well as coming to grips with the allocative failures attributable to the lack of some markets, and poorly functioning markets otherwise, for some considerable time to come in the PET's. Moreover, the natural order of things is based on interdependence. There will hence be hysteresis effects associated with what is now done well or badly (Pickel, 1992). As a result, the efficiency of resource allocation will have to be maximized under circumstances where one or more markets may be absent or function only poorly.[9] Improvements can be sought, of course. The key questions, then, are: How quickly can functioning markets be erected? and What should be done in the interim to mitigate transitional market failures?

Effective competition in contemporary trading of goods and related services can be ensured relatively easily: from abroad; by encouraging the establishment of new small and medium-sized enterprises (SMEs), including banks, provided adequate prudential

---

9 Incidentally, this underscores the importance of *completing* rather than *commencing* the transformation processes simultaneously.

regulation can be applied; by separating economic from other functions of SOE's; and by deconcentrating economic activities, especially in conglomerates that can be broken up without losing too much of their scale economies. This can advance, even though for some time to come serious obstacles inhibit the funneling of adequate information to individuals to bolster the growth of SME's, particularly in large countries with poor infrastructures (Sapir, 1993). Matters are quite different for factor markets, especially for capital markets. The latter's difficulty derives from the tasks that such markets should fulfill: ensure the efficient allocation of existing capital so as to obtain the maximum contribution to newly created national wealth; mobilize new capital to enlarge the reproduction process; and facilitate the privatization (including divestment) of assets owned by the state or privately to smooth exit and entry, and thus raise net worth through competition. Very little of this demanding construct is as yet functioning in a way conducive to market-based decisions.

Because maturely functioning markets cannot reasonably be expected to crystallize for some time to come, policy makers may in the interim seek to mitigate market failures, provided governance capabilities are in place to ensure that the magnitude of government failure will not exceed the market failure that it was designed to correct to begin with (Brabant, 1993a, b). Various types of regulation provide a useful intermediate format when imperfect information impairs competition, notably in the case of financial intermediation.[10] Note that even when intervention is deemed to be optimal at some point, this assignment with its attributes need not be indelibly etched in granite forever. Market building is one avenue by which the State can discharge its responsibilities and mitigate market failure (Brabant, 1993a, 220-226).

The real challenge for PET policy makers during the transformation, then, is to enable economic agents to reach reasonably efficient decisions while the entire infrastructure for market-based decision making is *in statu nascendi* over an indeterminate period of time. But some markets are likely to become operational sooner than others. In the meantime, emerging markets are bound to exhibit shortcomings. A key question thus arises: Should markets be complemented with other instruments, policies and institutions, perhaps through an industrial policy and good (economic) governance? One can hardly avoid a positive answer if it is recognized that there are market failures that do not necessarily coincide with government failures. That equation is not a given, but depends on the availability of minimum governance capabilities to build, maintain and integrate markets as well as to help identify, and at times foster, the foundations of a growth path that is sustainable over the long haul by mitigating uncertainty and buttressing realistic expectations (Brabant, 1995). It also depends on how these capabilities are mustered, including the ability to divest government of tasks that, as the transformation proceeds, can be better executed elsewhere as per a pragmatic subsidiarity rule (Brabant, 1993a, b; 1994a, b, e).

---

10 The recent calamity with speculative investment funds - classic Ponzi schemes dressed up in a Slavic format - offers a chilling illustration of the machinations of human greed in the absence of effective prudential regulation.

5.   Elementary banking and emerging capital markets

Effective intertemporal intermediation in resource allocation is a paramount task of the capital market in its broad sense, including credit markets.   Once a modicum of macroeconomic stability is restored, with liberalization and gradual divestment, stimulating the emergence of capital markets becomes crucial.   But this is a complex task, if only because the planned economy forcibly denied the vast majority of its economic agents access to a whole range of financial and real assets.   As a result, the inherited capital market in general and credit markets in particular lack depth and breadth (Calvo and Frenkel, 1991; Long and Sagari, 1991).   Nurturing along the key components of a capital market (such as merchant and investment banking, real estate, stock exchanges, and insurance companies for all kinds of risk) is better not viewed in a *deus ex machina* fashion.   Indeed, these and related features of a market economy will emerge gradually in conjunction with the establishment of the proper 'market institutions' with their enabling incentives.

Regardless of the difficulties and inadequacies of building functioning markets during the first transformation phases, the financial sector should play a special role almost from the transition's inception.   As monetized property-right transactions become more complex with modernization, effective intermediation among economic agents contemporaneously and intertemporally plays a critical role in driving the development process.   This is particularly so in economies, such as the PET's, where two precepts prevail.   One is that these societies cannot afford to retrogress to a low-level economic equilibrium, one from which the inefficiencies and inadequacies as legacies of the planning system would naturally be rooted out, thus affording agents a nearly completely 'clean slate'.   The other priority is regaining a positive growth path that is sustainable at an adequate pace for a protracted period of time.   This *sine qua non* for securing sociopolitical support for the transition agenda and for blotting up its unavoidable burdens in an orderly manner is at least of equal importance to avoiding retrogression to a primeval equilibrium.

A banking sector provides the most elementary components of the capital market.   To permit it to discharge its quintessential market functions as quickly and efficiently as circumstances afford, it deserves assiduous support.   I see three primary tasks of the banking sector that need to be taken care of expeditiously:

* reliable and prompt clearing of reciprocal claims;
* effective intermediation between (short-term) savers and (longer-term) investors (Hardy and Lahiri, 1992, 781); and
* marketing new financial assets for individual and corporate wealth portfolios, including government instruments to finance any deficit and indeed to mobilize savings for development purposes.

Note that the economist-transitologists are by no means unanimous on the tasks of banks during the initial phases of the transition.   Most recognize the above three as elementary tasks.   Some would like to deny even these, constraining banking activity essentially to the clearing of payments (as in Rostowski[11], 1994), which can hold only under extremely adverse conditions, and not engaging in any kind of credit operations to decentralized units (McKinnon, 1991a, 6-7; 1991b, 118-121) or to do so only within very strict quotas (Kornai, 1990, 47-9). But one wonders then whence, for example, the skills to assess credit worthiness will emerge; certainly not magically from privatization, as some contend. It is by definition learned on the go at the expense of those making the wrong allocation. Others want to move well beyond that and transform banks, among other aspects of German-style universal banking (Buch, 1993), into pragmatic agents of privatization (Bonin, 1993); into self-interested conciliators with SOE's that have 'bad debt' (Belka, 1994, Slay and Vinton, 1994); into agents that exert corporate control over privatized enterprises and, at least temporarily, over SOE's as well; and into institutions that take care of all kinds of risk in the emerging market economy (Guitián, 1993).

It would indeed be useful to have available the capabilities to ensure essential coordination of economic decisions through other layers than the compromised or inept bureaucracy. It might even be instructive to explore the respective merits of an Anglo-American (given the transparency and contestability) versus a German-Japanese (given the economies of scope and informational advantages) banking systems (Smith and Walter, 1993). But this cannot be something that should inspire or motivate behavior in the short run, although it might have to be studied because the legal environment, when prematurely set up, is bound to precommit future behavior. In fact, banking skills in the PET's are extremely scarce; the kind of formal training and assistance that can be delivered quickly does not as a rule provide much of a solid backdrop for managing 'economic risk' in its diverse dimensions; restructuring the enterprise sphere far transcends the skills and resources available in the banking sector; and, in any case, much of the *métier* of banker, as a sophisticated financial intermediator and trusted counselor in many economies (but much less so in the Anglo-American variant), will have to be learned on the job, largely from mistakes and by building further upon successes attained by taking risks for which adequate, market-delivered rewards and sanctions must be in place. The need to bridge the latter phase is sufficient reason to reject the excessively restrained function of banks that some observers claim needs to be observed during the first years of transformation. In what follows, I therefore focus on the three cited tasks, but I return to the other aspects in the conclusion. This does not mean, of course, that all 'commercial banks' would be clones. Rather, there will be room for various specialized institutions, including savings banks, agricultural credit cooperatives, and credit unions (Hannig, 1994).

With a view to encouraging the restructuring of economic activity, the key role of banks certainly during the initial phases of systemic transformation is effective intermediation between savers and investors. At first, this will chiefly call for collecting fairly short-term deposits and lending them for longer-term productive investments with a reasonable intrinsic risk. The qualifier depends on the assessed merit of the venture and the way in which its management is judged to be capable and motivated to capitalize on

---

11 He erroneously asserts that effective clearing has been the primordial task of banks during capitalism's evolution. A clearing house is simply a different institution from a bank.

these resources for profit, given the general uncertainty and volatility in the very nature of transformation policies. This affects the expected value of assets, the nature and extent of 'bad debts,' the reliability of commitments made by the former communist regime, technology, ownership, moving towards a new growth path, and a myriad of other facets inextricably associated with, and indeed produced by, societal change.

There is therefore a built-in moral hazard in deciding what to do with existing commercial banks and how to encourage the emergence of new banks. No decision maker will find it easy to sort out the various aspects of uncertainty, for any decision is bound to affect the prospective behavior of agents, including the quality of the debt portfolio. Path dependency and hysteresis effects pervade the transition no matter how carefully the policy menu has been chosen or the patience with which a professionally responsible and sociopolitically dispassionate choice can be hammered out. It is therefore very important to avoid extreme views. Rather, stringent prudential regulations with the maxim "no bailout," once rules are on the book and basic cleanup of bad assets has been completed, should be applied with determination. This would penalize institutions that assume too much risk on the basis of their realistic assets. If anything, that should be more stringent for existing commercial banks, because they are state-owned, than for new private institutions. Whereas risk by definition will make some loans uncollectible, the banking sector should be able to work off such *ex post* losses through its statutory capital, retained earnings, and current profits accruing from its other loans made on the basis of the bank's own liabilities (deposits, borrowed money, capital and retained earnings). Of course, the application of standard prudential regulations, such as the Basle rules, to financial institutions in an environment that is anything but a standard mature economy may well fail to avert premature bankruptcy. That too would be part and parcel of a learning experiment.

Yet, the banking system must be given a startoff with some concept of what financial intermediation should be all about. As far as the role of the central bank as such is concerned, its responsibilities include as a minimum keeping treasury accounts; managing official international reserves; providing clearing facilities and, more generally, rendering assistance in the processing and settlement of payments; regulating bank liquidity; supervising bank operations and activities of other financial institutions; and taking responsibility for the conduct of monetary policy (Guitián, 1993, 117). In practice, by the nature of the transition, it also perforce includes ways and means of divesting the central bank of other functions, including those entrusted to commercial banks and being the State's fiduciary agent with a very close interlinkage between fiscal and monetary authority.

Just like the central bank should not act as the government's treasurer, commercial banks should finance endeavors at their own risk. For that constraint to bite with the establishment of independent commercial banks, it is necessary to put in place stringent prudential regulations and surveillance rules to be applied by the (independent) central bank; to clean out the loan portfolio inherited from the monobank and the questionable loans granted during the 'uncertain' phase of the transformation, including to private firms[12]; to capitalize new banks; to recapitalize existing commercial banks in a way that will not inhibit these institutions from performing their intermediating functions on a strictly commercial basis; and to enforce commercial behavior with hard budget constraints (Brainard, 1991; Carlin and Mayer, 1992; Corbett and Mayer, 1991; Rybczynski, 1991).

Yet, it should be clear that for now banks cannot afford to enforce bankruptcy proceedings against their borrowers in technical default even when the legal infrastructure for such exit is firmly in place for reasons examined in Section 5. This has inhibited these institutions from playing their proper intermediating role during the construction of the market economy for lack of both resources (Section 6) and banking *savoir-faire* or inability to apply their knowledge under the given circumstances (see Section 7). Aside from hamstringing the weak private sector, the commercial-banking situation has also hampered the privatization of state-owned assets, including notably of themselves; the adoption of sound regulatory policies and bank supervision; and the development of at least moderately robust financial structures. True, a redefinition of assets and liabilities would help to impart somewhat greater flexibility to banks as well as to overcome the identified obstacles; but those advantages should not, of course, be considered separately from other elements of the transformation agenda. It would, in any case, not make much sense to redefine all assets and liabilities of banks and SOE's (Bruno, 1992).

6. Resolving bad debts

Bad debts pose a major policy problem to the extent that they cannot be resolved or, if resolved, they would bankrupt virtually the entire banking system. Before deliberating on how to resolve bad debts, the nature of these debts, why they have arisen, why they pose such a problem, and what can possibly be done to rectify the situation must be clear. As regards their nature, the source is threefold. First of all, as described in Section 2, under administrative planning debts were contracted, since the 1960s mostly via one or a few state banks, to support SOE's according to criteria that, on the whole, were well out of truck with market conditions. That is not to say, however, that credits under the *anciens régimes* were granted for reasons wholly unrelated to the economics of administrative planning. That domain of discourse was simply different from a market environment, particularly at the extremes of decision making. Those debts are now part of the portfolios of the so-called commercial banks. Their counterpart is the questionable debt of SOE's not carried by other SOE's or the state treasury. In other words, "policies to deal with bank's balance sheets cannot be pursued in isolation from policies dealing with enterprises' financial situations" (Calvo and Kumar, 1993, 14), and indeed from other transformation policies affecting the economic buoyancy and the sociopolitical stability of the PET (Mates, 1992). What is collectible depends on the eventual quality

---

12 In several PET's, the relative acuity of bad debts experienced since the political mutations has in good part been stronger in the private than in the civilian state sector (Belka, 1994; Rostowski, 1994; Slay and Vinton, 1994).

of the loan portfolio, something that is inextricably a function of SOE restructuring. Only once this is taken care of, preferably through a well-thought-out industrial policy (Brabant, 1993a), can an informed assessment of potentially performing assets be undertaken.

In any case, old debts bear little relationship to how an enterprise will perform under new, emerging market conditions. That includes the ability of firms to service the debt while moving ahead with restructuring in line with market disciplines and incentives; it might be useful to entrust *prima facie* problem debt to a specially created state debt-resolution agency; this may assist banks but does not necessarily improve incentives for indebted SOE's. Likewise for the banks: With their present endowment and ability to mobilize resources, they are largely hamstrung, condemned to continue lending chiefly to their core clients in the hope that soon some solution can be found to the *de facto* insolvency of the majority of them, as explained later.

The second component of the debt has arisen in reaction to, in some PET's overly, stringent monetary policies and related, largely experimental transition policies pursued (as in Mongolia and Vietnam at some points). SOE's have granted each other credit simply by not honoring obligations, thereby rapidly escalating involuntary arrears. Similarly, SOE's have increasingly violated their loan obligations to banks and have flouted their fiscal and social-security fiduciary obligations.[13] This has continued during the first years of the transition in part because of bad policing of what is ostensibly still state property, as noted; inadequate prudential regulations and application of any regulatory regime in place; if available at all, a thoroughly inadequate legal infrastructure to enforce bankruptcy; and political apprehension about massive SOE failure. In addition, especially during the first phase of the transition, existing banks have on the whole continued to lend to their established customers - by and large the less solvent SOE's with whom the banks had built up firm relationships over an extended period of time.

A third component needs to be added. In many PET's, inflation at the transition agenda's inception all but destroyed the real value of debts inherited from communist administration. Because of substantial interest rates levied on arrears thereafter as well as punitive penalties for delinquency (Slay, 1992, 36), total (including arrears and tax delinquency) outstanding debts have been piling up rapidly (Calvo and Kumar, 1993). True, in many cases, interest rates have remained negative in real terms, thus reducing the real present value of the debt. However, given the marked deterioration of the financial strength of many borrowers due to the transition's depression, it is not clear whether the ostensible reduction in the measured 'real value' of an enterprise's debt really signals that the SOE finds itself now in a better position to service outstanding debt. In any case, it is only in countries where interest rates have remained low (and will continue to be held down) in spite of inflation that the stock of debt inherited from communist planning has all but resolved itself.

---

13 The really volatile component in several PET's has been indefinite deferment of delivery obligations rather than explicit violations of loan obligations (for Russia, see Pitiot and Scialom, 1993, 148-150).

Inasmuch as the vast bulk of loans granted under administrative planning were extended only within the state and cooperative sectors, these are literally liabilities of one economic agent in the socialized sector to another, hence granted largely for reasons embedded in the logic, including abuses, of administrative planning. The problem should accordingly be tackled against this backdrop, particularly now that new decision-making arrangements rank high among policy priorities. Of course, it cannot even be addressed until the commentator has formed some idea about what precisely is 'bad debt.' This involves two rather arbitrary issues. One is the point in time at which managers of the transition decide that henceforth commercial banks should be responsible for their decisions and will be held to that constraint. Note that, inasmuch as the jump from administrative planning to market building cannot be accomplished from one day to the next, the cutoff date is essentially arbitrary.

The other is what portion of the portfolio identified as being 'weak' should actually be cleaned up. Here two radically different approaches have been pursued: All debt before the cutoff is bad or contaminated and should be removed from the books or bank assets should be marked to market. On the first approach, many observers asserted, rather whimsically particularly during the early phases of the transformation, that virtually all 'old debts,' loosely understood to encompass all debts prior to a decision to come to grips with the problem, are bad. This is most certainly wrong. Whereas it is difficult to estimate the size of problem debts, sheer logic suggests that it depends on the course of the transformation, including any attempt to resolve the perceived debt problem. Furthermore, the banking sector in the PET's does not claim that all are problematic. Nonperforming assets are defined and measured variously, some on the basis of questionable approaches (for examples, see Brabant, 1994c, 24ff.).

Though it would be useful to find a quick solution to the problem debt, there would be little merit in bankrupting banks unless other financial institutions were to emerge quickly, which is doubtful for reasons examined in Section 6, and the value of discretionary assets, which is the real bread-and-butter of bank capital (Buch, 1993, 81), were to be close to zero. In other words, the case for destroying what is in place is not particularly compelling. Indeed, something can best be initiated with existing institutions if governance capabilities are available and preferably in such a way that future options are not too much preempted; wherever possible, an evolutionary approach towards prudential regulation and banking laws deserves to be adopted.

In a regular market economy, with some notable exceptions (*viz.* the S&L crisis in the United States in the early 1990), banks should enforce contractual loan obligations. Why are banks in SOE's not doing so with their long-standing customers? The answer cannot be confined to the argument that banks are simply perpetuating the passive adjustment of finance to planned targets of the real economy as under administrative planning. In any case, governments should explicitly finance loss-making SOE's that are chosen to be kept afloat through *ex ante*, precommitted subsidies and not by forcing banks or other SOE's to finance losses. Nor would it be correct to say that the problem arises simply for lack of political will or of managerial expertise.

Under prevailing circumstances, there may indeed be persuasive arguments for banks not to enforce loan obligations. First, the expected value of the assets that can be collected may be less than the cost of enforcing the contract through cumbersome bankruptcy proceedings. Second, there may be an option value in waiting, given the pervasive uncertainty, particularly during a severe downturn that government will have to help reverse, in which case new lending to 'bad debtors' may rationally be justified. Third, taking action against bad debtors may so weaken the structure of the bank that enforcement will be postponed. Fourth, any such action may alarm policy makers and regulators sufficiently to do something about the 'signaled' problem for the sector as a whole. Finally, banks may simply anticipate that there will be a bailout by government, in which case the incentive to proceed is very small. Indeed, by making the collective problem more cumbersome to come to grips with, waiting with enforcement of discipline may compel government to bail out the banking sector (Brainard, 1991, 102-103).

Many observers of the PET's have argued that the state should quickly come to grips with outstanding debts essentially by 'taking over,' socializing, or confiscating these loans in true shock-therapy mode. The main purpose would be to enable both SOE's and banks, possibly newly established ones (Phelps et al., 1993), henceforth to function on their own account without being burdened by legacies from the past for which, in most cases, the indebted economic entity was not responsible; but neither was the new government or the rejuvenating society! SOE's that carry no debt and banks that carry only performing assets on their balance sheets would not only be able to respond more constructively to emerging market signals; they would also be more attractive vehicles for privatization once the decision to divest them is taken. Otherwise, it is argued (for example, Levine and Scott, 1993), there will be endless debates on the true value of the debt, hence on the purchase price of firms to be privatized or reconstructed. Likewise, piecemeal debt resolution does not eliminate moral hazard.[14]

Nonetheless, the proffered, ostensibly clean and encompassing, solutions seem to render the problem deceptively tractable (Begg and Portes, 1992, 20; OECD, 1992, 48-50), almost as if the magic pencil-and-eraser of the classical accountant of yore could simply 'doctor' the books with impunity. Of course, matters are not quite that straightforward; the problem debt must necessarily be identified fully within the context of the needs for the whole society, including the economy, given the PET's' aspirations and core features. Many observers (see IMF, 1993; Levine and Scott, 1993) have actually argued that debt could be transferred to the state without, in fact, yielding sizable obligations that will eventually have to be covered from fiscal revenues. To anyone with a double-entry bookkeeping mind, once the renationalization option is precluded as unrealistic, this cannot be true (Brabant, 1994c, d). It is an illusion that fundamentally confounds stocks and flows, and perceives the debt of a SOE, whether with respect to the bank or another SOE, as something that will not be serviced. The latter derives from a misconception: Questionable debt depends in good measure on the progress with transition, or the speed at which 'normal' economic conditions for any firm, old or new,

---

14 Levine and Scott (1993) and Eduardo Borensztein (IMF, 1993) argue that debt forgiveness should be undertaken when an SOE is sold. Whereas this might facilitate the sale of the firm, it would not necessarily compromise moral hazard, and might be justified if the seller had 'better' information on the true value of the debt than the potential buyer. But it would manifestly not solve the problem of the banks, unless the government were to place a 'real' value on the obfuscated debt and reimburse the relevant bank whose debt has now been conflated with the sale of the SOE for the appropriate amount.

can be regained. Only then will it become evident that some assets are worthless, and hence could be offset against some liabilities. But others will not be so, and hence should not be written off.

The alternative approach recognizes that some assets are probably bad and some are probably good, and so to forge ahead with proper banking behavior, assets should be 'marked to market,' even if that entails some marginal calls. This usually is assumed to involve marking the state's net wealth position down on the tacit assumption, as in the *tabula rasa* solution discussed earlier, either of there being an anthropomorphic state or that unambiguous market valuations can be constructed. This is hardly likely to be the case (Brabant, 1994c, d). Let us start with the anthropomorphic state. True, as in the heyday of strict central planning, when the state's budget included all revenue and expenditures of all SOE's, the distinction between fiscal and credit financing of SOE's was hard to draw (Hardy and Lahiri, 1992, 780). To an omniscient planner or a sole western evaluator the washout solution would therefore seem self-evident based on an assessment of the state's net worth. This can be attained only when one omniscient planner or his successor rules over the entire accounting system, in which case renationalization should be simple. The same applies to attempts to net out interenterprise debts beyond what can be accomplished voluntarily in a bilateral fashion. But in that case one is not really addressing the debt problem! In any case, even though this solution essentially calls for a transfer within the state sector and might strengthen corporate governance as a result of bolstering retained earnings, this would clearly apply only to successful firms and it would be meaningful solely if otherwise 'market discipline' were to be enforceable. This is hardly likely to be the case, including because of diffuse property rights; bad monitoring; and poorly functioning markets, as discussed.

In addition, although this solution would not have any implications for public-sector debt, it would affect the ability of firms and banks to operate to the extent that net assets of actually or potentially profitable firms and banks are offset against the liabilities of actually or potentially unprofitable firms and banks, thereby hampering the transformation. In any case, wiping out deposits would not only hamstring SOE's in their day-to-day operations, it might also debilitate them so severely that massive and largely premature bankruptcy would, in fact, be engineered in the process. Whether the policy is enacted one or two years down the road in the transformation agenda is immaterial, except that some of the deposits of the earlier 'potentially profitable' SOE's would have arisen from actual profits under the admittedly convoluted transitional situations.

The washout solution will, then, normally have fiscal implications that cannot be belittled, given the tight budget constraints under which most PET's labor and the growing number of tasks entrusted to them. Otherwise, it would adversely affect the credibility of any stabilization program. Furthermore, there is no reason to presume that the legacies of chronic principal-agent problems typical of administrative planning will now completely vanish. Given PET realities, agents entrusted with SOE's during the transition are unlikely to be monitored much better than under administrative planning, unless public-sector governance is quickly renovated (Brabant, 1993a, b; 1994b). In some cases, divestment will ensure such better use of resources. But since this process cannot be completed quickly for a host of legitimate reasons (Brabant, 1992), reform of the public sector is a dire necessity that has not so far been adequately explored. Without this, who then can be expected to make a wise decision about the washout (the stock problem) or by way of preventing the problem from recurring by having all agents henceforth act responsibly on behalf of owners (the flow problem) - by necessity overwhelmingly still the state?

Though the 'bad debt' problem has not been ignored in most PETs, no country has thus far resolved the issue, let alone peremptorily. All have at least tacitly condoned the aggravation of the problem by imposing high nominal interest rates with a wide margin between lending and deposit rates to enable banks to form contingent reserves for bad loans; by allowing banks to continue to serve their 'best' customers, which are the traditional SOE's; and by aequiescing in the buildup of arrears by SOE's, including in relations among themselves. This stark contrast between rhetoric and real choice is paradoxical, at the very least. And an illuminating explanation must encompass more than lack of insight in what needs to be done on the part of the managers of the PETs agenda.[15] The seeming contradiction can be resolved only against the broader backdrop of the transition agenda and transformation policies. Only then will it become clear that cleaning up the 'old debt' simply *cannot* be an isolated component of transformation policies. On the contrary, it is but *one*, albeit in some cases a critical, element of a much more convoluted economic, political and social situation in which unsettling uncertainty is very pervasive.

7. Tackling recapitalization

As described, not only is the loan portfolio of existing commercial banks at the transition's inception of dubious value, it is bound to deteriorate during the first few years of the transition, particularly as a result of the transformational recession. This has various origins, including enforced domestic austerity, rerouting trade ties towards western markets, inelastic supply response and policy errors, some due to advice issued by international economic organizations (Brabant, 1993c). Whatever its origin, the drop in output of and demand for domestic products, compounding the uncertainty derived from the weird property-rights situation in PET's, is likely to induce banks to roll over credits even for weak SOE's, and indeed to capitalize interest, rather than to provide funds based on sound risk-based judgments. Furthermore, given the general uncertainty and the transition's vacillations, even established customers will lose their incentive to service their debts. Moreover, the entirely labile situation strengthens the case for involuntary interenterprise debt, which has been surging throughout the PET's during the early phases of transformation, and recurs unless hard budget constraints can be enforced without too much wavering. In the end, the uncertainty about property rights and controlling them is likely to force governments to bail out banks that are about to fail (Blommestein, 1993). None of these outcomes is desirable. A good many of them are unavoidable. But by far not all are necessary.

---

15 For a review of the recent experiences in Bulgaria, the Czech Republic, Poland and Slovenia, see *MOCT-MOST* (1994, 3).

Since bank intermediation is critical in greasing the wheels of market-based operations, on the one hand, and banks find themselves with limited resources to do so, on the other hand, the logical inference is that existing banks need to be recapitalized or that incentives should be created to constitute new banks from domestic and foreign sources. From a purely technical perspective it would be useful simply to bankrupt and eliminate the existing problem banks - those whose net worth is negative or below minimum capitalization levels - if new financial institutions could be expected to emerge quickly. But there would be little merit in doing so otherwise. Domestic voluntary sources are highly limited and there exists acute aversion to risky investment. Likewise, external interest in engaging in banking operations, other than those required for foreign direct investment (FDI) and ordinary foreign trade, during the initial phase of the transformation is restrained in part because their risk aversion is arguably even larger, given the uncertainty in PET's and their unfamiliarity with doing business in these countries. It is therefore doubtful whether new viable financial institutions will emerge quickly. A second logical inference, for all practical purposes, is that the initial impetus to financial-sector reform will have to take the form of recapitalization of existing banks, chiefly from the public purse. Those resources could conceivably be used to establish new state-financed or cofinanced institutions, but that would not be desirable unless one were to advocate a dual-track commercial-banking system, presumably because government in effect cannot adequately monitor existing imbalances, but it might be able to do so for new financial institutions held to more rigorous surveillance rules. This too is easier said than done.

Since the essence of proper commercial-banking behavior is to attract deposits, even if short term, and onlend them, even if for a longer period, at some risk, part of which must be covered through the bank's own resources, any operation designed to cleanse 'bad debts' without fully replacing their 'market value' in the affected portfolios is bound to weaken the bank's capital base. The latter might already have been dubious to start with, in which case it is rather hopeless to depend on the commercial banks' being in a position to fulfill their tasks in an emerging market environment. An inadequate or eroding capital base in conjunction with rather sluggish savings' behavior, and even averse predisposition of savers to augment their bank deposits in most cases, inhibits commercial-banking operations. Special incentives for savers in 'familiar' institutions may provide some fillip (Hannig, 1994).

Given their narrow resource base, banks can engage only in the most secure projects, of which there are likely to be few during the most volatile phase of transformation, when bank intermediation would be most helpful in eliciting market-based restructuring. This puts a damper on private-sector entry, slows down the divestment of state-owned assets, inhibits the effective adoption of sensible regulatory policies and bank supervision (EBRD, 1993), encumbers the development of a sound financial infrastructure for modernization, and complicates the restructuring of SOE's, including notably of the commercial banks themselves. Furthermore, because existing assets are of poor quality, with borrowers wantonly disregarding their debt obligations, exit is being impeded. This in turn inhibits the restructuring required to regain a new growth path.

Banks cannot afford to enforce bankruptcy proceedings against their borrowers in technical default even once the legal infrastructure for such exit is firmly in place. This has compounded the difficulties that these institutions encounter in playing their proper intermediating role during the construction of the market economy. The prevailing stalemate is particularly debilitating in that banks cannot, in fact, mobilize short-term savings and ensure their allocation to long-term investment in profitable ventures, including notably for new SMEs. The latter's emergence and health are critical for the expeditious transformation of these economies, and they are thus expected to become the real carriers of switching these economies onto a new, endogenous growth path. Most so-called commercial banks are in any case not involved in retail financial services as most households for now prefer to keep their savings either 'under the mattress' or at institutions - the savings banks in some form - that are expected to provide a near-ironclad, if only implicit, deposit insurance because savers expect the state sector to be backed up by the good faith of the reform-oriented Government. Whether this will, in fact, prevail is a different matter. At least for now, then, people's expectations are such that banks either have to attract the placement of the institutions that collect savings or that they have to confine their lending to what is prudently loanable against their own resources (capital, reserves, borrowed funds and highly limited deposits). Since capital and reserves are generally very low as all banks are undercapitalized and have low profitability (and in some cases they intrinsically have a negative net worth), efficiency considerations have played at best a marginal role in bank lending to date. This is particularly inhibiting the emergence and restructuring of the private sector, which for now depends largely on 'family' assets.

Coming to grips with this problem in one way or another involves a destruction of part of bank assets. Whether this is punishment for bad bank behavior or the simple cleaning up of bookkeeping magnitudes that do not reflect underlying realities relevant to the transformation is something that I shall not further discuss here (Brabant, 1994c, d). The point is that in the purification process (through bankruptcy, conciliation, transfer to a state agency, setting aside contingent reserves and other ways) the capital base of the banks is bound to be severely eroded. Barring private initiative, the State needs to issue special financial assets in exchange for the debt to be serviced out of future fiscal revenues and ensure that further capitalization takes place, perhaps by bringing in a foreign partner, as the Czech Republic and Poland have recently explored. This would recapitalize the banks to some extent and thus enable them henceforth to begin to discharge their critical intermediating role in constructively moving ahead with the transformation agenda.

By now, virtually all PET's have enacted some form of recapitalization of existing banks, of allowing the creation of new banks (in some PET's, however, with thoroughly inadequate prudential regulations (Pitiot and Scialom, 1993), particularly as practiced and enforced), and of encouraging the entry of foreign partners for domestic banks, possibly in conjunction with privatization. To date only a limited impact on domestic banking operations, as distinct from the two functions noted earlier, has been exerted. The most common recapitalization format has been the transfer of 'bad assets' from the commercial banks to the government or a government-created agency against some government-backed debt instrument, but at less than face value and below-market interest rates. The replacement of nonperforming loans, however identifiable at some stage of the transformation, on banks' books with interest-bearing government debt (such as bonds or treasury paper) poses several technical questions (Calvo and Kumar, 1993, 14), but these need not detain us here. This approach would have the unquestionable merit of making the banks' asset base sounder. An alternative would be capitalizing new banks unencumbered by the legacies of incompetence, institutional inertia and principal-agent problems (Phelps et al., 1993, 23ff.). It would also clean up the situation for SOE's and thus facilitate restructuring and divestment.

This type of asset substitution, even if well below face value of the bad debt, is advocated on the ground that banks will now have 'better assets' against which they can contract new loans, particularly to new firms. When these loans have to be paid out, banks should be able to do so by mobilizing their liquid resources. When the latter fail, they should utilize the state's debt instruments in secondary markets, just like in the case of turning enterprise debts into negotiable instruments (Aglietta and Moutot, 1993, 92). Of course, the latter have as yet to emerge. To the extent that the new instrument has an intrinsic value exceeding the recognized 'market value' of the bad assets, recapitalization occurs and the banks can mobilize these resources for their lending activities provided there is a liquid secondary market in which these debt instruments can be readily traded.

A particular twist on this scenario has been pursued in Bulgaria: Government bonds emitted at well below market interest rates can be acquired and used *at face value* in the privatization process (Dobrinsky, 1994). Note that this entails the *de facto* destruction of assets that, in fact, belong to the State (or Society as such). Elsewhere, notably in the case of Hungary and Poland, some debt-swaps have been arranged, the banks in effect becoming part owner of the SOE that was indebted to them. In Poland, this way of proceeding has been tied directly to the privatization of the banks as well as the reconciliation of the debtors with the banks' outlook; failing that indebted SOE's are placed in bankruptcy or liquidation - the two following different legal procedures but leading up to the same result (Belka, 1994; Slay and Vinton, 1994). Also in this case the government's wealth is deliberately sacrificed and other claimants on SOE's entering into conciliation procedures lose their priority claim, and often their assets altogether. Whether credible hard budget constraints can henceforth be enforced and this type of 'investment' in cleaning up the foundations for economic transformation will in the end prove its worth remains to be seen from more than one point of view.

Some countries have tried to enforce prudential regulations by requiring banks to set aside contingent reserves for bad loans, largely by permitting them to maintain a sizable gap between deposit and lending rates. This is one of the reasons why lending interest rates continue to be very high in several PET's. Because private borrowers cannot reasonably afford such high real positive interest rates and traditional borrowers, who are not genuinely held to a hard budget constraint, do not really care too much about interest charges, banks have continued to lend to their traditional clientele. None of this is very useful given the context of the desirable transformation agenda.

Whatever the form of recapitalization and cleaning up of bad assets pursued, usually conjointly, it should not detract from the observation that the volume and variety of loanable funds at commercial banks remain highly confined for now, and that commercial banks, whether privatized or not, remain in need of additional capital infusions. These can hopefully be procured from abroad, at least in some cases. But greater confidence on the part of savers, to augment the mass of savings kept in the formal sector, and of depositors, to funnel their savings through the commercial-banking system, remains a high priority.

8.   Strengthening commercial bank behavior

As described in Section 2, (commercial) banks under administrative planning were not really banks but funnels to accommodate the monetary streams associated with, and subordinated to, the plan's physical flows of goods and services. This differed in many important respects from engaging in intermediation on commercial grounds, effectuating swift settlements of reciprocal claims that are now no longer guaranteed by the plan, and marketing financial instruments with various degrees of risk for which banks must take responsibility in return for an expected profit margin. The overriding goal at present is commercialization of activities, and this requires first and foremost the development of skills to deliver on the three basic tasks outlined here. Of course, if banks are to perform other functions, such as those advocated by other commentators (see Section 4), the requirements for effective behavior will rise *pari passu*.

One curious side effect of virtually all proposals regarding the cleaning up of bad debt or the creation of new financial institutions is the presumption that there is a layer of competent bankers available who for some reason are presently unable to take charge of existing banks or to found their own. Furthermore, it is assumed that such new banks would be able to function properly even though the new institutions would be state-owned, at least initially. These far-fetched assumptions remind me of the exceedingly naïve claims made at the inception of privatization (see Brabant, 1992). Whereas cleaning up bad debts, recapitalizing existing banks, and the creation of new banks are useful activities, none guarantees that there will be proper 'commercial' behavior on the part of banks, that is, that transformed financial institutions will cope better with risk and at lesser transaction costs than other economic agents. Though foreign banks, including through joint ventures, may offer useful banking experience, their ignorance of local conditions and of the extraordinary circumstances of the transition guarantee that, as for existing banks, vital commercially-motivated bank behavior will, in fact, emerge only through experience and even then only over a fairly protracted period of time. Training and transfer of banking technology may bolster experience and cut down on the learning period required. But it cannot eliminate the latter or close the time gap overnight.

As regards effecting smooth settlement of reciprocal payments, the fact remains that the transmission of payments within countries, and even more among countries, remains extremely slow. Certainly, the acquisition of modern technology and automation may help. But more is required particularly in terms of organization and management so that up-to-date technology can be put to best use. Only then will the reciprocal payments system function at low transaction costs and contribute to formalizing part of the transactions that are now conducted in the informal sector in cash or at usurious informal credit rates.

Because commercial banks in principle collect savings from multiple depositors and lend these funds to few investors, the safety of deposits depends on the ability and willingness of the banks to administer the funds in the depositors' best interest. Since this principal-agent problem is often overloaded with moral hazard, a substantial role devolves to the State to protect depositors through its supervisory functions as well as through various prudential regulations, such as deposit insurance or minimum reserve requirements. These might reassure depositors in the absence of other capital markets, provided the risk that commercial banks take is not too onerous, for that would require government bailouts.

Furthermore, commercial banks as shell institutions under administrative planning did not have an incentive to invest in building up 'information capital.' Proprietary information is arguably the bread and butter of financial institutions, including commercial banks. If only in that sense, there is presently a very substantial backlog on gathering, processing, and applying elementary information and related skills. The latter's application will be critical in compressing transaction costs, and making a profit on onlending funds, in all PET's. Moreover, impersonal transactions require costly specification and enforcement mechanisms such as rating and supervisory systems for banks. The informational needs transcend those invoked earlier. Because these systems are, as so many things in the PET's, *in statu nascendi*, the transaction costs of impersonal exchanges are high and many actors are for now sticking to old, well-established business routines with known clients (Buch, 1993).

Finally, even as concerns the marketing of new financial instruments, the drive to innovate beyond the commercialization of government debt instruments has remained surprisingly inert. Banks will not only have to gain the confidence of savers. They will also have to innovate financial-asset instruments in which savers will want to maintain some of their wealth. The road that remains to be traveled in this respect, particularly until other credible capital-market intermediaries will appear, remains long and arduous. But progress should be made quickly. Training and the transfer of basic technical assistance on these matters would be very useful indeed.

Besides taking deposits and extending credit, banks normally carry out a number of other activities, such as in the areas of payment settlements, custody of assets, and management of investments (Guitián, 1993). These can give rise to serious conflicts such as mismatch of assets and liabilities, low capitalization, and unduly risky asset portfolios. For that reason, bank are usually subject to official supervision and regulation. The aim is to promote bank safety and soundness and to maintain confidence in the financial system as a whole. PET's suffer from inadequate regulation, poor prudential regulation, and lack of experience with applying and enforcing rules, when they are at all on the books. This is perhaps less the case for market-entry requirements and capital-adequacy rules than for balance-sheet control and concrete application of prudential regulations. Depositor protection is frequently poor and systemic support from the central bank as lender of last resort suffers from the fact that it cannot be confined, as it should, to emergency situations and provided at a relatively high price, if only as an effective deterrent.

Even though banking skills may be slowly emerging, the importance of adequate prudential regulations and of the application of strict banking supervision cannot be overemphasized. Both the central bank and commercial banks for now lack reliable information about the financial condition of SOE's and the banks themselves. They have limited experience in risk analysis of potential borrowers. Furthermore, they have limited knowledge about the intrinsic worth of their past borrowers, inadequate tax regimes for making loan-loss provisions, lack of experienced supervisors and auditors, and prudential regulations that leave a lot to be desired (Blommestein, 1993).

9. Conclusions

To forge ahead with the creation of market-based resource allocation, existing commercial banks need to switch from being passive agents associated with physical planning towards becoming major contributors to the discovery and successful treading of a new growth path in these countries. This requires the establishment of new 'institutions,' and of formal and informal rules, the reinforcement of the central bank as a surveillance organ and modulator of monetary and credit policies, and imbuing depositors with a sense of confidence while permitting commercial banks to explore selective tasks whose ambit is expanded as experience is gained and the process of structural transformation is credibly solidifying.

Whereas it is widely recognized that the weak commercial-banking infrastructure in PET's has been one central factor clouding the atmosphere for the transition, the remedies to rectify the situation proposed to date are by no means self-evident, except in highly simplified frameworks that rely on assumptions that eschew some of the PET's' core realities. Many take a partial approach, essentially falling into line with other advocates of ensuring that the environment for microeconomic decision making be cleansed as quickly and as thoroughly as possible by hiving off all obligations to the government. It is plainly pernicious for advisers to pretend that the State can assume responsibility for virtually all adverse legacies of communism when at the same time it is being slimmed down erratically as a result of a shrinking revenue base (for example, because of a call for low import duties, for keeping domestic fiscal systems pro-competitive, for quickly divesting state-owned assets, and because of the inability of the new governments to enact fiscal reforms and collect adequate revenues to finance mandated tasks). It may be an insurmountable task for government to discharge these liabilities under weak market arrangements. Whatever social consensus on the state's role may henceforth be identified, it will have to be reconciled with adequate financing. Freeing up the private sector to engage in 'ostensibly clean' operations unloads onto the state a burden that would all but paralyze it precisely at a time when it must muster all resources to manage the transition.

Such an option is neither feasible nor desirable. It would, therefore, be preferable to purposefully muddle through in a gradual, but purposeful way in whatever format available governance capacities permit. Whereas debt resolution and recapitalization could, in principle, be undertaken in shock-therapy mode, the critically important acquisition of useful banking *savoir-faire* materializes only by learning from doing, including from making containable mistakes. Indeed, much of the strength of financial institutions, including the banks as the rock bottom upon which the remainder of the capital market may in time be erected, depends on embodied knowledge and information that can simply not be acquired otherwise, regardless of how favorable FDI flows or western-financed technical-assistance efforts might be.

Whereas one could be ambitious and aim at assimilating the entire gamut of skills that universal banks in some mature economies play, I have argued that the capacities existing in the PET's are simply too limited to be usefully diluted in this manner. Concentration of effort on the essential tasks of bank intermediation is of far greater importance than speeding forward at any cost towards building the essential vestiges of, say, universal banking. This applies also to the widening of the activities of commercial banks as experience is gained with elementary financial intermediation and the transformation process proceeds.

References

Aglietta, Michel and Philippe Moutot (1993); Redéployer les réformes; *Economie Internationale*, 54, 67-103.

Begg, David and Richard Portes (1992) Enterprise debt and economic transformation: financial restructuring of the state sector in Central and Eastern Europe, Discussion Paper Series No. 695, London: CEPR, June.

Belka, Marek (1994); Financial restructuring of banks and enterprises in Poland; *MOCT-MOST*, 3.

Blommestein, Hans J. (1993) Financial sector reform and monetary policy in Central and Eastern Europe, in Fair, Donald E. and Robert J. Raymond (eds) *The new Europe: evolving economic and financial systems in east and west*, Dordrecht, Boston, MA and London: Kluwer Academic Publishers, 145-67.

Bonin, John P. (1993); On the way to privatizing commercial banks: Poland and Hungary take different roads; *Comparative Economic Studies*, 4, 103-19.

Brabant, Jozef M. van (1992) *Privatizing Eastern Europe - the role of markets and ownership in the transition,* Dordrecht, Boston, MA and London: Kluwer Academic Publishers.

Brabant, Jozef M. van (1993a) *Industrial policy in Eastern Europe - governing the transition,* Dordrecht, Boston, MA, London: Kluwer Academic Publishers.

Brabant, Jozef M. van (1993b) Governance, the state, and industrial policy in Eastern Europe, paper prepared for the Third American-Polish Round Table, Charleston, SC, 15-16 September.

Brabant, Jozef M. van (1993c); Lessons from the wholesale transformations in the East; *Comparative Economic Studies*, 4, 73-102.

Brabant, Jozef M. van (1994a) *The transformation of Eastern Europe - joining the European integration movement*, Commack, NY: Nova Science Publishers.

Brabant, Jozef M. van (1994b) Governance, evolution, and the transformation of Eastern Europe, in Poznański, Kazimierz (ed.) *The transformation of Eastern Europe and evolutionary economics,* Boulder, CO: Westview.

Brabant, Jozef M. van (1994c); Bad debts and balance sheets in transforming Eastern Europe; *Russian and East European Finance and Trade*, 2, 5-33.

Brabant, Jozef M. van (1994d); Transforming the bank and enterprise balance sheets in Eastern Europe; *MOCT-MOST*, 3.

Brabant, Jozef M. van (1994e); Privatization, industrial policy and governing the transitions; *MOCT-MOST*, 1, 63-85.

Brabant, Jozef M. van (1995); Restructuring, the State, and technological change; *Cuadernos del ESTE*, 14, forthcoming.

Brainard, Lawrence (1991) Strategies for economic transformation in Central and Eastern Europe: role of financial market reform, in Blommestein, Hans J. and Michael Marrese (eds) *Transformation of planned economies: property rights reform and macroeconomic stability*, Paris: Organisation for Economic Co-operation and Development, 95-108.

Bruno, Michael (1992) Stabilization and reform in Eastern Europe - a preliminary evaluation, IMF Staff Papers, 4, 741-77.

Buch, Claudia M. (1993); Banking reform in Eastern Europe: an institutional approach; *MOCT-MOST*, 3, 73-94.

Calvo, Guillermo A. and Jacob A. Frenkel (1991) Obstacles to transforming centrally-planned economies: the role of capital markets, IMF Working Paper No. WP/91/66, Washington, DC: International Monetary Fund.

Calvo, Guillermo A. and Manmohan S. Kumar (1993) Financial markets and intermediation, in Calvo, Guillermo A., Manmohan S. Kumar, Eduardo Borensztein and Paul R. Masson (eds) Financial sector reforms and exchange arrangements in Eastern Europe, Washington, DC: The International Monetary Fund, Occasional paper 102, 1-33.

Čapek, Aleš (1994); The bad debts problem in the Czech economy; *MOCT-MOST*, 3.

Carlin, Wendy and Colin P. Mayer (1992); Enterprise restructuring; *Economic Policy*, 15, 311-52.

Corbett, Jenny and Colin P. Mayer (1991); Financial reform in Eastern Europe: progress with the wrong model; *Oxford Review of Economic Policy*, 4, 57-75.

Dobrinsky, Rumen (1994); The problem of bad loans and enterprise indebtedness in Bulgaria; *MOCT-MOST*, 3.

Dunning, John H. (1992); The global economy, domestic governance, strategies and transnational corporations: interactions and policy implications; *Transnational Corporations*, 3, 7-45.

EBRD (European Bank for Reconstruction and Development) (1993); Banking reform in central and eastern Europe; *EBRD Economic Review - Current Economic Issues*, July, 8-16.

Guitián, Manuel (1993) From the plan to the market: banking and financial reform aspects, in Fair, Donald E. and Robert J. Raymond (eds) *The new Europe: evolving economic and financial systems in east and west*, Dordrecht, Boston, MA and London: Kluwer Academic Publishers, 113-29.

Hannig, Alfred (1994); Die Rolle von Sparkassen im Finanzsystem der Transformationsländer; *Konjunkturpolitik*, 1, 67-99.

Hardy, Daniel and Ashok Kumar Lahiri (1992); Bank insolvency and stabilization in Eastern Europe; IMF Staff Papers, 4, 778-800.

Hussain, Athar and Nicholas Stern (1993); The role of the state, ownership and taxation in transitional economies; *Economics of Transition*, 1, 61-87.

IMF (International Monetary Fund) (1993); Reforming centrally planned economies: what have we learned?; *IMF Survey*, 16, 241, 247-51.

Kornai, János (1990) *The road to a free economy - shifting from a socialist system: the example of Hungary*, New York and London: Norton.

Kregel, Jan A. (1990) Market design and competition as constraint to self-interested behaviour, in Groenveld, Klaas, Johannes A.H. Maks and J. Muyskens (eds) *Economic policy and the market process - Austrian and mainstream economics*, Amsterdam: North-Holland, 45-57.

Levine, Ross and David Scott (1993); Old debts and new beginnings: a policy choice in transitional socialist economies; *World Development*, 3, 319-30.

Long, Millard (1993) Financial aspects of enterprise restructuring, in Fair, Donald E. and Robert J. Raymond (eds) *The new Europe: evolving economic and financial systems in east and west*, Dordrecht, Boston, MA and London: Kluwer Academic Publishers, 131-44.

Long, Millard and Silvia B. Sagari (1991) Financial reform in the European economies in transition, in Marer, Paul and Salvatore Zecchini (eds) *The transition to a market economy - Vol. II: special issues*, Paris: Organisation for Economic Co-operation and Development, 430-42.

Mates, Neven (1992); Does the government have to clean bank balance sheets in transitional economies?; *Communist Economies and Economic Transformation*, 3, 395-409.

Mayer, Colin P. (1993) In the image of the west: creating financial systems in Eastern Europe, in Fair, Donald E. and Robert J. Raymond (eds) *The new Europe: evolving economic and financial systems in east and west*, Dordrecht, Boston, MA and London: Kluwer Academic Publishers, 61-8.

McKinnon, Ronald I. (1991a) *The order of economic liberalization - financial control in the transition to a market economy*, Baltimore, MA and London: The Johns Hopkins University Press.

McKinnon, Ronald I. (1991b); Financial control in the transition from classical socialism to a market economy; *Journal of Economic Perspectives*, 4, 107-22.

OECD (Organisation for Economic Co-operation and Development) (1992) *Reforming the economies of Central and Eastern Europe*, Paris: Organisation for Economic Co-operation and Development.

Phelps, Edmund S., Roman Frydman, Andrzej Rapaczyński and Andrei Shleifer (1993) Needed mechanisms of corporate governance and finance in eastern Europe, London: EBRD Working Paper No. 1, March.

Pickel, Andreas (1992); Jump-starting a market economy: a critique of a radical strategy for economic reform in light of the East German experience; *Studies in Comparative Communism*, 2, 177-91.

Pitiot, Hélène and Laurence Scialom (1993); Système bancaire et dérapage monétaire; *Economie Internationale*, 54, 137-56.

Ribnikar, Ivan (1993); Rehabilitation of banks in Slovenia; *Est-Ovest*, 5, 79-94.

Ribnikar, Ivan (1994); Investment, bank debt, and bank rehabilitation in Slovenia; *MOCT-MOST*, 3.

Rostowski, Jacek (1994) The banking system, credit and the real economy in economies in transition, paper prepared for the conference 'Banking Reform in FSU and Eastern Europe: Lessons from Central Europe', Budapest, 14-15 January, mimeographed.

Rybczynski, Tadeusz M. (1991); The sequencing of reform; *Oxford Review of Economic Policy*, 4, 26-34.

Sapir, Jacques (1993); Formes et nature de l'inflation; *Economie Internationale*, 54, 25-65.

Slay, Ben (1992); The banking crisis and economic reform in Poland; *RFE/RL Research Report*, 23, 33-40.

Slay, Ben and Luisa Vinton (1994); Bad debts and the Polish restructuring program; *MOCT-MOST*, 3.

Smith, Roy C. and Ingo Walter (1993) Bank-industry linkages: models for Eastern European economic restructuring, in Fair, Donald E. and Robert J. Raymond (eds) *The new Europe: evolving economic and financial systems in East and West*, Dordrecht, Boston, MA and London: Kluwer Academic Publishers, 41-60.

Steinherr, Alfred and Pier-Luigi Gilibert (1994); Six proposals in search of financial sector reform in Eastern Europe; *MOCT-MOST*, 1, 101-14.

UNECE (1993) *Economic survey of Europe in 1992-1993*, New York: United Nations publication, sales no. E.93.II.E.1.

Comment on Jozef M. van Brabant

Mechthild Schrooten

In light of van Brabant's comprehensive treatment of the emergence of financial markets in economies in transition, it is not easy to add a new perspective. Therefore, I would like to concentrate on remarks regarding certain specific aspects which the author has mentioned.

Undoubtedly, the character of the banking sector began to change at the eve of the transformation process in Central and Eastern Europe. In view of the challenges of financial intermediation in a market economy, where commercial and private banks are important agents in coordinating individual saving and investment plans, a new legal framework was installed in all these economies. This has brought with it the creation of a two-tier banking system, with a more or less independent central bank. Simultaneously, commercialization of the existing banks took place, while privatization of this sector was postponed. Due to the legacies of the past, and because transformation is an ongoing process, a banking sector comparable to that of any western country could not be created as rapidly as was necessary. One of the most urgent struggles with the legacies of the past is to overcome the passive role which the banking sector played in the former system. However, the expansion of possibilities of taking responsibility for their own choices has initiated an increased rationality in the behavior of individual banks.

Given that the rationality of individual behavior is dependent upon actual institutional frameworks, the implemented incentive structure is widely responsible for the result of the decision making process. Thus, individual behavior can be rational, even if the outcome does not seem to be consistent with that under market conditions or, in other words, does not appear to be efficient. This may be the case in most of the economies in transition. When this is evident, further development in the direction of a market-oriented institutional and legal framework must be an important goal while aiming at a higher degree of efficiency in financial allocation. Furthermore, this fortification may accelerate the necessary improvement of the low degree of competition within the banking sector observed in these economies. Under the well-known weak economic conditions, a breakdown of the existing market entry barriers for foreign banks could support domestic efforts. As a side-effect of human capital transfer and technical assistance related to Foreign Direct Investment, an improvement of the incentives for domestic commercial banks could occur in order to broaden their offered services, and consequently, to ease financial flows.

Some of the key problems of the transformation process are the weak and uncertain macro-economic conditions under which financial intermediation can take place. The relationship between macro-economic stability and the emergence of financial intermediaries creates a dilemma: In the mentioned economies there is often great uncertainty about the realization of announced governmental stabilization programs; high and

177

volatile inflation rates hamper the emergence of a smoothly functioning financial sector. At the same time, the existence of a well operating financial sector seems to be a prerequisite for the introduction of indirect or market oriented instruments of monetary policy. The implementation of these instruments is important to stabilize the monetary and economic development, i.e. stabilize inflationary expectations or even to break the underlying inflationary mentality.

Because of the difficult conditions under which financial intermediation takes place in these economies, there is a lack of adequate financial institutions and intermediaries, especially at the eve of the transformation process. Therefore, state-owned commercial banks often operate as the most important interface between micro- and macro-levels of these economies. It is remarkable that these commercial banks have a considerable lower influence on the overall credit allocation in comparison to banks in developed market economies. An illustrative example of this is given by the widespread existence of directed and preferential credits often characterized by real negative interest rates. These credits are granted by the government to the state-owned or former state-owned enterprises, channelled through the state-owned commercial banks. These highly subsidized credits are a symptom for close linkages between the different sectors of economies in transition. They are the main reason for the persistence of the "soft budget constraint" of the public sector.

Favored by these credits, the pressure for structural change in the often over-staffed and inefficient operating state-owned companies is at an endemic low. While the political logic behind these credits is to hamper high unemployment figures, they operate like a safety net of state bail-out. To secure the liquidity of these loss-making enterprises, transfers from the budgetary sphere are often granted in addition to the already mentioned preferential credits. This means that in most of these countries a mixture of monetary and fiscal policy instruments operate as a substitute for a comprehensive social policy based on a broad social consensus. In particular, the responsibility of the fiscal and monetary policy for the situation in the labor market - which seems to be largely protected in most of these economies - has often reached a high degree. Substitution as mentioned is in many cases financed by money printing. This kind of financing hampers the breakdown of the inflation expectations, increases the uncertainty about the future stabilization process and will cause incredibly high social costs in the long-run. As a consequence the credibility of governmental stabilization programs is low; the saving and investment behavior of economic agents is widely disturbed.

Thus, to enable the banking sector to cope with the important task of financial intermediation, especially to co-ordinate domestic saving and investment decisions, a liberalization of the interest-rate seems to be an important precondition. Because of that, a simultaneous revision of the widely-spread subsidizing programs for the state-owned enterprise sector appears necessary. Although a social consensus about the consequences of a cut of these directed or preferential credits seems in many cases unavailable, a lot of the difficulties in the micro- as well as on the macro-level of these economies could be overcome by this cut. Thus, the persistence of these credits in reality as well as considerable problems in lending behavior of the state-owned commercial banks, brings us to the next issue - bad debt.

Although there have been fundamental changes in the institutional framework, a massive burden of the past lies on the emerging financial markets - especially on the often modernized state-owned commercial banks, which were built up to finance the economic activities of special branches of the old system. Until now, a close linkage between the different sectors of the economy has been structural phenomenon in all of these countries. These linkages appear to be amid the main reasons for the difficulties to distinguish between problems caused by the past and present generated disturbances. In addition to the granted governmental credits and subsidies to the enterprise sector, commercial banks often give new loans to companies which are often even unable to service existing credits. However, the separation of different reasons responsible for the existence and persistence of bad debt, seems to be necessary for analyzing stock and flow problems of this phenomenon.

Due to the lack of information, full clarity about the real structure and magnitude of the bad loan problem is clouded. Although there is a lack of precise data regarding the bad loan problem, it is clear that its magnitude differs widely from country to country. Because of the considerable varied situations evident in each transitorial economy, divergent strategies must be addressed to solve the problem. A few indicators might be of primary importance, as e.g. the ratio of bad loan to banks' loan portfolio and the ratio of the cumulated bad loans in the banking sector to the GDP. But low quality of the data base could counteract the development of adequate strategies. As van Brabant points out, a "one-for-all strategy" for all these economies is not available and even appears to be ineffective. Although the micro- and macro-economic dimension of the bad debt problem varies, the results of the yet implemented restructuring programs can be taken into consideration before creating an own strategy.

For instance, the Polish experience shows us that even if there is a high burden of non-performing loans on the balance sheets of the banks, an effort could be made by a relatively small involvement from the state budget. In this particular case, a decentralized strategy was preferred, which tried to simultaneously tackle the restructuring of the banking sector and the restructuring of the enterprise sphere. As a consequence of the program, the state-owned companies were forced to calculate under a hard budget constraint. The combination of remarkable success and small cost could make the implemented program attractive for other economies in transition. Therefore, the peculiarity of the Polish program, as well as the characteristics of its starting point, has to be taken into consideration. One can argue that the Polish case was possible because of the low level of monetization in the Polish economy, which brought with it a specific low ratio of credits to the GDP and, as a consequence, a particular small ratio of bad loans to GDP.

However, if the result and the costs are dependent upon initial conditions and the chosen strategy, there is nothing to substantiate the thesis that the restructuring costs will gradually be lowered. This is not only because, as time goes on, it would be more and more laborious to identify granted loans as being good or bad. Additionally, enhanced gradually, incentives are offered for a close cooperation between banks and state-owned companies which bring themselves into a good financial position before privatization. This could take place by over-rolling an unacceptable share of their non-performing loans to the governmental sector. Therefore, it is important to abandon these encumbrances as soon as possible and to implement a so called "shock therapy" for the financial sector as well as for the state-owned companies. This would not only facilitate avoiding the explosion of the long-term social costs of the transformation but it would also help bring the banking sector as well as the state-owned companies rapidly into a position of self-determination and self-responsibility.

Closing, I would like to emphasize that certain dangers exist in a universal banking system of economies in transition. However, there are widely accepted advantages of universal banking: the special owner structure, the lack of experience with financial intermediation and the rudimentary developed institutional framework lead to a higher risk, which could increase inefficient lending. Consequently, universal banking is more likely to intensify existing problems than help to overcome them in most of these economies in transition.

11 Evolution and emergence of markets in a developing post-socialist economy: the case of Kyrgyzstan

John Garland

1. Introduction

In terms of generally accepted measures of economic development, the five Central Asian republics[1] of the former Soviet Union (FSU) lag far behind the other ten former Soviet republics. Indeed, some historians have described the Soviet-Central Asian relationship in terms of colonialism and dependency theory, traditionally used to explain capitalist exploitation of less developed countries (see for example Gleason, 1991). In any event, these countries' economic performance has long relied primarily on extractive industries, agriculture, and Soviet subsidies.

None of the Central Asian republics actively sought independence. Instead, it was more or less thrust upon them by events beyond their control, and perhaps prematurely. Their national borders, arbitrarily determined by Stalin, do not well reflect strong national heritages. Rather, the governments are dominated by shifting patchworks of tribes, kingdoms, and clans, which frequently overlap national borders, and to whom many citizens still see their first loyalty (Tett, 1994). Two countries, however, Kyrgyzstan and Kazakhstan, stand out from the others in their tolerant (sufi) rather than fundamentalist Islam, and in their progress made along the road to a market economy. This paper addresses the case of Kyrgyzstan.

2. Adverse circumstances upon gaining independence

As one of the poorest former Soviet republics, Kyrgyzstan accounted for less than one percent of Soviet GNP. When Kyrgyzstan gained its independence in Autumn of 1991, however, the country faced additional adverse circumstances (IMF, 1993a, 322-324). The country was over-specialized and heavily dependent on trade with the FSU, and the collapse of trading relationships resulted in a loss of markets for Kyrgyz outputs as well as a loss of imported raw materials, intermediate goods and components. Union budgetary transfers, which had amounted to approximately 10 percent of GDP, were discontinued,[2] as was additional direct financing for enterprises from their affiliate

---

1 Kyrgyzstan, Kazakhstan, Tajikistan, Turkmenistan and Uzbekistan.

2 Most of the factors apply to virtually all of the FSU outside of Russia, but Kyrgyzstan's greater specialization and dependence makes its circumstances particularly damaging. However, note that, outside

organizations elsewhere in the FSU. There was a sharp deterioration of terms of trade, especially in view of Kyrgyzstan's high dependence on imported oil and gas (whose suppliers began a gradual move to market-based pricing). The collapse of the centrally planned regime had occurred so quickly that no market-based institutions were in place to fill the vacuum. Moreover, natural disasters (earthquakes and mud slides) took heavy tolls. Russians, who comprised over 20 percent of the population of 4½ million, began leaving the country on a scale of about 90 000 per year; they were concentrated in urban areas and in the more advanced administrative and industrial sectors, so that their functional importance was greater than that reflected merely by their demographic weight (Barylski, 1994, 389-416). Finally, I am reminded of the alleged words of a Ukrainian politician several years ago: "Why do we have to be independent? We didn't do anything wrong!" A similar attitude, perhaps fear of the unknown, seems widespread among the populace in Kyrgyzstan regarding the transition to the market,[3] in spite of the fact that the pro-reform President is extremely popular (especially for Central Asian standards). These problems have been partially (or perhaps "marginally") alleviated by Western assistance. In May 1993 Kyrgyzstan became the first recipient of the IMF's new Systemic Transformation Facility, and Kyrgyzstan so far has received more financial aid on a *per capita* basis from the West than any other FSU republic. This surely reflects the West's assessment of the Kyrgyz commitment to both democratization and marketization, compared to its perception of commitments elsewhere in the FSU.

3. Macroeconomic stabilization

Because macroeconomic stabilization is crucially important to the success of the transition process, let us note Kyrgyzstan's situation in this regard before considering more specific elements of the country's marketization. In May 1993 Kyrgyzstan left the rouble zone in order to pursue an independent monetary policy and reasonable macroeconomic stabilization, the latter including a reduction in the fiscal deficit (mainly by limiting both transfers and lending to state enterprises), a sharp tightening of monetary policy, and price liberalization. There were early difficulties in keeping this program on track (IMF, 1993b, 353 ff.) but the Figure below suggests a reasonably successful effort.

Real GDP fell by 19 percent in 1992 and 16 percent in 1993, with inflation at 855 percent and 600 percent for the two years, respectively. But the worst seems clearly to have passed, and in late 1994 inflation, at only 1.7 percent per month, was the lowest in the FSU (cf. Figure 11.1), and the new currency, the Som, the most stable currency (at

---

the FSU, Mongolia's position was perhaps much worse. Mongolia has proceeded more rapidly with successful reform, after former Soviet assistance was reduced in 1991 from an amount equal to 53 percent of its GDP (1989) to only seven percent. See Boone (1994, 330).

3 During my visit to Kyrgyzstan during May-June 1994, while discussing foreign trade relations, a Kyrgyz economist told me, out of frustration, "We don't have any comparative advantage! We don't do anything well!" While most economists would immediately object that all countries, by definition, must have some comparative advantage, the statement reflects a psychological phenomenon found in many of the less developed countries.

10.7 to the dollar) (Lloyd, 1994, 4). This of course substantially enhances the prospects for further (and necessary) structural reforms.

Figure 11.1   Consumer prices percent increase on previous month

Note: * 4.9 percent in June 1994.
Source: United Nations.

The comprehensive medium-term program for 1994-97 (in agreement with the IMF, which in September 1994 approved a three year "enhanced structural adjustment facility" of $ 104 million) aims at creating a non-inflationary environment conducive to the restoration of economic growth. Objectives for 1997 include five percent output growth (from minus five percent in 1994); a reduction of inflation to 6.5 percent annually; reducing current account deficits to about nine percent of GDP; and raising gross international reserves to 2.1 months of imports (IMF, 1994b, 273-274).

The earlier (May 1993) systemic transformation facility had provided for sharp reductions in the budget deficit (from 15 to 7 percent of GDP in 1993) and in the growth of broad money and domestic credit. Several measures taken instantly by the Kyrgyz government had been the elimination of most exemptions to the VAT system and the minimization of exemptions to the personal income and profits taxes. Moreover, the program envisaged no central bank financing of the fiscal deficit, that being funded instead and entirely by external financial inflows.

The figures are of course rough approximates. Statistical reliability suffers from the increased reliance on barter, the underrecording of private production, substantial corrective price adjustments, and the fact that only 27 percent of cash roubles were exchanged for Som when the new currency was introduced (causing recorded reserve money and broad money to plunge). However, price stabilization measures are surely taking hold, and there is a welcome and growing reliance on auctions to allocate foreign exchange and refinance credit among banks (IMF, 1994c).

At the same time, the World Bank has strongly argued that

- further revenue enhancing measures should include:
  - reinstating excise taxes of fuels,
  - increasing taxes on tobacco and alcohol,
  - raising user fees for services (e.g., transportation, telecommunications, irrigation) to cover the economic costs of these services, and
  - increasing rents to cover at least the operating and maintenance costs of housing; and
- expenditure cuts should include:
  - phasing out transfers to nonviable enterprises,
  - limiting public sector wage increases,
  - reducing consumer subsidies on items still subject to price controls,
  - passing on fully to industry and consumers the increases in imported energy prices, but
  - protecting expenditures on critical social services (World Bank, 1993).

The World Bank also encourages the promotion of exports and the revitalization of interrepublic trade, which we cover below.

4.   Monetary policy and the banking sector

In May 1993, Kyrgyzstan became the first FSU republic outside the Baltics to introduce its own currency, the Som. Until then the IMF had generally opposed the introduction of new currencies in the FSU, on the grounds that a) macroeconomic stability and structural reforms had not yet been sufficiently achieved, and b) the introduction of new currencies would probably lead to even further collapse of interrepublic trade (see for example, IMF, 1992a, 41-42). However, the collapse of the rouble zone in 1992 and Russia's lack of monetary discipline led the IMF to reconsider the issue (IMF, 1992c, 363).

Moreover, Kyrgyzstan has maintained a liberal exchange regime for both current and capital accounts transactions. Current account convertibility is essential for exposing domestic producers to foreign competition and for correcting price distortions, both of which stimulate efficiency regarding production and allocational decisions. This is particularly important in Kyrgyzstan, where the domestic market is clearly too thin to support numerous producers in the same sectors. There are generally four preconditions for the successful introduction of convertibility (see Greene and Isard, 1991):

- An appropriate exchange rate (i.e., one that is broadly consistent with equilibrium in the balance of payments);
- Adequate international liquidity (to avoid large swings in exchange rates or interest rates resulting from short-term fluctuations in the price of volume of tradeables);

- Sound macroeconomic policies (to prevent, among other things, speculative pressures); and
- Proper incentives and ability of enterprises and households to respond to market prices (without which, markets will not function properly).

Kyrgyzstan has performed very well on the first three of these, the adequate liquidity being provided by IMF funds specifically targeted for the purpose.

Kyrgyzstan opted for floating rather than fixed exchange rates, under IMF advice. Some argue that fixed rates would have been more appropriate, primarily because they facilitate a more rapid price stabilization. However, fixed rates require substantial reserves (which none of the FSU republics has) and the coordination of fiscal and monetary policies among FSU republics (which has been politically impossible) (Gomulka, 1994, 95). These problems are exacerbated by the still unclear trading arrangements among members of the Commonwealth of Independent States (CIS), and by the continuing terms of trade shock associated with the gradual increase of energy prices to world market levels. In any event, a rouble zone currency union type of arrangement requires certain conditions which do not apply in the Kyrgyz case, namely high labor and capital mobility, diversified industrial structures, nominal wage and price flexibility, and similar abilities to respond to external shocks (IMF 1992b, 321ff.). Kyrgyzstan passed a Central Bank Law in December of 1992, which gave the Bank increased independence and authority to supervise financial institutions, license commercial banks, oversee the functioning of the payments system, and conduct monetary policy. A well-functioning market economy requires especially a relatively efficient payments system, which in turn requires, among other things:

- that the market be open (including a clear divorce between lender and borrower, so that borrowers are not able to corner the market);
- that full information is available (so lenders are able to judge the credit-worthiness of individual borrowers); and
- that borrowers must repay or face the full consequences of not repaying (Bruno, 1993, 5-19).

None of these conditions holds in the case of Kyrgyzstan. First, the commercial banks are typically owned by the enterprises who are their major customers, and as high as 90 percent of individual banks' loans go to these shareholders (World Bank, op. cit., xix). This is an area that needs urgent attention, for it contributes to the softening of budget constraints for state enterprises while making access to funds more difficult for non-shareholders. Second, both inexperience in assessing credit worthiness and generally chaotic conditions distort the usefulness of the limited information that is available. Third, the legacy of nonperforming loans in the portfolios of commercial banks seems to defy solution, especially given inexperience with, and great reluctance to use, genuine bankruptcy proceedings.

The proposed Kyrgyz solution to this last problem (of nonperforming loans) apparently aims at having the government create a liquidation or restructuring agency to which the management of a limited number of the most distressed enterprises is transferred. These enterprises would be effectively isolated from the banking system, restructured, downsized, and perhaps even liquidated. This approach would lend credibility to the government's efforts to impose hard budget constraints on enterprises, but the selection of distressed enterprises would be extremely difficult. Irrespective of the method chosen, "reducing the share of nonperforming loans to an acceptable level will be a process, rather than an event, given the difficulty of corporate restructuring, the costs of recapitalization, and the dependence on sustained economic recovery". (Dhar and Selowsky, 1994, 44-47)

Closely associated with banks' nonperforming loans is the problem of inter-enterprise debt. The problem has been noticed also in Eastern Europe, but it is in the states of the FSU, Kyrgyzstan included, that the problem has reached alarming proportions. What distinguishes the much worse situation in the FSU are technical and macroeconomic phenomena, which include: the breakdown of payments mechanisms (especially for interrepublic payments); the inconvertibility of non-cash roubles into cash; the near hyperinflationary environment; and, perhaps most importantly, the lack of credibility of the stabilization programs (Rostowski, 1993, 131-159).

Inter-enterprise credit is a rational response at the enterprise level to the many major shocks in recent years - e.g., the collapse of regional trade, the downward shift in domestic demand due to the reduction of government purchases and to price liberalization, input dislocation making it impossible for purchasers to complete and sell their own output, etc. But it circumvents restrictive monetary policy and thus makes macro-economic stabilization more problematic, and it is a way of avoiding necessary but unpleasant corporate restructuring, including the downsizing of the labor force. Among the consequences are self-fulfilling inflationary pressures, systemic risk due to the creation of an interlocking network of enterprise commitments, and the redistribution of liquidity from sound to potentially unsound enterprises (ibid). Indeed, the inter-enterprise debt problem had become such a problem in Russia by mid-1994 that it had the potential of paralyzing the economy, and had become the government's top political concern (Freeland, 1994a, 2).

5.   Trade within the commonwealth of independent states

The Soviet Union ceased to exist on January 1, 1992. The former Soviet republics (except Georgia and the Baltic states of Estonia, Latvia and Lithuania) subsequently established the Commonwealth of Independent States (CIS) to harmonize economic policies among its membership (and to provide the West with some assurance that the former USSR's formidable nuclear arsenal was under effective joint control). The CIS is not a state or confederation, but rather a voluntary community of fully sovereign states bound together by the high level of regional specialization and inter-dependence resulting from their previously united and centrally planned economic system. To date, the CIS has been fully ineffective in coordinating its members' economic policies.

First, we should note that it is terribly difficult to quantify interrepublic trade. We are all familiar with the earlier difficulties associated with unreliable and incomplete data, secrecy, the omission of services transactions data, budgetary rather than actual balance of payments flows, etc. These problems were exacerbated during the Gorbachev era (in spite of Glasnost) through the steady erosion of all-union authority and the deterioration of state enterprise discipline in reporting transactions. The collapse of the FSU into 15 independent states poses a great need for completely new information at the same time that institutional responsibilities for statistical compilation changed. Meanwhile, enterprises intentionally underreport transactions in order to avoid both domestic taxation and the obligatory foreign exchange repatriation and surrender. There is confusion associated with the introduction of new currencies, as well as with the decentralization of foreign exchange transactions in the commercial banking systems. Many of the (growing) barter transactions go falsely or not at all reported, and this is confounded also by the breakdown of bilateral payments arrangements. In some cases, clearly including that of Kyrgyzstan, often customs border controls simply do not exist.[4]

However difficult it is to quantify CIS trade flows, it is clear that Kyrgyzstan (and all other CIS members) has suffered a severe drop of trade with other republics of the FSU. Observers of the former centrally planned trade regimes are very well familiar with the autarkic and trade-inhibiting tendencies within the former CMEA. For the newly independent republics of the FSU, however, precisely the opposite problem arises. Overspecialization among these republics created an unusually high dependence on other Union republics for both input and output markets. Thus, Kyrgyzstan's interrepublican trade (exports and imports) as a percent of GNP was approximately 80 percent in 1989 (compared to Britain's 22 percent or Germany's 27 percent trade within the European Community as a percent of GNP) (Economist, 1992, 84).

To be sure, the decline of interrepublican trade is partly a very beneficial consequence of natural adjustment to the previously abnormally high dependence on trade with the FSU, which was based on bureaucratic and political preferences as much as on mainly economic considerations. However, the drop in trade levels has contributed substantially to the disruption of production and decline in national income for Kyrgyzstan.

It has been reported that in October of 1994, most Kyrgyz enterprises were working at only 25 percent capacity (Economist, 1994, 38-40), and one major reason for this has been the effective end of central planning, which has disrupted both the supply of, and demand for, exportables (see Michalopoulos, 1993). Kyrgyzstan's economy lacks sufficient diversification to adjust rapidly to the fundamental changes being undertaken. Her huge Frunze agricultural machinery plant, for example, made one type of machinery for the FSU, but has now all but stopped production. The equipment is no longer in demand, and at any rate the necessary imports of steel for the machinery are no longer available (Lloyd, 1993, 2).

Other factors include the slowness of market institutions to fill the void left by the collapse of central planning, the sharp fall in income that has reduced Kyrgyzstan's demand for imports, the adverse terms of trade resulting from the FSU's progressive movement toward world prices (however beneficial this will be in the long run, since it is essential for improving resource allocation), and the altogether serious payments problems among republics of the FSU. The payments problems (associated with the use of a highly inflationary rouble, bureaucratic delays in interrepublic settlements, the earlier ability of each central bank to issue rouble credits, and the increasing autonomy of the separate

---

4 A good discussion of these problems may be found in Christensen (1994).

republics) led every FSU republic to impose export controls, in order to minimize the exchange of real goods for relatively worthless roubles. In any event, the breaking off of regional trade flows of supplies had devastating effects. The lack of alternative suppliers or purchasers, enterprises too heavily and irrationally concentrated (both geographically and technologically), and the commensurate lack of small and medium-sized enterprises capable of responding to the changed economic conditions, exacerbated the already chronic under-utilization of enterprise capacities (Benini, 1991, 33-50).

During early 1992, an extensive network of intergovernmental bilateral trade agreements led to the categorization of three types of trade. "Obligatory" trade entailed the intergovernmental barter of 100-150 of the most important energy and raw material products; governments were committed to fulfill these contracts (but not enterprises), and maximum allowable prices were typically specified. "Indicative" trade involved slightly over a thousand products, such as machinery, agricultural goods, and consumer products; here states would agree to provide licenses for enterprise contracts up to the quota amounts specified, but no trade would take place unless individual enterprises agreed on price, credit, and other terms. All remaining products, in the third category, could be freely traded among enterprises, but in fact little is traded free of restraints (Michalopoulos and Tarr, 1993, 22-25). In fact, a large proportion of the agreements even on obligatory trade have simply not been implemented, and the level of protectionism (mainly through export controls) has increased steadily.

Virtually every month, or so it seems, new trade agreements are reached (but with no implementation mechanism) among FSU groupings. In January 1994, for example, Kyrgyzstan, Kazakhstan and Uzbekistan agreed to form an economic union. The move was apparently motivated by the common desire to reduce dependence on Russia. It might have been mostly political posturing, however, given Russia's increasingly vocal demands for part of the wealth generated by oil and natural gas deposits in the area (as well as Russian demands for dual nationality for Russians living in the area). The proposed economic union would coordinate economic, monetary and labor policies among the three members, as well as abolish customs procedures and tariffs (LeVine, 1994, 4).

More recently, in October 1994, the 12 CIS members agreed to form a supranational economic committee in the hopes of eventually forming a payments union as well as a customs union. Here again, however, many of the smaller states express strong reservations about the agreement, and retain the right to opt out of CIS accords (Freeland, 1994b, 2). Some Western consultants have also proposed a payments union akin to the EPU following World War II. However, none of the potentially surplus countries seems interested in extending the inevitable credits, and to date there is little evidence that the countries can muster the political will to stabilize their currencies sufficiently.

Trade liberalization is important to both macroeconomic stabilization and structural transformation, and in Kyrgyzstan's case this will entail especially the elimination of export controls and the gradual change of state trading agencies. A gradual change is recommended (by the World Bank, 1993) because of the need to ensure adequate trade flows in the interim, although compulsory state orders at government mandated prices should clearly be replaced (rather soon) by market-based transactions. Furthermore, the Bank recommends that Kyrgyzstan should take efforts to make the profitability of hard-currency exports as great as for rouble exports (at least until recently, both the surrender requirements and the applied exchange rates have been prohibitively punitive). Besides eliminating price controls, it is especially important to phase out quantitative export restrictions, state trading, and import subsidies. It should thus be only a medium-term goal for Kyrgyzstan to become integrated into the multilateral trade system, at which time there could be established a firm link between domestic and world prices (IMF, 1994a, 56-59).

6. Structural adjustments

Brezinski and Fritsch note in this volume that entries and exits are main characteristics of a functioning market (Brezinski and Fritsch, 1997), and in the case of Kyrgyzstan, there remain substantial barriers to both. Privatization began in early 1992, with initial rapid progress in the consumer services and retail trade sectors. Late in 1992, the government removed barriers to the entry of private firms into agricultural production, marketing, transportation, and external trade. However, the May 1993 constitution did not allow private ownership of agricultural land (although long-term leases providing for inheritance rights were introduced for agricultural land), and the state order system was not dismantled. The principle of privatization, however, has been clearly accepted, and by mid-1994 approximately 30 percent of GDP was accounted for by the private sector (A. Robinson, 1994, 15).

The privatization program was introduced in December of 1991, and in July 1992 the State Property Fund was established to manage it. The first phase of the program involved privatization of small-scale retail and service enterprises, and by the end of 1993, 35 percent of the assets of these had been sold (some say "given away") to workers' collectives, enterprise directors and other "insiders". The transfer instrument (SMP, or Special Means of Payment, which could be - and was widely - used also to buy housing) was not widely used by the general public because it was non-transferable, required highly complicated exchange procedures and was thus not well understood, and allowed only for the purchase of shares in one's own enterprise.

A new program was introduced in January of 1994, based on 500 "points" rather than currency, and a mass privatization program beginning in mid-1994 will continue through 1996 (J.R. Robinson, 1994, 1ff.). This second phase targets 600 enterprises for privatization, 25 percent of each being sold for coupons in bi-weekly auctions. The number of shares received by each coupon bidder depends upon the number of bidders and number of coupon points bid. (If only one person "coupon bids" for an enterprise, he receives all the shares offered for coupons, i.e., 25 percent of the enterprise; if ten coupon bids are made, each with an equal number of points, each bidder receives shares representing 2½ percent ownership.) By September 1994, 15 auctions of regional enterprises for coupons and three republic-wide auctions of national enterprises for coupons had been held for 108 enterprises. After each coupon auction, cash auctions are to be held for the balance of the state's shareholding in each enterprise; to date, nine such cash auctions have resulted in full privatization of 68 enterprises. No other country in Central Asia has initiated such a radical and rapid privatization effort.

However, there are still serious barriers to enterprise restructuring. In May 1994 the Kyrgyz government established the Enterprise Reform and Resolution Agency (ERRA), which is to oversee the restructuring and perhaps liquidation of up to 30 large state-owned enterprises which are in serious financial difficulty (U.S.-Kyrgyz Business Report, 1994a, 1ff.). The restructuring is needed not only to respond to relative price adjustments, but also to correct the distortions resulting from priorities established earlier to suit the needs of the FSU - machine building had been over-emphasized, for example, whereas mining and metallurgy had been neglected. An associated factor of high relevance is that 70 percent of Kyrgyz industrial output came from FSU controlled industries, many of them related to military defense purposes; here the need for radical restructuring is quite obvious.

A number of factors are slowing the restructuring process. There still prevails a lack of "real" owners as advocates for capital, due to the de facto takeovers by managers, workers, ministries and concerns - all competing for control, but none with ultimate responsibility. The ownership of banks by the enterprises who are their major clients undermines serious efforts to introduce hard budget constraints. There is seldom sufficient technical, managerial and financial capacity for the necessary restructuring. Moreover, the transfer of state assets to workers' collectives, which often own up to 70 percent of the shares of their enterprises, retards restructuring due to the reluctance to shed labor when necessary (World Bank, 1993, 77). There is also clearly too much vertical integration, and thus a severe lack of competitive sourcing and distribution networks to provide materials, supplies, capital, marketing and sales.

Yet much "unplanned" restructuring is occurring. In the first half of 1994, industrial production fell by 31.8 percent, and production in the engineering and metal-working industry by 61 percent, compared to the first half of 1993. The production of large electric machines, spare parts for motor cars, personal computers and non-related wire stopped completely, and coal output dropped by 53 percent (U.S.-Kyrgyz Business Report, 1994b, 3).

The government has made relatively good progress in price liberalization, but here again numerous factors have inhibited adjustment at the enterprise level to the changing prices. The industrial structure is highly concentrated. There are restrictions on labor mobility, for example through housing constraints and through local work permit requirements. There are clearly remaining deficiencies in the legal framework and financial mediation, as well as general skepticism regarding the privatization program itself. Until these problems are resolved, the full impact of price liberalization, which is critically important for the appropriate allocation of resources, will not be realized.

Finally, compared to other states in Central and Eastern Europe and in the FSU, Kyrgyzstan's progress in agricultural reform has been judged "limited" in land reform, privatization, and trade liberalization, and "insignificant" in regard to price reform. The few state and collective farms that have reorganized themselves are said, for all practical purposes, to remain state and collective farms that are highly inefficient (Bosch-Lenoir, 1993, 489-502).

7. What might one conclude?

Markets for both inputs from, and outputs to, the other republics of the FSU have collapsed, which has especially dire consequences for any country so heavily dependent on them as Kyrgyzstan. The interrepublic payments mechanisms have also collapsed, causing a surge of inter-enterprise arrears and a widespread resort to barter. Union budgetary transfers to Kyrgyzstan have ceased, and the country additionally faces increasingly adverse terms of trade. These developments have contributed substantially to a fall in production and in national income. They are also developments largely beyond Kyrgyz control.

What Kyrgyzstan *can* control, however, is its own macroeconomic policies and structural adjustments at the enterprise level. Generally (and in sharp contrast to many of the other FSU republics), the Kyrgyz government's macroeconomic policies seem to be well-designed, correctly targeted, yet somewhat insufficient. Firmer action is especially needed in regard to the capital and labor markets. On the other hand, it appears as if clearly insufficient structural adjustment has been noticeable at the enterprise level, and it is here that the very slow emergence of market-based infrastructure and institutions constrains the transition process.

To be sure, the costs of fundamental transformation are always immediate, while the positive consequences are felt only in the medium and long runs. The J-curve effect is already apparent in Eastern and Central Europe. For Kyrgyzstan, some predict instead an L-curve - that is, a drastic drop in output and income that will be possibly permanent. Here, "the danger is not of the 'creative destruction' envisaged by Schumpeter, but just of destruction, de-industrialization, with nothing creative taking place." (Nove, 1994, 863-869)

Granted, the market economy will emerge much, much more slowly in Kyrgyzstan than in Eastern and Central Europe, with its rich entrepreneurial, pre-war capitalist, and technological traditions. Some, therefore, suggest that the Kyrgyz leadership not move too quickly to dismantle the structures of the command economy.

I demur.

Some in Kyrgyzstan, as in all the transition economies, insist on a return to the old system to address the altogether serious problems that the country faces. However, those problems are unequivocally the result of shortcomings of the old system itself. They are not, and cannot be, a result of the new, "market-based" system, because this new system is simply not yet in place.

References

Barylski, Robert V. (1994); The Russian Federation and Eurasia's Islamic Crescent; *Europe-Asia Studies*, 46, 3, 389-416.

Benini, Roberta (1991); The Soviet Union After the Failure of Five Years of Economic Reforms: Towards A New State of Transition; *MOCT-MOST*, 2, 33-50.

Boone, Peter (1994); Grassroots Economic Reform in Mongolia; *Journal of Comparative Economics*, 18, June, 329-356.

Bosch-Lenoir, Anne (1993); Round Table on Agriculture; *Economics of Transition*, I, 4, December, 489-502.

Brezinski, Horst and Michael Fritsch (1997) *Spot-Markets, Hierarchies, Networks, and the Problem of Economic Transition*, in this volume.

Bruno, Michael (1993); Stabilization and the Macroeconomics of Transition - How Different is Eastern Europe?; *Economics of Transition*, I, 1, January, 1993, 5-19.

Christensen, Benedicte Vibe (1994) *The Russian Federation in Transition: External Developments*, Washington, D.C.: IMF, February.

Dhar, Sanjay and Marcelo Selowsky (1994); Dealing With the Bad Debt Problem in Transition Economies; *Finance and Development*, June, 44-47.

The Economist (1992) *Of Dollars and Roubles*, 1 February, 84.

The Economist (1994) *The Reliable Referendum*, 29 October, 38-40.

Freeland, Chrystia (1994a); Russian Debt Plan for Promissory Notes; *Financial Times*, 25 August, 2.

Freeland, Chrystia (1994b); CIS States Inch Towards Integration; *Financial Times*, October 22-23, 2.

Gleason, Gregory (1991); The Political Economy of Dependency under Socialism: The Asian Republics in the USSR; *Studies in Comparative Communism*, XXIV, 4, December, 335-353.

Gomulka, Stanislaw (1994); Economic and Political Constraints During Transition; *Europe-Asia Studies*, 46, 89-106.

Greene, Joshua and Peter Isard (1991) Currency Convertibility and the Transformation of Centrally Planned Economies, IMF Occasional Paper # 81, Washington, D.C.

IMF (International Monetary Fund) (1992a) *World Economic Outlook*, Washington, D.C.: International Monetary Fund, 41-42.

IMF (International Monetary Fund) (1992b); IMF Study Explores Major Issues Related to the International Monetary System; *IMF Survey*, 26 October, 321ff.

IMF (International Monetary Fund) (1992c); New Currencies Need the Support; *IMF Survey*, 26 October, 363.

IMF (International Monetary Fund) (1993a); Kyrgyz Republic: Further Structural Reforms Are Vital To Macro-economic Stability; *IMF Survey*, 25 October, 322-324.

IMF (International Monetary Fund) (1993b); New Currencies Need the Support of Sound Policies; *IMF Survey*, 29 November, 353ff.

IMF (International Monetary Fund) (1994a); From Central Plan to World Market; *IMF Survey*, 21 Febuary, 56-59.

IMF (International Monetary Fund) (1994b); Kyrgyz Republic: ESAF; *IMF Survey*, 12 September, 273-274.

IMF (International Monetary Fund) (1994c) *Annual Report*, Washington D.C.: International Monetary Fund.

LeVine, Steve (1994); Central Asians Cut Loose From Moscow; *Financial Times*, 27 January, 4.

Lloyd, John (1993); IMF Watches as Kyrgyzstan Fights the Battle of the Som; *Financial Times*, 21 May, 2.

Lloyd, John (1994); Kyrgyz Fear Their Tiny Nation Will Fall Into Iron Hands; *Financial Times*, 16 September, 4.

Michalopoulos, Constantine (1993); Trade Issues in the New Independent States, *Studies of Economies in Transformation*, Washington, D.C.: World Bank.

Michalopoulos, Constantine and David Tarr (1993); Energizing Trade of the States of the Former USSR; *Finance and Development*, March, 22-25.

Nove, Alec (1994); A Gap in Transition Models? A Comment on Gomulka; *Europe-Asia Studies*, 46, 5, 863-869.

Robinson, Anthony (1994); Painful Rebirth From The Ashes; *Financial Times*, 11 November, 15.

Robinson, John R. (1994); Kyrgyzstan: Role Model for Privatization in Central Asia; CIS, *U.S.-Kyrgzy Business Report*, September, 1ff.

Rostowski, Jacek (1993); The Inter-enterprise Debt Explosion in the Former Soviet Union: Causes, Consequences, Cures; *Communist Economies and Economic Transformation*, 5 (2), 131-159.

Tett, Gillian (1994); Elegant Exorcism of Central Bogeymen; *Financial Times*, 29 July, 10. (Book review of Ahmed Rashid's The Resurgence of Central Asia.)

U.S.-Kyrgyz Business Report (1994a) *World Bank Grants $ 95 million Credit*, September, 1ff.

U.S.-Kyrgyz Business Report (1994b) *Latest Facts on Kyrgyz Economy*, January, June, September, 3.

World Bank (1993) *Kyrgyzstan: The Transition to a Market Economy*, Washington, D.C.

12 Recent developments in international currency derivatives

Lucjan T. Orlowski

1. Introduction

The floating exchange rate system that prevails today among key international currencies of industrial countries brings a considerable degree of uncertainty into exchange rate movements. In order to hedge the risk of unfavorable appreciation or depreciation of a single currency, exporters, importers and financial investors have developed a vast range of currency derivative instruments that allow advance locking-in the rates of a future currency conversion. These financial instruments are also used by speculators willing to arrange future currency selling (or buying) contracts while hoping to buy (or to sell) the currency at favorable anticipated exchange rates in the future, thus exposing their financial position to the risk of currency fluctuations.

This paper examines the critical problems of international currency derivatives that have emerged in international financial markets over the past two years, emphasizing the departures of spot exchange rate movements from the macroeconomic fundamentals among the "triad" currencies: the U.S. Dollar (USD), the German Mark (DM), and the Japanese Yen (YE). The macroeconomic variables that theoretically play a predominant role in the exchange rate movements are: differences in comparable market interest rates among the countries (interest rate differentials), differences in the rate of growth of real GDP (income differentials), and differences in the rates of inflation (inflation differentials). The changeable sensitivity of exchange rates to these key variables is tested in this paper for the "triad" currencies in two periods: 1991-1993, and 1994-1995. In the latter period, some considerable misalignments between forward rates and changes in spot exchange rates are observed. This is contrary to the historical evidence of the validity of the so-called "unbiased forward rate hypothesis" claiming that forward rates are the best predictor of adjustments of spot rates. It is argued that the recently observed failure of the relationship between forward rates and lagged spot rates has contributed to significant losses of investors and speculators in international currency derivative markets.

The examination of these relationships and the recent empirical developments provides useful lessons for the transition economies of Central and Eastern Europe in their attempts to construct viable modern financial markets. This study limits the scope of recommendations for developing financial markets to the conditions of Poland. It assumes that currency-based derivative transactions may play a pivotal role in reducing systemic risk of external trade and financial contracts in the Polish economy presently undergoing considerable structural adjustments aimed at promoting export and net capital inflows. It further argues that an introduction of financial derivatives in Poland shall be

194

preceded by a construction of sound underlying security markets. A stable currency accompanied by low inflation are necessary prerequisites for a successful functioning of currency-based derivatives.

Currency-based derivatives are complex financial instruments that are "derived" from the underlying currency exchange rates. They include currency forward "buying" or "selling" contracts, "buy" or "sell" currency futures, call and put options, currency swaps, and various combinations of these instruments. Their growth in the international economy has been enormous in recent years. The total notional value of the currency-based derivatives in 1994 exceeded 12 trillion USD (Goldstein and Folkerts-Landau, 1994, 10) up from 7.8 trillion in 1993, which itself was more than twelve times the total in 1986 (Mussa et al., 1994, 14). One may notice that the current notional value of the currency derivatives in 1994 was roughly twice the size of the United States GDP.

Despite the enormous growth of the currency-based derivatives their market was by no means "efficient" in 1994. Forward rates and strike prices of most currency futures and options contracts departed considerably from the actual changes in spot exchange rates. The reasons for these departures and recommendations for preventive actions are discussed in Section 3 of the paper following the brief overview of the currency-based derivative instruments in Section 2. Section 4 summarizes the examination of the currency-based derivative markets by drawing concluding lessons for the construction of the efficient entry of the transforming economy of Poland into modern international financial markets.

2. Currency-based derivatives: a brief overview

As indicated above, currency-based derivatives are defined as complex financial instruments that are "derived" from the underlying exchange rates. As any financial derivative products, they can be used for risk hedging or speculation when the underlying security (the exchange rate) exhibits a high degree of fluctuations, thus generating a considerable financial risk. Therefore, the currency-based derivatives are not applicable in the system of fixed exchange rates. They play a significant role as hedging or speculative instruments under the system of floating exchange rates, especially when the currency spot rate demonstrates high volatility[1].

Currency-based derivatives are used by exporters invoicing receivables in foreign currency, willing to protect their earnings from the foreign currency depreciation by locking the currency conversion rate at a high level. Their use by importers hedging foreign currency payables is effective when the payment currency is expected to appreciate and the importers would like to guarantee a lower conversion rate. Investors in foreign currency denominated securities would like to secure strong foreign earnings by obtaining the right to sell foreign currency at a high conversion rate, thus defending

---

[1] The empirical literature proves that volatility among the leading international currencies has been increasing since the inception of the floating exchange rate system in 1973. See Mussa et al. (1994, 18 - 22) for a detailed examination of this phenomenon.

their revenue from the foreign currency depreciation. Multinational companies use currency derivatives being engaged in direct investment overseas. They want to guarantee the rate of purchasing foreign currency for various payments related to the installation of a foreign branch or subsidiary, or to a joint venture with a foreign partner.

A high degree of volatility of exchange rates creates a fertile ground for foreign exchange speculators. Their objective is to guarantee a high selling rate of a foreign currency by obtaining a derivative contract while hoping to buy the currency at a low rate in the future. Alternatively, they may wish to obtain a foreign currency forward buying contract, expecting to sell the appreciating currency at a high future rate. In either case, they are exposed to the risk of currency fluctuations in the future betting on the pattern of the spot exchange rate adjustment consistent with their initial expectations. Speculative actions may have a stabilizing character on exchange rates when the observed trend of the exchange rate is expected to be reversed. Specifically, when the foreign currency has been depreciating in domestic currency terms but it is expected to appreciate in the foreseeable future, speculators will aggressively buy it, thus contributing to the currency advanced appreciation. Adversely, when the foreign currency has been appreciating but it is expected to depreciate, speculative selling may speed up its depreciation or stabilize the currency rate. By contrast, foreign exchange speculators destabilize exchange rates when their recently observed pattern is expected to continue. Expecting a further depreciation of the foreign currency, they normally sell it, thus triggering the excessive currency depreciation (or undervaluation). They aggressively buy the currency for appreciation is expected to continue, contributing to a destabilizing currency appreciation (or overvaluation).

To alleviate destabilizing speculative attacks on the domestic currency, foreign exchange traders must see signals that the domestic currency is expected to stabilize in foreign currency terms. The country's monetary authority should enforce anti-inflationary efforts and monetary tightening to reverse the trend of the domestic currency depreciation. Adversely, monetary easing is desirable in order to prevent an excessive appreciation of the domestic currency. In practice, it implies that the monetary authorities of the United States, Japan and the European Union ought to coordinate the directions of their monetary and fiscal policies in order to stabilize the "triad" currencies. Consequently, the stability of exchange rates between the three leading world currencies will help to accomplish a relative stability of many other currencies which patterns depend more or less on changes of the leading currencies exchange rates. However, skillful and sound monetary and fiscal policies pursued by governments of smaller nations are essential to achieve this task.

The most fertile ground for destabilizing speculative attacks on international currency derivative markets is caused by rising unbalanced inflation among the world economies. If domestic inflation increases unproportionally to the inflation trend among the leading economies, speculative selling of the domestic currency will occur, leading to the currency excessive undervaluation and to the net capital outflow. Consequently, currency derivative contracts will settle at lower strike prices and more expensive premiums. Similar effects occur when the national inflation is "stalled" at a high level, showing symptoms of high inflation inertia in the form of high wage demands and strong parallel price hikes by domestic producers and trading companies. In essence, lowering inflation and reducing speculative selling of domestic currency are necessary conditions for the introduction of viable derivative contracts for domestic currency in foreign currency terms.

The most commonly used instrument among the currency derivatives are currency *forward contracts*. These are large notional value selling or buying contracts obtained by exporters, importers, investors and speculators from banks with denomination normally exceeding 2 million USD. The contracts guarantee the future conversion rate between two currencies and can be obtained for any customized amount and any date in the future. They normally do not require a security deposit since their purchasers are mostly large business firms and investment institutions, although the banks may require compensating deposit balances or lines of credit. Their transaction costs are set by the spread between the bank's buy and sell prices.

Exporters invoicing receivables in foreign currency are the most frequent users of these contracts. They are willing to protect themselves from the currency depreciation by locking-in the future currency conversion rate at a high level. A similar foreign currency forward selling contract is obtained by investors in foreign currency denominated bonds (or other securities) who want to take advantage of higher foreign that domestic interest rates on government or corporate bonds and the foreign currency forward premium. They hedge against the foreign currency depreciation below the forward selling rate which would ruin their return from foreign financial investment. Investment in foreign securities induced by higher foreign interest rates and accompanied by the forward selling of the foreign currency income is called a *covered interest arbitrage*. It is feasible when the return on foreign investment shown by the right-hand side of the equation (1) is greater than the return on domestic investment (the left-hand side of the equation).

(1) $$K(1 + i) < K(1 + i^*) \, F/S$$

where K is the amount of capital invested, i is the domestic interest rate, i* is the foreign interest rate, F is the forward rate and S is the spot value of the domestic currency in foreign currency terms.

The forward selling contract is also used by speculators expecting a strong depreciation of the foreign currency. For instance, speculators may want to obtain the forward selling contract of DM at 1.39 DM per USD, hoping that the USD may depreciate well below this level, say, to 1.35 DM per USD, thus generating a profit of DM 0.04 on each USD invested.

The forward currency buying contract is widely used by importers invoicing payables in foreign currency, willing to protect themselves from the excessive appreciation of the foreign currency when it would become too costly to satisfy the foreign currency payments. International investors allocating their capital in domestic currency and willing to show profits in foreign currency (for instance, in order to pay lower foreign taxes) also hedge against an excessive foreign currency appreciation using the forward currency buying contracts. The speculative use of these contracts makes sense when the foreign currency is expected to strongly appreciate. Speculators will exercise the buying contract hoping to sell the foreign currency at a higher spot rate in the future. For example, speculators may wish to obtain the USD forward buying contract at 1.39 DM per USD expecting the USD to appreciate above it and to sell it at 1.42, thus generating a profit (before transaction costs) of DM 0.03 on each USD in transaction.

Forward contracts are the most commonly used currency-based derivative instrument in international financial markets. Their conversion rates are set by banks to their clients on the basis of simple formulas related to nominal interest rate differentials (differences between domestic and foreign market interest rates on comparable fixed income securities). For instance, if U.S. three-month Treasury bills are rising in nominal terms above the German three-month government bills, the USD will be set at a forward premium equal to the change in the nominal interest rate differential.

A simple method of determining the forward rate based on the nominal interest rate differential is illustrated by the following formula

(2) $i - i^* = (360/n) (F-S)/S$

where n is the number of days in the forward contract.

For instance, a bank offering a three-months forward contract in DM per USD would like to set the forward rate when the German nominal interest rate is 5.5 percent and the U.S. rate is 6 percent (annualized) on comparable three month T-bills, and the current DM per USD spot rate is 1.4. It may solve the problem by substituting these values to the equation (2) :

$$0.060 - 0.055 = (360/90) (F-1.4)/1.4$$

Solving the equation for F gives the value of the three months forward rate in DM per USD equal to 1.40175, which implies that the USD is at 0.005 (or 0.5 percent) annualized three month forward premium in DM terms (the right-hand side of the equation), equal to the annualized interest rate differential (the left-hand side of the equation).

The empirical literature (Levich, 1985; Tucker, Madura and Chiang, 1991, 259-261) presents strong evidence supporting the claim that forward rates are the best forecast of spot rate adjustments due to speculative actions taking advantage of the exchange rate arbitrage (buying currencies at the currently available lower rates on international financial markets and immediate selling at higher available rates)[2]. The phenomenon of forward rates serving as a good predictor of future spot rates known in the literature as an *unbiased forward hypothesis*. The forward rate levels which serve as a basis for *market-based exchange rate forecasting* have been assessed as a more accurate forecasting instrument than complex econometric models developing regression functions of exchange rates, or technical forecasting methods involving use of historical exchange rate data to

---

2 A contrary opinion stating a weak relationship between forward rates and future adjustments of spot rates is expressed, among others, by Hansen and Hodrick (1980), Fama (1984), and Tucker, Madura and Chiang (1991, 263).

predict future values[3]. The principle behind spot rates following closely the pattern set by forward rates is related to the market clearing mechanism of speculative actions. For instance, when the three months forward rate shows a premium for DM in USD terms, speculators will take advantage of arbitraging opportunities by arranging forward selling contracts of DM while buying DM spot as long as spot rates are below the three months forward rate pattern. By generating a stronger demand for DM in the spot market, they will lift the spot rate to the forward level. Adversely, if the DM is at a forward discount, speculators will arrange forward buying contracts hoping to sell DM at a higher spot rate. The action will be feasible as long as the spot rate is above the forward pattern. By selling the DM spot, they will adjust the exchange rate downward to the forward trend.

The belief in a strong association between forward rates and anticipated adjustments of spot rates has been well established in international financial markets and confirmed by their practice until 1993 (Madura, 1995, 249-252). Because of the perceived strong relationship between the forward trend and the actual changes in spot rates, strike prices of currency futures and options have been also very closely related to the forward rate trend, and ultimately, they have been strongly tied to nominal interest rates differentials.

Currency futures are financial contracts specifying a standardized volume of currency that is to be exchanged at a specified settlement date. The rate of the future currency conversion (the strike price) is locked in upon contract origination, although the premiums (prices paid for the contract) vary all the time. Currency futures have fixed denominations and fixed settlement dates upon which they can be exercised. The largest market for currency futures is the International Money Market - a branch of the Chicago Mercantile Exchange. Blocks of currency units per contract traded on this market include: 100 000 Canadian and Australian Dollars, 125 000 DM and Swiss Francs, 62 500 British Pounds (BP), and 12 500 YE. Standard delivery dates are limited to the third Wednesday of March, June, September and December of each year. There is a security deposit requirement for these contracts. They are regulated by the Commodity Futures Trading Commission of the U.S. Government, in contrast to forward contracts which are self-regulating. Although they are traded on the centralized exchanged floor in Chicago, the access to this marketplace is available through world-wide communication. The currency futures selling or buying contracts are obtained by exporters, importers, banks and international investors, and also by qualified public speculators. Their strike prices different from spot rates attract speculative transactions in a similar way to the differences between forward rates and spot rates. Speculators may generate substantial gains as long as the futures strike price differs from the spot rate and no gains are feasible when both rates are roughly equal. Currency futures contracts must be exercised on the settlement date. Because of the high degree of inflexibility - fixed settlement dates, fixed amounts in one block, the obligation of delivery - they are becoming less popular then currency options.

Currency options are contracts that guarantee the right to buy foreign currency (a call option) or the right to sell foreign currency (a put option) on a specified date in the future

---

3 For a comprehensive examination of technical, fundamental and maket-based forecasting see, for instance, Madura (1995, 239 -257).

and at a strike price fixed by the contract. They do not have to be exercised if spot exchange rates are more favorable to their holders. For instance, an international exporter invoicing receivables in DM may want the DM put option at a strike price of 0.70 USD per DM and the premium of 2 cents per each DM to expire if the spot rate of the DM rises to 0.73 USD or above. The Philadelphia Exchange is the major international market of both call and put options on international currencies, although currency options contracts are available in Amsterdam, Montreal, Chicago CME, Chicago Board Options Exchange, New York Mercantile Exchange and other markets as well. The blocks of currency call and put options available in Philadelphia are half of those of the Chicago futures (62 500 DM and SF, 50 000 CanD and AusD, 6 250 000 YE, 31 250 BP). Options on the French Franc (250 000 in a single bloc) and on the European Currency Units (ECUs) (62 500) are also available. These contracts have monthly settlement dates.

Currency call options are used mostly by importers invoicing payables in international currencies, investors in domestic securities (say, USD) who want to exercise gains in foreign currencies, speculators anticipating a sharp appreciation of the foreign currency above the level of the call's strike price plus premium. Perhaps the most desirable use of these contracts is by multinational companies engaged in foreign direct investment projects which still may not go through, or companies exploring possibilities of such projects through market research and feasibility studies in foreign countries. They need to hedge certain "sunk" costs in foreign currencies, that is, costs that must be incurred regardless whether the project will or will not materialize.

Currency put options are used by exporters invoicing receivables in foreign currencies, investors in foreign currency - denominated securities, and speculators anticipating a strong foreign currency depreciation so that they are able to purchase the currency at a weak anticipated spot rate in the future reselling it by exercising the put option contract with a higher strike price.

There are two types of currency options that depend on settlement time conditions. The "American-style" currency options can be exercised at any time before or on the expiration date. The "European-style" options can be exercised only on the expiration date. The "American-style" options offer the holder more flexibility since they can be sold to a third party or exercised prior to the expiration date if the direction of spot exchange rate does not favor waiting for the options maturity date.

The level of premiums on currency options depends generally on three factors. The most influential among them is the difference between the strike price and the current spot exchange rate. In the case of call options, the higher the strike price is in relation to the current spot rate, the lower the option premium will be. This is because the speculative demand for the least expensive call options is normally the strongest. They are the most beneficial and valuable for the speculators, therefore, their premiums will be the highest. Adversely, for currency put options higher premiums are set for options with higher strike prices in relation to the current spot rate. Again, put options with higher strike prices are more beneficial to speculators willing to sell the foreign currency at the highest conversion rate. Consequently, they have normally higher strike prices. These relations are illustrated by Table 12.1, where premiums for the BP calls in USD terms decline with higher strike prices and premiums on puts rise as the strike price increases. The second factor affecting option premiums is the length of time until the expiration date. Options, both calls and puts, for a longer time duration are associated with a higher degree of uncertainty of the spot exchange rate forecast, thus their premiums will be higher. Table 12.1 shows that August 1995 options premiums for the BP are more expensive than July 1995 options. The third influential factor affecting options premiums is the degree of currency volatility. Premiums on both call and put options are higher for more volatile currencies, since the risk of departures of spot rates from the options strike prices is higher in their case.

Table 12.1 British Pound options in US Dollars on June 7, 1995 in Philadelphia Exchange (premiums in cents per BP; BP 31 250 in a single option)

Strike Price	Call Options		Put Options	
	July '95	August '95	July '95	August '95
1.575	1.83	3.26	0.42	2.03
1.600	0.55	2.09	1.57	3.23
1.625	0.07	1.22	3.54	4.83

Source: Financial Times.

Currency options provide to their holders a very high degree of flexibility of applications. They can be obtained at different levels of strike prices, considerably departing in many instances from the current spot rate. If the adjustments of spot rates assume unfavorable directions to investors and speculators, they may always consider reselling these instruments to a third party even before the expiration date. Because of the variety of strike prices and a the wide extent of duration ranging from one month to two years or recently even more, investors may apply in their financial schemes various combinations of currency options instruments creating more complex, sophisticated currency-based derivative securities. The scope of this paper does not allow for a more detailed coverage of complex derivatives, although some of their basic types are worthwhile to signalize in order to grasp the coverage of recent developments in these markets presented in the next Section[4].

The simplest among option-based currency derivatives is a *straddle* which is a combination of a call and a put option with the same strike price and the same expiration date. It normally has two different premiums. It is particularly beneficial when the underlying currency has a high degree of volatility. Holders of a straddle benefit when the spot rate departs considerably from the strike price by a higher margin than the combined premium on a call and a put option. Depending upon the direction of this departure, investors may decide to exercise one of them and forego the other paying both premiums.

---

4 A highly recommended examination of complex derivative securities can be found in Hull (1993, 415 - 432) and in Kolb (1994, 387 - 640).

The combination of a call option and a put option on the same currency with the same expiration date but at different strike prices is called a *strangle*. In this case the investor expects the spot rate to fall within the margin between the call and the put strike price in order to benefit from exercising both the low-value call and the high-value put. The profit is equal to the difference between them minus the premiums on both options.

The forecasted pattern of adjustments of spot rates decides whether the investor prefers to apply a *bull spread* or a *bear spread*. The bull spread is a combination of currency options with different maturity dates designed to profit when the spot value of the underlying currency is expected to rise, for instance, a combination of a short call (in one month) and a long call (in several months) option. The bear spread is applied when the underlying currency is expected to depreciate and it will normally involve short and long put options in order to lock in currency selling rates within the next few months. Such an option is highly desirable to hedge a continuous revenue stream in a currency expected to considerably depreciate. Similar directions of expected changes in spot rates decide about the choice between a *strip* and a *strap*. A strip is the combination of a long position in one call and two put options with the same strike price and expiration dates, designed to benefit the investors betting on the currency depreciation in the future. A long position in one put and two call options with the same strike price and expiration date is called a strap, aimed at benefiting the investors when the underlying currency is expected to appreciate considerably.

When the direction of changes in the spot rate is highly uncertain, importers invoicing their payment in a foreign currency ought to consider applying a *butterfly spread with calls*. This instrument involves three calls with the same expiration date on a given currency at three different strike prices. Correspondingly, exporters and investors in foreign currency-denominated securities may consider a *butterfly spread with puts*, again, when the expected direction of the spot rate is highly uncertain. They may obtain a combination of three puts with the same expiration date but at three different strike prices. Since these instruments involve a larger number of options at different strike prices their combined premium is normally very high, they are certainly very expensive to their holders.

The above listed instruments are only the very basic combinations of currency options used predominantly for hedging purposes. From the standpoint of this analysis it shall be emphasized that designing all of these financial instruments very much depends on the direction of the spot exchange rate forecast. The viability of these derivatives exists only if they are centered around the actual future pattern of the exchange rate. They completely fail if the actual adjustment of the spot rate departs considerably from the forecasted level. Although these options do not have to be exercised and they may be resold to other investors, their premiums to be paid are normally very high and may be a source of considerable losses. Therefore, it is essential to correctly predict future changes in spot rates to benefit from these derivative instruments.

As discussed before, the available forward rates have been perceived as the empirically-proven best indicator of future changes in spot rates. Consequently, they have served as a basis for forecasting spot exchange rates by "derivative product engineers" at financial institutions. Until the early 1990s, the spot rates among the leading international currencies did follow forward rates, which, as indicated above, were closely related to nominal interest rate differentials. This situation contributed to a relative success of more complex currency-based derivatives. However, recent departures of spot rates from the forward trend and from the macroeconomic fundamentals, especially from interest rate differentials, tell a different story.

3. Recent developments in derivatives of the "triad" currencies

There has been a number of failures of investments in currency-based derivatives reported since mid-1993. Several leading international investment banks reported heavy losses from investments in derivative securities. American investment institutions such as Merrill Lynch or Bankers Trust reported losses from currency-based derivatives in 1994. Barings of London lost close to USD 1 billion on wrong betting on Tokyo market futures as a result of a tremendous risk exposure created by the investment schemes of the bank's trader, Nicholas Leeson. One of the leading international investors - Mr George Soros, and his investment fund, who were once able to benefit USD 2 billion from correct speculation on the BP depreciation on the day of the European Exchange Rate Mechanism crash on September 19, 1992, reported a heavy loss of USD 600 million from wrong betting on the Japanese Yen's alleged depreciation against the USD in February 1994. Many other financial institutions also admitted losses in these markets.

Perhaps the most useful lessons for the discussion on the scope of international regulation of derivative markets can be learned from the cases the Chilean copper mining company Codelco, and the German mining and metals conglomerate Metallgesellschaft AG (Goldstein and Folkerts-Landau, 1994, 11). Codelco reported a loss of USD 207 million in January 1994 from trading in copper futures. The head futures trader of the company apparently entered incorrectly some of the futures transactions in the computer system, generating an original loss of USD 30 million, and did not inform his supervisors about his error. Later, he attempted to regain the loss by speculating on the futures markets. But with the declining copper prices this speculation multiplied the original loss. In the beginning of 1994, Metallgesellschaft had to admit its financial fiasco. The company sold long-term contracts to customers to provide petroleum products at fixed prices with an option to terminate the contract by the customers at the cost equal to half of the realized profit at any time, if the spot price of petroleum was above the forward price. To cover this risk exposure, the company hedged its position in long-term futures contracts. The scheme was beneficial to the company as long as the market was in the so called "backwardation" position related to the advantage of spot prices over the forward prices. In the "contago" position, when spot prices were lower than the forward price, the contract was disadvantageous. This position prevailed in international futures markets contributing to a loss of DM 1.9 billion reported in January 1994. The company traded 55 000 of these contracts in the New York Mercantile Exchange (Nymex) and since the amount was twice the allowed limit, Nymex requested a margin call that could only be covered through the rescue package of DM 1.5 billion from Deutsche Bank and Dresdner Bank.

These failures have contributed to an extensive discussion among the U.S. lawmakers and governments of other countries on the methods and the scope of possible regulation of international derivative markets. However, their deliberations have produced almost no concrete results. It is impossible to introduce an extensive regulatory framework for these markets. They are too complex and too global to be restrained by a single government regulation. For instance, hedging or speculation on Philadelphia currency options and their complex combinations can always circumvent possible domestic restrictions on currency-based derivatives outside the U.S. American investors may also go to international derivative markets in response to possible regulatory efforts in the U.S. There is a high degree of liquidity of international capital which can always bypass attempts of regulation escaping to financial centers where restrictions on capital flows do not exist.

Nevertheless, some general rules for companies engaged in derivative instruments shall be applied as a lesson from the Codelco, Metallgesellschaft, Barings and other companies' mistakes. Among them are full disclosure rules to the management or, perhaps even to shareholders of firms on the mechanism and the degree of risk of transactions involving derivative securities. Most of the international banks have already such rules in place but they do not always follow them, especially in the cases where very complex currency-based derivative instruments are applied by portfolio managers and they are not fully understood by senior executives. It seems that extensive training of executives in modern financial products conducted by qualified professional companies and consultants and co-sponsored by government regulatory agencies shall be also recommended. Most of the leading financial companies in the U.S. have established "product engineering" divisions aimed at introducing complex derivative schemes for which they hire mathematicians and physicists with doctoral degrees, but with limited economic training. Another desirable regulatory effort is the introduction of high margin requirements for investors in derivative securities so that smaller, more risky players/speculators are discouraged from these markets.

If the regulation of these markets is to be successful it must be coordinated internationally by the most qualified agencies, preferably by the Bank for International Settlements of Basel, Switzerland. The BIS has already accomplished solid steps toward partial regulation of international capital through the 1988 Capital Adequacy Directives (CAD) modified and extended in April 1993 by the BIS Committee on Banking Supervision introduction of a new set of capital requirements for banks. Corresponding measures have been also endorsed by the European Union Capital Adequacy Directives in March 1993 which modified the Solvency Ratio and Own Funds Directives of 1989. In brief, these measures include:

- the rules for capital requirements for market risk
- measurement of interest risk
- recognition of netting schemes
- separation of bank's loan and trading books
- the isolation of market risk from specific risk (which includes credit risk, settlement risk, liquidity risk, and the risk of adverse movements of underlying securities)

- rules of conversion of fixed-income securities into more liquid debt-related securities.

These efforts will never compensate for the factors that are essential for the stability of international derivative securities. Perhaps the most critical among them is international coordination of monetary policies leading to a relative stability of floating exchange rates. Such coordination is essential since "dreams" of returning to the global fixed exchange rate system are simply unrealistic. Foreign exchange reserves of central banks reaching up to USD 120 billion for Japan and Taiwan are a tiny fraction of daily capital turnovers of approximately USD 600 billion in international financial markets. There is no reserve money to support such a system especially under the present conditions of growing trade and fiscal imbalances among the leading economies. Stable market-determined exchange rates will undeniably reduce the ground for destabilizing speculation and lower the risk of currency fluctuations. This, in turn, will reduce the cost of complex currency derivatives. For instance, butterfly spreads with call or put options will no longer be feasible if the spot exchange rate is expected to fluctuate within a narrower range. Instead, simple straight and less costly call or put options will be preferred.

The reality of foreign exchange markets in the recent two years has not shown an improved stability of exchange rates between the leading international currencies. Consequently, correctly forecasting changes in spot rates and to set strike prices of most currency-based derivatives has become increasingly difficult. As a result, significant errors and losses in investing in international derivatives have emerged. At least three general factors that contributed to these losses deserve a closer examination. They include:

- departures of spot exchange rate from the macroeconomic fundamentals
- a growing instability of spot exchange rates
- departures of spot rates from the forward level that historically serves as a best-fit forecast for spot rate adjustments

To illustrate the relationship between spot exchange rate fluctuations and changes in the macroeconomic fundamentals, a multivariate regression function of spot rates, as a dependent variable and income (GDP) differentials, interest rate differentials, and inflation differentials can be applied. The function which serves as a basis for technical or econometric forecasting of current exchange rates can be written:

$$(3) \qquad S = a + b(y - y^*) + c(i - i^*) + d(p - p^*)$$

where S is the spot exchange rate expressed in a foreign currency value of a unit of domestic currency, y is the rate of growth of domestic GDP, y^* is the rate of growth of foreign GDP, i is the domestic market interest rate, i^* is the foreign market interest rate, p is the domestic rate of inflation and p^* is the rate of inflation overseas.

All of the variables are coincident in time t and no lagged adjustments are incorporated in this simple function. Parameters a, b, c and d are regression-fitted coefficients.

Since the purpose of this analysis is to examine the most recent relationships between spot rate and macroeconomic fundamentals, the empirical testing of this function has been conducted in two series of weekly observations. The first sample of observations covers the two-year period between November 15, 1991 and February 15, 1993 and the second sample investigates the most recent period between March 2, 1994 and July 18, 1995. The examination is restricted to the "triad currencies" (USD, DM, YE) in relation to the GDP differentials between the United States, as a "domestic" variable and, separately, Germany's and Japan's GDP growth rates as "foreign" variables. The same countries' differentials are applied to short-term (three month government securities) interest rates, and inflation rates. Spot exchange rates and interest rates are monitored on the end-of-week basis, and GDP growth rates and CPI inflation rates are carried over respective weeks based on the most recently reported national statistics.

The results of these tests are presented in Table 12.2 The empirical testing is based on two general modifications of formula (3). The investigated function is a log-lin relationship, which has been proven by the empirical literature to have a higher deterministic value (Frankel, 1989; Marrinan, 1989). This form also holds better in tests applied for the purpose of this analysis yielding higher R-squared and F-statistics. The applied function has been also modified in all cases by the first-order autoregressive correction AR(+1) aimed at neutralizing the substantial positive autocorrelation of unadjusted functions reflected by their Durbin-Watson (DW) d-statistics ranging between 0.31 (for the DM per USD test in the early series) and 0.43 (for the YE per USD series in the early test). The modified function that served as a basis for empirical testing which results are shown in Table 12.2 is represented by the equation (4):

$$(4) \qquad LnS = a + b(y - y^*) + c(i - i^*) + d(p - p^*) + e\, AR(+1)$$

where LnS is the natural logarithm of spot rates in DM per USD and, separately, in YE per USD terms.

Based on the theory of determination of exchange rates, coefficient b ought to assume a negative sign if one believes in the adjustments between international demand in commodity markets and spot exchange rates. Namely, if the U.S. economy grows at a faster rate than the Japanese (or the German) economy, the American demand for foreign goods increases and the spot value of the USD in YE terms (or in DM terms) falls. The stronger U.S. demand for foreign goods results in the stronger U.S. demand for foreign currencies which are expected to appreciate, thus the USD ought to depreciate. Adjustments in capital markets have an adverse effect. If the U.S. GDP is expected to grow faster than the foreign GDP, the international demand for U.S. securities should rise, thus contributing to the USD appreciation. Therefore, b would assume a positive sign. Coefficient c is normally expected to have a positive sign, since rising U.S. nominal interest rates above the corresponding foreign rates generate higher interest yields on USD-denominated fixed-income securities and result in a stronger foreign demand for these securities and for the USD. Consequently, the USD will appreciate, showing a direct relationship between the interest rate differential and the spot exchange rate. Coefficient d is expected to be negative reflecting an inverse relationship between the inflation differential and the spot exchange rate. Specifically, if the U.S. inflation grows faster than overseas, the USD is expected to always depreciate.

Table 12.2 Regression estimates of the log-lin functions of DM per USD and YE per USD exchange rates and income, interest rate, and inflation differentials (end-of-week data)*

Coefficients		Nov 15, 1991 - Feb 15, 1993 Series		March 2, 1994 - July 18, 1995 Series	
		DM per USD	YE per USD	DM per USD	YE per USD
a	(constant)	0.6948 (10.94)	4.7604 (28.43)	0.3834 (16.64)	4.4252 (2.86)
b	(income differentials)	0.0052 (1.53)	0.0045 (0.91)	0.0153 (2.02)	-0.0039 (-0.32)
c	(interest rate differ-entials)	0.0501 (4.51)	0.0131 (1.09)	-0.0024 (-0.15)	-0.052 (-0.35)
d	(inflation differentials)	-0.0338 (-4.74)	0.0054 (0.82)	-0.0418 (-1.71)	0.0104 (0.89)
e	(first-order autoregressive correction)	0.8140 (12.16)	0.9768 (25.02)	0.7608 (6.41)	0.9760 (25.91)
R^2		0.92	0.85	0.92	0.94
F-stat.		156.92	74.56	121.05	164.18
DW-stat.		1.64	1.97	2.06	1.51

* t-statistics in parentheses

The empirical results presented in Table 12.2 show very low values of statistical significance (low t-statistics) of sensitivity coefficients b, c, and d. Only in the first series of observations, the DM per USD exchange rate shows statistically significant sensitivity of spot rates to interest rate and inflation rates differentials between the U.S. and Germany. The second DM per USD regression does not comply with this degree of significance. For the YE per USD exchange rate both series have extremely low significance of b, c and d coefficients proving a weak adherence of spot exchange rates to these key macroeconomic variables. The highest statistical significance is assigned to coefficient e and to the autoregressive correction AR(+1) reflecting a very strong role played by expectations of future spot rate movements in the determination of current exchange rates. The departure of the DM per USD rate from interest rate differentials and inflation differentials proves that in the recent period spot exchange rates have exhibited a weaker sensitivity of spot rates to macroeconomic relationships than before.

It is worth explaining the reversal of the sign of the c coefficient between both periods. The coefficient is positive in the first period both for the DM per USD and the YE per USD regressions, being consistent with theoretical assumption of the determinants of exchange rates. But in the second period it assumes negative values. It is not surprising.

In 1994 and in the first quarter of 1995 the U.S. Federal Reserve applied seven rounds of monetary policy tightening while the USD actually experienced a sharp depreciation. Consequently, U.S. three months T-Bill rates gradually increased to the peak level of 6.3 percent in the beginning of January 1995, being only slightly adjusted downward by mid-July of 1995 to 5.7 percent, while comparable German rates gradually fell from the peak level at the beginning of the series in March 1994 of 5.8 percent to the lowest level of 4.3 percent at the end of the series. Japan's rates, operating at very low nominal levels due to some deflationary pressures, peaked at 2.35 in mid-January 1995, falling to a mere 0.82 in mid-July. Correspondingly, the USD gradually fell in DM terms from 1.73 in the beginning of the series to 1.38 in the beginning of July 1995, and in YE terms it fell from 105 in March 1994 to 84.2 in the beginning of July 1995. The sign reversal of c and the subsequent departure of spot exchange rates from the nominal interest parity condition is an unprecedented phenomenon. It strongly distorted the relationship between forward and spot rates since forward rates, always strongly tied to nominal interest rate differentials, showed a much stronger USD than spot rates.

Another intriguing finding is the difference in the sign of the coefficient d between the DM per USD and the YE per USD series. The coefficient of sensitivity of spot rates to the inflation differential for DM per USD series is negative, thus consistent with theoretical assumptions. However, the coefficient has a positive value for the YE per USD series. This development is complex to explain and an answer to this puzzle would require additional investigations. However, throughout the 1990s the USD was continuously depreciating in YE terms while at the same time the U.S. inflation was declining by a stronger margin than the Japanese inflation. This stems from the fact that inflation in Japan already operates at a very low or negative level, while the U.S. inflation had a higher starting point with the beginning of the current economic recovery.

The reversal of the sign of the coefficient b in the second series of observations for the YE per USD rate deserves a further explanation. For the remaining series, b is positive indicating that the U.S. GDP outperforming the growth of German and Japanese economies contributed to the USD appreciation. This relationship is usually transmitted via adjustments in capital markets, since faster U.S. economic growth contributes to a stronger international demand for U.S. securities and, consequently, for the USD. The negative sign of the coefficient b for the YE per USD in the second series implies that the growing U.S. income created a strong U.S. demand for Japanese goods and for the YE. The sustained deep U.S. trade deficit with Japan confirms this relationship. Therefore, it may be argued that the recent changes in the YE per USD rate have been very sensitive to the inability of the U.S. to improve its trade imbalance with Japan and despite the positive income differential for the U.S., it is the Japanese currency which has actually appreciated.

In summary, spot exchange rates between the "triad" currencies are recently showing a relatively weak sensitivity to income, interest rate and inflation differentials[5]. They are, therefore, increasingly related to determinants of exchange rates that are not incorporated

---

5 An interesting alternative analysis of recent departures of exchange rates from macroeconomic fundamentals is presented by Clark (1994).

in the basic model prescribed by formula (4). One may speculate that the relative weakness of the USD has been recently tied to a low confidence of international investors and currency traders in the U.S. ability to control its fiscal and trade imbalances. Among them, the persistent deep U.S. trade deficit with Japan is particularly relevant for the determination of the YE per USD exchange rate. It contributes to a significant undervaluation of the U.S. currency (Krugman, 1992, chapters 1 and 2).

The second general factor that contributed to failures in currency-based derivatives is the growing degree of instability of exchange rates between the leading international currencies. As argued before, larger fluctuations of exchange rates contribute to higher premiums paid for currency futures and options making them more expensive for investors and speculators. The empirical literature on the subject of stability of floating exchange rates generally proves a growing degree of volatility and misalignments of spot rates between key currencies as the system of floating rates evolves (Mussa et al., 1994, 18 - 24). To some extent, the development of currency-based derivatives has cushioned the growing volatility of spot exchange rates by providing a vehicle for hedging the increasing risk of currency fluctuations. But the augmented volatility also means that costs of hedging with derivatives are higher due to more expensive premiums. Mussa et al.(1994) provide convincing evidence that since the inception of the floating exchange rate system in 1973 fluctuations of exchange rates among the "triad" currencies have gradually become larger and less predictable. This finding can be enforced by the examination of recent developments in spot exchange rates between these currencies. In both series of weekly observations that served as a basis for the tests presented in Table 12.2, the growing volatility of spot exchange rates can also be detected. In the first series of observations covering the period between November 15, 1991 and February 15, 1993, the coefficient of variation (the ratio of standard deviation to the mean value) of the DM per USD spot rate was 4.0 percent (0.04). For the YE per USD spot rate the coefficient of variation was only 2.8 percent. The coefficient rose sharply for both currencies in the second series of weekly observations covering the period March 2, 1994 - July 18, 1995, reaching 6.9 percent for the DM per USD and 7.9 percent for the YE per USD exchange rates. In essence, spot exchange rates between the "triad" currencies are not only departing from the macroeconomic fundamentals but they are also experiencing a growing degree of volatility and unpredictability. Under such conditions, the risk of failures in investing in currency-based derivatives becomes more apparent.

The third factor contributing to jitters in currency-based derivative markets are misalignments between forward rates and future changes in spot exchange rates in the recent period of time. As discussed above, the unbiased forward rate hypothesis requires that the spot rate ought to follow the trend set forth by the forward rate level[6]. But the empirical evidence in 1994 and 1995 does not support this rule. For instance, the one-year forward rate available on July 1, 1994 showed a mere 0.52 percent USD discount in DM terms and a 3.27 USD discount in YE terms. In fact, the DM per USD spot rate fell from 1.583 on July 1, 1994 to 1.390 on July 1, 1995, which indicates a 12.2 percent

---

6 Refer particularly to Fama (1984) for a dissident voice expressing doubts about the evidence supporting the unbiased forward rate hypothesis.

depreciation of the U.S. currency. At the same time, the YE per USD spot rate fell from 98.68 to 84.22 showing a 14.7 percent depreciation of the USD. In both cases the USD scored much lower than the forward rate would imply. The USD spot rate on July 1, 1995, weaker than the one-year forward rate available on July 1, 1994, reflects negative savings from hedging DM receivables in USD terms (expressed as a difference between the lagged spot rate and the forward rate). If the exporters and investors in DM securities did not hedge with the forward DM selling contract they would generate higher USD returns by converting the DM at a lower spot rate. The same rule applies to receivables from exports or investments denominated in YE. Correspondingly, speculators betting on the USD appreciation above the forward level obtained DM or YE forward buying contracts (or buy futures and call options) to be exercised on July 1, 1995. Their forecast of spot rates stemming from perceived adjustments in monetary policies would be consistent with theoretical principles of exchange rate determination since the Federal Reserve tightened monetary policy more than Bundesbank or the Bank of Japan. To those who assumed such an investment position, the steep depreciation of the USD in both DM and YE terms turned out to be a disaster.

The sharp depreciation of the USD below the forward rate level was beneficial to importers of goods invoicing payables in DM or in YE, or to investors in USD securities exercising benefits in foreign currencies if they hedged with the forward DM and YE buying contracts with the USD stronger than in the spot market. Exercising forward contracts, DM and YE buy futures and call options cost them less USD for each unit of DM or YE than the purchase of these two currencies in the July 1, 1995 spot market. On the contrary, if importers invoiced their payables in USD hedging with the USD forward buying contract was less beneficial. One may presume that this position was widespread among international importers since most of the international trade transactions are still paid in USD and unhedged transactions are rather rare.

In summary, departures of exchange rates from macroeconomic fundamentals, growing volatility of key exchange rates and misalignment between forward rates and the spot adjustments have generated a higher degree of risk in international financial markets. They also have contributed to a failure of exchange rate forecasts which in turn generated a higher degree of uncertainty of investing in currency-based derivatives. All of the currency-based derivatives are designed on the basis of forecasted underlying spot exchange rates. Specifically, if the USD is expected to appreciate in terms of other leading international currencies, forward buying contracts, buy futures, USD call options or any combinations of options with calls prevailing shall be applied by international investors. Their application may turn out to be catastrophic if the USD actually depreciates.

4.   Conditions for involvement of Polish firms in currency-based derivative markets

An effective currency risk management shall be a part of financial strategies in transforming economies of Central and Eastern Europe. The examined increasing volatility of exchange rates among the world's leading currencies, growing inaccuracy of exchange rate forecasts and misalignments between forward rates and actual changes in spot rates contribute to an accelerating degree of currency risk in international trade and financial transactions. On the one side, an exposure to the currency risk can be harmful for expanding trade transactions, international financial investing and foreign direct investment projects which are critical for constructing a modern open economic systems. But on the other side, developing hedging mechanisms of currency risk may promote international exchange of goods and capital, as well as enhance gains from trade, and international financial and foreign direct investment. A greater involvement of Poland and other former centrally-planned economies in international currency-based derivative markets allows the establishment of an effective mechanism of currency risk hedging.

This involvement does not mean that the transforming economies of Central Europe ought to establish options and futures contracts for their own currencies. Such contracts would be very limited in total trading on international capital market due to a small volume of their national currencies in world-wide circulation. This restricted liquidity would not guarantee a proper pricing mechanism of options and futures. A high degree of instability of strike prices and premiums would invite speculative transactions and destabilizing attacks on exchange rates. At the present stage of the capital markets evolution in Central Europe's transforming economies, it is too early to offer options and futures currency contracts. A lack of such contracts certainly limits hedging methods for exposure to exchange rate fluctuations. However, Polish and other Central European exporters, importers and investors may still use currency forward contracts that are gradually emerging in the region. In addition, the exposure of domestic currency equivalents of export earnings and import payments to currency fluctuations, in the presence of relatively flexible exchange rates, will be diminished if Poland (and Hungary) undertake aggressive efforts to trim domestic inflation. A comprehensive disinflation policy is a strong prerequisite to achieving stable exchange rates and avoiding a real appreciation of domestic currency.

For the purpose of an effective entry of the Polish Zloty (ZL) into forward contracts with other currencies, Poland needs to establish a relative stability of underlying spot exchange rates. This stability does not mean an application of a currency peg at the present stage of the economic transformation. Rather, somewhat more flexible formulas of the exchange rate ought to be favored so that the country's monetary policy is not fully based on the exchange rate target. The stage of transformation which requires active structural adjustments induced by the realignment of relative prices ought to be accompanied by the exchange rate flexibility, so that the mechanism of adjustments of relative prices is not distorted. At the same time, monetary policy ought to be targeted on domestic credit and based on predetermined feedback rules. Such orientation will help to facilitate domestic credit necessary for structural adjustment and will create a ground for construction of domestic security markets (Orlowski, 1994).

The currency stability shall be accomplished through a sustained, non-discretionary monetary policy oriented on controlling inflation. A steady course of anti-inflationary monetary policy will eventually improve credibility of the National Bank of Poland (NBP) and reduce "inertial" inflation, that is, the one which is self-propelled by rising inflation expectations of firms and consumers. At the same time, the environment of lower inflation will diminish the degree of real appreciation of the ZL when the spot exchange rate fluctuations are limited to the permitted band under the adjustable peg formula. The task of stabilizing the exchange rate shall not be based on a completely flexible adjustment of the spot rate to the galloping inflation in an open market, but on the achievement of price stability in the first place.

The development of the exchange rate policy in Poland and other Central European transforming economies increases the need for foreign exchange risk hedging. In the beginning of the Polish transformation program in 1990, the ZL was pegged to the USD as a tool of reducing the "residual" or "corrective" inflation. Policy makers introduced the peg with the intention to change it later into more flexible exchange rate formulas in order to prevent excessive overvaluation of the ZL, which was a routine policy solution of heterodox stabilization programs (Bruno, 1992). It remains debatable whether this solution was really essential in the former centrally-planned economies where the tradition and the magnitude of "inertial" or "chronic" inflation did not initially play a critical role in contrast to Latin American economies. The fixed rate in Poland was eventually changed into the crawling peg in May 1991 and, with the further success with disinflation, into the crawling band in May 1995. The program of expanding flexibility of the exchange rate has been designed and gradually enacted, although its implementation has been too slow in Poland. Nevertheless, by expanding the band of permitted currency fluctuations Poland has achieved a much higher degree of currency flexibility than the Czech Republic and has avoided negative effects of the real currency appreciation. It seems paradoxical, but further adjustments of the exchange rate system will have to bring it back to fixed exchange rate formulas. This direction is required in the context of preparations for accession to the European Union. Even if Poland and other Central European states do not become automatically members of the European Monetary System upon their future official membership in the European Union, they would have to adjust their monetary policy onto exchange rate targeting with the ECU or the DM (Orlowski, 1995). If they are unable to significantly cut their annual inflation to, say, less than 5 percent, they will risk bearing extensive negative effects of a real currency appreciation.

If the underlying spot rate is more stable and more predictable, it will be easier to offer forward contracts with more accurate ZL per foreign currency conversion rates and with a longer time horizon. Such contracts will improve the quality of hedging export receivables, import payables and income from international investment. Their longer time span will help to hedge funds necessary for foreign direct investment in Poland and direct investment of Polish companies abroad, ultimately leading to acceleration of these activities.

It shall be noted that several commercial banks in Poland have already established forward contracts, mostly in ZL per USD and ZL per DM transactions. They are, however, experiencing difficulties with setting proper forward rates and expanding their time horizon. Specifically, it is difficult to set proper forward rates on a longer time forward contracts under the present conditions of high inflation running around 20 percent annual rate and, therefore, more unpredictable real interest rates. Nevertheless, the only feasible solution is that forward rates shall be based on interest rate differentials.

They will have the same degree of error as forecasted interest rates. Relating them to spot exchange rate forecasts would be more risky. The expected pattern of spot rates is even more unpredictable with the May 19, 1995 departure from the crawling peg to the crawling band formula having a wider band of permitted fluctuations of plus-minus 7 percent. Since the present formula incorporates more risk of spot rate fluctuations, the need for forward contracts is even stronger. In essence, their accuracy depends on stabilization of the spot exchange rate which is closely tied to lower inflation accomplished through coherent programs of fiscal and monetary convergence.

Forward contracts are the only type of currency derivatives in which the ZL shall be involved. It is impossible to enter the Polish currency into currency futures and options trading before the underlying security markets are well developed. Such involvement may be considered in the very remote future or, perhaps, it shall not be debated at all since the Polish monetary system will have to be gradually more aligned with the DM or the European Currency Unit (ECU) when the program of accession to the EU is under way. Consequently, the ZL will have to be closer tied to the future European currency and Polish banks will be able to use futures and options for hedging purposes between the European currency and other leading international currencies. Furthermore, the program of accession to the EU may also help to stabilize the ZL by the unavoidable reorientation of monetary policy targeting on stable ZL per ECU (or DM) rates (Orlowski, 1995).

Regardless of the limited scope of involvement of the ZL in currency derivatives, Polish exporters, importers and banks when invoicing payments in DM, USD or other leading currencies ought to be engaged in international options markets using other currency options contracts. For instance, it would be particularly beneficial to obtain the DM per USD put option by exporters invoicing receivables in DM if for any reason the USD were expected to considerably appreciate in DM terms above the put option strike price. This type of cross-currency hedging would significantly increase ZL gains from the transaction. Certainly, exporters shall always attempt to apply invoicing in the currency expected to appreciate the most, in this case in the USD. This hedging transaction shall be considered if the exporters do not have a bargaining position to invoice payments in the most desirable currency, which would be a likely case of Polish firms exporting goods to Germany.

Correspondingly, Polish importers would significantly benefit from the DM per USD call option while invoicing payables in DM and expecting a considerable appreciation of the DM above the call option strike price. By exercising the option, the effective payment would be realized through the USD as a relatively weak currency. It would be, therefore, less expensive for Polish importers. In both cases, American-style options shall be preferred since they can always be exercised in advance or sold to a third party if spot rates assume unfavorable directions.

Although similar effects could be calculated from hedging with currency futures, their markets shall not be advised to Polish firms willing to hedge payments. As discussed before, futures markets are less flexible in terms of settlement dates, the size of blocs of foreign currency in a single contract, and they are mostly used by speculators.

In general terms, Polish exporters shall always make efforts to invoice receivables in the currency expected to appreciate the most and importers ought to follow the rule of invoicing payables in the currency expected to depreciate. If they do not have bargaining power to do so, they may maximize their gains by cross-hedging via currency-based derivatives, primarily forward contracts and currency options. In any case, the correct choice of their hedging or currency investment strategy very much depends on their accurate forecasts of key exchange rates not only between the ZL and other currencies, but also the rates between the leading international currencies. It is also advisable that Polish companies develop systems of accounting of exposure to currency fluctuations not only in the domestic currency, but also in USD, to allow to design most beneficial risk hedging schemes.

The access to international currency-based derivative markets shall be also expanded for Polish banks and investment funds. Using currency derivatives gives them an opportunity to hedge the risk of converting foreign currency earnings into ZL. Existing barriers on international capital investment and high capital gain taxes shall be reduced to allow them to profit from international investing and accumulate capital funds. At the same time, speculation by Polish firms in international derivatives markets ought to be discouraged. Speculative transactions generated considerable losses in 1994/95, especially to inexperienced participants. These losses are likely to persist if underlying currencies spot rates continue to exhibit increasing volatility and misalignment.

Polish international trade companies shall be fully aware that the risk of exposure to exchange rate fluctuations can be also hedged with methods not involving currency-based derivatives. This is particularly important when the ZL per foreign currency exchange rates show an increasing degree of volatility and unpredictability. Among such methods *the money-market hedge* is highly recommended. Specifically, if an exporter sells goods to Germany and invoices receivables in DM, he/she may borrow a DM loan from a German bank at the time of signing the contract. Simultaneously, the Polish exporter will exchange borrowed DM into ZL at the current spot rate and invest the amount in ZL denominated interest-bearing assets. It will generate a desirable ZL income for the time of duration of the export contract. At the end, the collected receivables in the future will be used to repay the German bank loan. This transaction is risk-free since it involves all parameters (the German credit rate, the ZL deposit rate and the current spot exchange rate) known upon the contract origination. The income will, therefore, depend on the amount of earning from the ZL-denominated assets. It can be easily observed that this operation is beneficial if the ZL real interest rate or, eventually, the DM deposit rate in a Polish bank exceed the real rate of interest on the German bank loan.

A similar scheme can be also applied by Polish importers. If they invoice payables in DM, they may consider borrowing ZL from a Polish bank, converting the amount to DM today, and investing in DM interest-bearing securities for the duration of the import contract. The DM assets will be later cashed-in and used to cover DM payables. At the same time in the future the Polish bank loan will be repaid in ZL, which in effect will be a cost of the import transaction. This time, the ZL credit real interest rate must be lower than the DM asset interest rate to exercise relative gains from this transaction.

In summary, international currency-based derivative products open vast opportunities for firms in the emerging market economy of Poland. Yet, they bring a growing degree of risk for speculative transactions. It is desirable for Polish companies to engage in these markets to enhance hedging opportunities and to maximize profits from international investing. To a limited degree, forward contracts on the ZL exchange rate shall be expanded. But building derivative security markets in transition economies must be preceded by strengthening of underlying security markets, whose success strongly depends on the ability of the economic authorities to reduce inflation. The policy adjustments that are inevitable in rational programs of preparation for accession to the EU will help to strengthen domestic security markets, stabilize inflation and the exchange rate and, ultimately, assist in a future construction of derivative security markets.

References

Bruno, Michael (1992) *Stabilization and Reform in Eastern Europe: A Preliminary Evaluation*, Washington, D.C: International Monetary Fund, Working Paper no. WP/92/30, May.

Clark, Peter B. (1994) *Exchange Rates and Economic Fundamentals: A Framework for Analysis*, Washington, D.C.: International Monetary Fund, Occasional Paper no. 115, December.

Fama, Eugene (1984); Forward and Spot Exchange Rates; *Journal of Monetary Economics*, 319-338, November.

Frankel, Jeffrey (1989); Flexible Exchange Rates: Experience versus Theory; *Journal of Portfolio Management*, 45-54, Winter.

Goldstein, M. and D. Folkerts-Landau (1994); International Capital Markets: Developments, Prospects and Policy Issues; *World Economic and Financial Surveys*, Washington, D.C.: International Monetary Fund, September.

Hansen, Lars Peter and Robert J. Hodrick (1980); Forward Exchange Rates as Optimal Predictors of Future Spot Rates: An Econometric Analysis; *Journal of Political Economy*, 829 -853, October.

Hull, John C. (1993) *Options, Futures and Other Derivative Securities*, Englewood Cliffs, New Jersey: Prentice-Hall.

Kolb, Robert W. (1994) *Futures, Options and Swaps*, Miami, Florida: Kolb Publ. Co.

Krugman, Paul R. (1992) *Currencies and Crisis*, Cambridge, Massachusetts: MIT Press.

Levich, Richard M. (1985) Empirical Studies of Exchange Rates: Price Behavior, Rate Determination and Market Efficiency, in Ronald W. Jones and Peter B. Kenen (eds.) *Handbook of International Economics*, Amsterdam: North-Holland Publ. Co., Chapter 19.

Madura, Jeff (1995) *International Financial Management*, St. Paul, Minnesota: West Publ. Co.

Marrinan, J. (1989); Exchange Rate Determination: Sorting Out Theory and Evidence; *New England Economic Review*, Boston, Massachusetts: Federal Reserve Bank of Boston, 39-51, November-December.

Mussa, Michael et al. (1994) *Improving the International Monetary System: Constraints and Possibilities*, Washington, D.C.: International Monetary Fund, Occasional Paper no. 116, December.

Orlowski, L.T. (1994); Spanish Monetary Policy Before and After the Inclusion into the European Community: Lessons for Poland; *Reperes - Bulletin Economique et Financier*, Luxembourg: Banque Internationale a Luxembourg, 39, 4-14, November.

Orlowski, L.T. (1995); Preparations of the Visegrad Group Countries for Admission to the European Union: Monetary Policy Aspects; *The Economics of Transition*, 3, 3, September, 333-353.

Tucker, Alan L., Jeff Madura and Thomas C. Chiang (1991) *International Financial Markets*, St. Paul, Minnesota: West Publ. Co.

Author Index

217

Subject Index

agents 20, 32, 40-56
allocation 3,11-16, 22, 40f., 56, 75
arbitrage 14, 51, 88f.
AT&T 87-94

bad debts 161ff.
banking reform 3, 149-180
banking supervision 171, 204,
bankruptcy 127, 130, 138, 154, 160-169, 185
behavioral change 2, 3, 11f., 14, 20-36, 55f.
British Telecom 88, 94
broker 60-77
brokerage fee 60
budget constraint(s) 45, 49
Bulgaria 2, 133-148

capitalization 3, 59f., 80f.
Central Bank Law 133, 185
Central Eastern European Country (CEEC) 133
centrally planned economies (CPE) 7, 55f.
Chlorofluorocarbons (CFCs) 2, 99-112
Codelco (Chilean copper mining company) 203f.
Commonwealth of Independent States (CIS) 185f.
competition 2f., 8-11, 13, 16, 22-28, 44f., 49, 52, 83, 87f., 90-98, 133
competitiveness 2, 16, 22, 34, 49, 59, 87, 89f., 90, 97
consumer 15, 29f., 32, 40, 42, 46, 50f., 53, 55, 94
- goods 13-15
- preferences 40, 50
- taste cluster 41f., 44
contract 3, 10, 12, 21, 27, 33, 63, 73f.,
- forward 3, 10, 12, 15, 21, 27, 33, 63, 73f., 77
- relational 12, 15, 21, 27
cost 2-4, 7-15, 20-33, 41-49, 85
- organizational 2, 45
- transactional 2, 4, 7, 10-12, 15, 21, 23, 28, 85-96
credit 29, 60-64, 67, 71
currency 3, 54
- derivative instruments 3, 194
- forward contract 197, 211
- futures contract 199
- options 199-203, 213

decentralization 1, 11, 16, 41, 55
demand elasticity 96
distribution 26, 32, 33, 40-42, 53f., 56

economic
- agent 3, 32, 40
- competition 23, 24, 83
- elements 21
economy
- centralized 13ff., 40, 42f., 45f., 49, 53, 55, 80f.
- command 11
- market 7, 9f., 16, 20f., 31, 34, 37f., 40, 42, 44
- mixed 26
- moral 24, 28
enterprise → firm
Enterprise Reform and Resolution Agency (ERRA) 190
entrepreneur 3, 10, 14-17, 29, 32f., 53f., 77, 81
equity markets → markets, stock markets
EU-Commission 96, 98

223

HAW.

AiLT
30

DiV 1/10 ET